THE MINNESOTA LIBRARY ON STUDENT PERSONNEL WORK

EDITED BY E. G. WILLIAMSON

---

*Published before titles were assigned numbers.

THIS IS VOLUME SEVEN
IN THE MINNESOTA LIBRARY ON STUDENT PERSONNEL WORK

TOWARD A PHILOSOPHY
OF ORGANIZED
STUDENT ACTIVITIES

by HERBERT STROUP

University of Minnesota Press, Minneapolis

To

HARRY DAVID GIDEONSE

*in commemoration of his twenty-fifth year
as President of Brooklyn College*

⤙ Foreword

FOR far too many decades the literature describing and appraising student activities and programs has been limited to small group discussions, to task accomplishments, and to organized recreation. In this book Dean Stroup presents a mature, philosophic, and historical reorientation to extra-curricular activities. He traces briefly various stages of evolution, some of them continuing into the present day, from the traditional disruptive conflict that characterized the medieval universities, through the emphasis in recent times on recreation and togetherness as fringe benefits, and onward to the present restructuring of activities as educative in their own right. Although, as he points out, student activities has been too long confined to trivialities and pleasurism, organized activities — as one of the many emerging student personnel services — possesses great relevancy to higher education. In defining this relevancy, Dean Stroup reinstates two ancient Greek modalities of man's behavior, the Dionysian and the Apollonian — pleasurism as contrasted with rationality.

Readers interested only in how-to-do-it techniques will find parts of Dean Stroup's discussion difficult, since it is historically and philosophically grounded in the complex nature of man. Others will recognize his matured societal philosophy as *the* foundation of student personnel work. His interpretation of the role of student activities in the college or university will be most welcome to many as filling a serious gap in our professional literature. To still others in the field, this book will be helpful in securing wider understanding and acceptance of our work within the institutions of higher learning. Moreover, his analysis of values in education and his concept of freedom will make for a clearer delineation of our role in higher education.

I am delighted to include this book in our student personnel series because it is a pioneering venture and one that has long been needed. Student activities can become more than simply hedonistic, can develop objectives other than those of mere pleasurism, important though activities so categorized may be for alternation from a curricular to an off-duty modality of behavior. That the student need not turn anti-intellectual or lapse into immaturity on leaving the classroom for the extra-curriculum is a message Dean Stroup has stated most convincingly.

E. G. WILLIAMSON

⤜ Preface

AS AMERICAN higher education has grown in scope and complexity, many relatively new specializations have arisen among its functions and personnel. One of these, the field of student personnel work, is the subject of this book. Although this study is concerned with only a particular complex within that field, that of student activities, the vagaries and ambiguities within student personnel work are such that it scarcely seems amiss to discuss questions which in one light fall within the narrower subfield of student activities, but which in their implications reach out into all sectors of student personnel work. Many of the assertions made here are therefore directed not only to student activities as a subspecialization, but to the totality of student personnel work.

Like the whole of student personnel work, student activities is noticeably weak in its theoretical underpinnings, a condition owing to a number of fairly obvious circumstances. Comparatively new, historically speaking, the field has not yet had sufficient time in which to develop a mature philosophy. If a theory can be developed only after a long course of practical experience in which both the need and the bases for theory gradually become apparent, this is not wholly a defect. Moreover, the field is often deliberately conceived to be eminently practical in that student personnel workers have been primarily program builders and maintainers, for the most part serving a custodial function in higher education. Quite content with this limited conception of their operations, many workers have openly championed the custodial view, as though exercise of the speculative mind handicapped practical affairs. Furthermore, since student personnel work has been regularly classified as an applied science, and has borrowed from several different sciences, it has depended heavily on the theories — where found relevant and useful — of other disciplines. For these and other reasons, then, theory has not been coherently outlined in student personnel work and its subsections. Conceived as a step toward remedying that situation, this book is presented in the hope that it will serve its intended purpose, if only in a preliminary way.

No encyclopedic coverage is attempted within the modest dimensions of this study. No pretense is made of laying out systematically the whole subject, the theory of student activities. I hope that objective will be realized ultimately, even though a long succession of tentative efforts may be required to bring it about. At the present time, however, there is so little of the "why" in student personnel work that the task of the systematic theorist must be deferred until a richer assortment of materials is accumulated.

Rather than attempt to be all-inclusive, I have taken a number of loosely related themes and have tried to develop these as a painter might, with broad and daring brush strokes, seeking to convey a most complex reality beyond immediate and sensory observation. On none of these themes do I presume to be writing dogmatically, although I do wish to convey my own ideas. I readily recognize that one can choose among many possible approaches toward developing a supporting theory in student personnel work, and I can only hope that others will not only be critical of what is contained in this book, but will take the pains to state their own outlook in positive terms, in the interest of the development of the field.

Aimed at essentially two types of readership, this book is addressed, first, to those college and university administrators and faculty members who are not identified with the field of student personnel work. Often they openly wonder what "apologetics" guides the field, whence it derives its rationale, why it needs to be accorded a place within the intellectual community, what its relations are to other fields of learning. Second, this book speaks to workers within the field itself. Of necessity the questions of a theoretical character will appeal mainly to workers who have the benefit of long experience and thought, although perceptiveness regarding the intellectual undergirding of their field appears to be increasing among workers in all ranks.

Others less formally involved in the fact and fate of higher education may be interested as well.

I am deeply indebted to a number of persons for their aid in the development of this book. President Harry D. Gideonse and the faculty of Brooklyn College gave me my first responsibility for student activities many years ago. I appreciate the trust shown by the faculty, and the wise leadership provided by the President. Dean Thomas E. Coulton and Dean William R. Gaede, with whom I have worked closely for years, have been primary influences in the growth of my institutional and administrative understanding. My colleagues too, in the Department of Personnel Service, including the Office of Student Activities headed by Dean Margaret E. Sober, have taught me more about student personnel services than they will ever realize. And without the students of Brooklyn College, who have always been cooperative, challenging, critical, and stimulating, I would have had fewer occasions to develop my own mind on many subjects.

The text of this book has benefited from careful readings by several persons. In painstakingly and critically reviewing the work, Dean John Addley of the University of Hartford, and Dean Roy Senour, Jr., of Pratt Institute, have saved me from many errors and have generally improved the whole enterprise. The task of the reader has been eased by the skilled editorial efforts of Mr. Maurice Eastmond of the Department of English of Brooklyn College, and by Mr. Barry Josephson, who compiled the index.

I cannot forego a special word of appreciation for the assistance and encouragement of Dr. E. G. Williamson, Dean of Students and Professor of Psychology at the University of Minnesota. Concerned in many ways with this entire project, he has lent his time, skill, and stimulation in generous measure.

Of course, as every author readily says, no one but myself is finally responsible for the views presented in this book, and any deficiencies in it must be laid at my own door.

HERBERT STROUP

✕ Contents

TOWARD A PHILOSOPHY OF
ORGANIZED STUDENT ACTIVITIES

-≮1

Perspective

IN MARCH of 1958 the staid and dignified Secretary of State, John Foster Dulles, was reported in the newspapers to say "he could not get excited about student riots in Indonesia because he used to be a student rioter himself . . . When he was a student at the Sorbonne, in Paris, Mr. Dulles explained, he used to riot from time to time. A reporter asked, on which side? Mr. Dulles chuckled and said that he could not remember and that this just served to prove his point."[1]

For our present purposes, student activities may be classified as unofficial and official. The type Mr. Dulles described is mainly unofficial — neither organized nor granted specific sanction by the university. The second type, described in the latter part of this chapter, is official — the university counts them among its approved activities. Although the two kinds may overlap on occasion, it is well for analytic purposes to consider them separately. Certain aspects of the unofficial kind will be reviewed first.

The continuous flow of exacerbating information about negative student behavior reported in the mass communications media is one of the primary characteristics of the current situation in higher education. Little is heard from today's youth regarding problems having to do with the academic side of student life in America's colleges and universities. Apparently, whatever courses and requirements are established

NOTE: This chapter is based in part on my article, "Role of Student Activities in the University," *Association of American Colleges Bulletin*, 41 (1955), 436–437, reproduced here in modified form with the permission of the publisher.

for certificates and degrees by faculty committees and governing boards are perfectly well accepted by the students. Only rarely do students organize to press for curricular changes, the expansion of the library, increased faculty promotions, and like matters. Educators themselves have issued a plethora of detailed reports on ways of improving higher education, but at few points is their enthusiasm for improvement paralleled in the student bodies of the land.

Students are strongly interested, however, in the nonacademic phases of college life; the newspapers contain reports of continual student agitation. Students at Marquette University in Milwaukee rise up in indignation because the officials ban "good-night kisses."[2] At the University of Michigan in Ann Arbor, five hundred rebel against "starchy, inadequate and improperly prepared meals."[3] Students at Lamar State College of Technology in Beaumont, Texas, draw up a formal petition protesting antisegregation picketing of the college by a newly organized white citizens' council.[4] Princeton University revises procedures for election to eating clubs when a charge of discrimination is made.[5] Three are found guilty at the University of Wisconsin of an attempted bombing of a Jewish student center.[6] Thirty-one at the Massachusetts Institute of Technology are arrested during riots protesting the quality of food and the increased cost of lodging.[7] At Cornell University, eight hundred demonstrate against the administration's ban on parties in students' off-campus apartments, and press other alleged grievances.[8] These few fairly representative examples of student agitation concerning noncurricular life illustrate the intense feelings of students about matters which, they think, vitally affect them. On the basis of spotty evidence it would seem that students feel more deeply about the nonacademic aspects of education than about what goes on in the classrooms, making the charges of professional surveyors and writers that today's students are a "gloriously contented" generation seem too pat.[9]

Others, too, would question the findings that college students are a conservative, pacific group. Every college town has its contingent of irate citizens ready to complain about sundry evils perpetrated by "those kids on the hill." Many are unwilling to condone what they term "sowing wild oats." At worst these critics believe the present generation is more obstreperous and lawless than any in the past. But on this score some cultural and historical perspective is required. Several years ago, in West Germany, the university and technical students threatened a nationwide strike to "bring their financial plight to the attention of public opinion." [10] Again, in 1956, a few days before President Eisenhower met his fellow presidents of the Americas at a historic gathering in Panama, student turbulence in several Central American countries caused widespread comment throughout the hemisphere.[11] In every section of the world, including that of the Soviet imperialism (Hungary's rebellion was led in a significant degree by university students), college students regularly engage in organized expressions of discontent and even of political rebellion.

Historically, too, students have at times proven to be unruly and in need of discipline. A university president of today who is approached by nervous trustees about the "unholy" and "dangerous" ways in which students deport themselves, needs to be well armed with the facts of the past. The behavior of their earlier counterparts often makes modern students at their worst look like pastoral nymphs dancing lightly across verdant fields sprinkling rosewater from sacred urceoles. Consider the following sampling of student problems encountered in medieval universities.[12] At New College, Oxford, an enactment prohibited the throwing of stones in chapel. At Leipzig there were graded penalties for the student who picked up a stone to throw at a professor, the student who threw and missed, and the student who threw and accomplished his objective.

The courts of the medieval period also dealt with cases of student restiveness, of which records remain. A student at Bologna was attacked with a cutlass in the classroom, to the hurt not only of himself but of those who had assembled to hear the lecture of "a noble and egregious doctor of laws." In 1289, in the same university, a student was set upon in the street in front of a lecture room by a certain scribe, "who wounded him on the head with a stone, so that much blood gushed forth," while two companions gave aid and counsel, saying, "Give it to him, hit him."

If the university president of today cannot convince his trustees of the idyllic character of his students on the basis of the evidence thus far offered, he can always ask: "Do you know anything about the Carnival Riot of 1228–1229 in Paris?" The trustee who can pass this examination should be awarded an honorary degree. At any rate, the president should be prepared to read to his trustees Rashdall's account of this historic event.[13]

Throughout America, far and wide in the world, in the distant past as well as today, students in higher education have regularly given vent to strong feelings of discontent with the noncurricular side of their educational life. In the face of such expression, there seems to be no reason to think that American students are morally better or worse than their predecessors; certainly they are not as violent as those elsewhere. Seldom is anyone seriously hurt or killed in the protest activities of American college students. Death, however, is a not infrequent concomitant of student riots in other parts of the world.

Thus far there has been no extended effort to study these student disturbances in a systematic and scientific way. More attention has been given to large-scale social revolutions, which have been investigated by social scientists, among whose studies Crane Brinton's *Anatomy of Revolution* stands out as one of the best.[14]

In the simplest analysis, student disturbances in American higher education may be described as consisting of three major phases. In Phase One an alleged or real event catalyzes alleged or real grievances, with the students challenging those who are assumed to be responsible for the irritation. Those deemed responsible are rarely fellow students. More commonly they turn out to be administrators, since administrators in the bureaucratic or hierarchical institution hold the next to final official authority. When feelings and actions are directed against community authority it is the mayor, the governor, or a similar person who becomes the symbolic scapegoat. In this phase also the growth of combatant ideology is apparent, combining within it the simplifications, distortions, and elaborate rationalizations which are characteristic of the demands of the rebels.

In Phase Two the conflict is joined. Those who hold authority in the contested situation, whether objects of student resentment or not, are required to take a stand for order at some stage. The "battle" is joined at this very point. Those who rebel seek "justice" by their own description. Those who resist want "order" in alignment with the conditions they believe necessary to their own official dignity, the requirements of the trustees, the demands of public relations. Phase Two is characterized by reaction, counterrevolution, and even violence against the challengers (through the action of law enforcing officials). The reactionists also have an ideology in which the nature of their particular interests is made apparent.

Phase Three consists of settlement. At some point in student rebellion the "tide is turned" in terms of the power forces available to the students, to the college, and to the community respectively. The adjustment may consist of a complete victory for one side or the other, though in most instances it is not so clear cut. The ultimate solution usually provides some satisfactions for both sides to the dispute.

This brief and superficial description of the natural history of student disputes is an admittedly incomplete outline of the problem of student rebelliousness. Undoubtedly, there are other ways of approaching the problem. Another method which has its own followers is the psychological or psychoanalytic. This view, in contrast to the primarily sociological view just presented, lays stress upon the developmental strains of adolescence when youth protests the controls of parents in a strenuous declaration of independence. Adolescence, it is said, is often a time of rebelliousness. Where students are not able, by reason of their physical distance, to assert their independence and assumed maturity against their parents, they "take it out" (a response called "displaced hostility") on whatever authority figures are at hand — university administrators, the police, local government officials, and so forth. Both the sociological and the psychological interpretations increase our understanding of this problem, although both are far from exact in their scientific documentation and conclusions.

To call the kinds of activity which have been under discussion "student activities" is to make a limited, specialized use of the term. They amount to only a small and even sporadic part of the totality generally known as "student activities," for the term also describes that segment of the total collegiate life which relates to its noncurricular aspects. In fact, the great bulk of what are properly called student activities are conducted under professional leadership and constitute no conflict or power challenge for the university.[15] Those activities which may be categorized as official, briefly analyzed below, bear the sanction of the university and aim in some degree to be directly congenial to the educational nature of the institution. A classification of the variety of groups currently found in student activities is attempted in Chapter 9.

Student activities as a "professional" field shares a number of principles, concepts, methods, goals, and ethics with such related disciplines as social group work, progressive education, recreation, adult education, and student personnel work. In its professional aspect, student activities utilizes social relations within relatively small groups as a means of encouraging individual growth. It also is concerned with the development of social responsibility as expressed toward fellow students, the group, the college community, and democratic society generally. Its philosophy, whatever its ultimate base, respects individual personality as a primal end in itself. Philosophically, furthermore, student activities respects the requirements of democratic social living. Individual personal expression is freedom; social responsibility is order. Freedom and order in creative tension is a fundamentally accepted tenet in professional student activities.

A characteristic of professional student activities work is its voluntarism.[16] In a university the student is required to take part in many activities — mainly those of a curricular character. He must present the proper number of academic credits for a degree. He must meet the requirements of the university for specializing in subject matter. He must complete the work of his courses to the satisfaction of his instructors. But in practically all universities there is no requirement that a student participate in student activities; he may or may not, according to his own whim or interest. He may take part in one or more of such activities; he may be interested in joining a fraternity; he may take part in the university's debate team. In some cases, universities limit the number of groups a student may join, or the officerships he may assume. But such restriction seeks to avoid a conflict between social and academic emphases in his education.[17]

Student activities programs, moreover, are generally guided in their professional aspects by a trained leader who may be called a student personnel worker, a resource person, an adviser, a student activities worker, or by some other special designation. The training of the leader may be minimal and indirect, or it may consist of subject courses in graduate schools, and supervised field experience leading to a doctorate. The role of the leader is to participate in and influence the group process so that the decisions come from the exercise of knowledge within the group rather than from domination by the leader, by members of the group, or by persons outside the group. The student activities leader also is concerned to develop those relations among student groups, and between the campus and the larger community which contribute to the development of responsible campus citizenship, the maximizing of personal and social benefits for those participating in the groups, and the general advancement of democratic values.

In his leadership the professional student activities worker depends upon two kinds of knowledge. First, he depends upon the knowledge of program activity. He has a "content" to his purposes as a leader. That is, the leader must know something, usually a great deal, about the subject matter on which the attention of his group is centered. If he is adviser to a group of students undertaking historical research, he should be familiar with historical method and studies. If the group he leads is the student governing body of the college, he should understand the nature of politics, of parliamentary procedure, and of other factors which make up his content. It is true that the student activities worker cannot be an expert in all contents, particularly those of a more specialized sort, because of the multifarious character of group interests. It is well that he does not pose as an expert, but functions rather as an "advanced fellow student," a resource person, or an adviser.

The breadth of content required by the worker gives an indication of the kind of person who ideally should consider student activities as a profession. He should be a person with wide-ranging interests, the ability to adapt easily to the new contents, the humility to respect the authentic specialists within the various content fields, and the deep-seated desire to work objectively with the program materials which form the basis for the group's formal existence.[18]

The professional worker, however, has another body of knowledge to master. It is that of interpersonal relations. The worker must possess an understanding of the nature of groups, the ways in which groups form and disband, the kinds of conflicts which arise in group life, the ways of settling disputes, the forms of indigenous leadership possible to groups, the procedures for the establishment of joint goals, the manner by which groups relate to other groups and to the campus and general community, the role of specially defined persons within the groups and their needs and aspirations. In these and other respects the professional worker also must be prepared in knowledge. While it is true that some part of his knowledge of interpersonal relations today must stand on an extemporized, intuitive, or experimental basis, yet the social sciences are increasingly throwing light upon the nature of interpersonal relationships, and giving leads by which the professional leader may act responsibly and effectively.

In addition to possessing these two kinds of knowledge, content and interpersonal relations, the professional worker must be adept in applying his knowledge to group situations. This aspect of his activity may properly be called creative or artistic, since it rests ultimately upon skills which in part are teachable, but which are largely dependent upon variables of personality and situation which cannot regularly be predetermined and controlled. Since skill is usually developed through various kinds of practical activities under qualified supervision,[19] the worker looks forward throughout his lifetime to the continuous development of his knowledge of content and interpersonal relations. It is within a social laboratory that he seeks to develop his skills of leadership. Obviously the two types of knowledge and the skill of the worker are interrelated and even intermingled in specific situations.

By and large, another feature of student activities is its dependence upon small groups to achieve its goals. Other forms of group influence are not necessarily restricted to small groups. An audience of thousands may be deeply moved by the motion picture *The Ten Commandments*. A group of three hundred may listen intently to a lecture on the width of Roman roads. A clergyman like Billy Graham may persuade a hundred or a thousand to seek forgiveness of their sins. These and other group experiences, found everywhere, are not to be valued merely for the numbers of people involved in them. Student activities, however, is focused primarily upon small groups. How small or large a group must be in order to qualify as a student activities group is impossible to say; many consist of from five to twenty-five students. Some run larger, and, as in student governments, may represent larger bodies. In others, such as interfraternity councils, size of the group may be determined by the number of subgroups.[20] Occasionally there may be definite value in organizing large groups, although the kinds of personalized relations which are considered desirable in student activities are less likely to develop in large groups. Certainly, every campus displays striking examples of large student activities groups.

Student activities in its professional aspects is conducted under the auspices of an agency, that is, the university. The nature and the responsibility of the university greatly modify the character of student activities. Contrary to "liberal" notions of extreme individualism under which every person enjoys absolute freedom to do whatever he pleases, the philosophy of student activities is fundamentally based upon acceptance of the university as the primary organizational datum of its existence and process. Not every sort of group activity is appropriate to student activities, however suitable they might be under the auspices of other agencies, for a university is unique, a distinctive social institution with a commonly agreed upon, formally stated set of objectives. For the university to achieve its specified goals, it is necessary to define the nature and extent of the activities which may be sponsored by it, whether curricular or noncurricular in kind. This point forms in large part the subject for discussion in Chapter 4.

Again, and more positively, student activities in the university is possible because the organized university exists, with its various physical, personnel, and community resources. A group seeking formation under the auspices of the university is the recipient of a vast and complex heritage, and a present system of advantages not available elsewhere to the forming group. Students of history who wish to know about the concept of history in preliterate societies, for instance, may call upon a faculty member who is an anthropologist for an explanation. Those students, moreover, who have the opportunity of attending a national meeting of student government leaders enjoy this privilege because they are a very definite part of a social institution, a university.

Student activities in the university is not conducted in an organizational vacuum. It exists because the university exists. Students who participate in it, as well as leaders who guide it, must take into account constantly the fact that they are members of an academic community with distinct and formal bases for existence and operation.

Finally, professional student activities is an educational process.[21] Some educators have shown a ready inclination to look upon student activities as a "fringe benefit" of a college education. They have considered it an appendage to university life of lower value than classroom activity or library study. They have thought that, by reason of the several characteristics previously attributed to student activities, it possesses no clear educational base. It is true that the educational value of student activities varies from university to university, and between groups within any given university. Student activities can show no guarantee to assure anyone of its high educational value. To an uncomfortably large extent student activities at present lacks a genuinely articulate basis in educational theory by which it could be generally justified as an important segment of the total life of the university. Its closest friends are often its severest critics. Yet, the claim may properly be made that student activities is an educational process. The educational nature of student activities rests primarily upon the educational goals to which the process is directed.

These goals require both knowledge and skill. With the professional leaders, the knowledge forming the educational process is knowledge of both content and interpersonal relationships. The student who engages under the direction of a faculty adviser in conducting a scientific survey to discover the nature and extent of student expenses may find in this relation certain gains in knowledge which may have eluded him in his economics classroom. The student who makes a special study of English statesmen to determine the correlation between collegiate debating skill and high political attainment has surely added to his general store of important information.

But content knowledge is only one part of the total; the student also learns about the nature of interpersonal relations. He may spend hours with his fellow students and his adviser in learning how to assess student spending. But as he does this he also learns through observation and participation about the boy, for example, who constantly strives for group recognition. He may learn about English statesmen from participating on the debate team, and at the same time discover that he must restrict his own ambition to dominate the team, among whom are talents superior to his own. So it goes; the student learns not only a content, but how to relate himself to others. Both, it is claimed, under proper leadership may make significant and lasting educational contributions to the student. As many college students can readily attest, experiences gained in student activities can sometimes be far more meaningful and truly educative than those secured in the classroom.[22] Actually, however, there is no necessary basis for the competition and distrust which occasionally arise between the curricular and the noncurricular. Students in higher education sorely need valuable educational experiences of this broadly ranging kind, from whatever source within the university they may come.

Another educational objective in student activities, aside from securing knowledge of content and insight into interpersonal relations, is that of developing skill in getting along with others. Skill in interpersonal relationships is given a practicum in which to flourish and grow. Student activities without growth in knowledge and skill is student activities of a low order. It deserves everybody's criticism. Student activities in which the leader and the group grow in knowledge and in the skill of relating themselves effectively to each other and to their advancing knowledge constitutes student activities of a higher order. The student, then, like his counterpart, the student activities worker, is a participant in a social process involving both knowledge and skill. In particular situations the same knowledge and skill are required of both, although the worker and the student may perceive them from somewhat different personal orientations and embody them in different degrees.

It is satisfying to note, in considering student activities as an educational process, that both the leader and the students must be conjoined with similar backgrounds and aspirations. So conceived, there is no chasm or natural antipathy between leader and group. Both are following the same principles in the interest of achieving the same goals. Furthermore, it is of value to note that student activities so conceived is not in conflict with the curricular phases of university life. Both have a generic basis for existence; together they seek the same goals. To use a familiar figure, they are two sides of the same coin.

-⨍ 2

Background

ALTHOUGH student activities comprises a quasi-independent field of professional activity in itself, it is nonetheless closely related to such service occupations as social group work, adult education, and student personnel work. In the organization of American higher education, a large part of the noncurricular life of the university is commonly classified as student personnel work. There is in fact, however, no clear basis for defining the scope of student personnel service at the present time, since the activities included within the term vary widely from university to university. Borderline activities, such as many of the services of registrars' offices, fit neither into the curricular nor the student personnel phases of the institution. In the main, however, student personnel services widely consist of the following: loan and aid programs, general counseling, psychological and vocational counseling, job placement, certain medical activities, student housing, discipline, freshman orientation, admissions, and student activities.

Student personnel work is a hodgepodge of university-directed student services which derive their existence from the fact that in one form or another they are necessary to the efficient functioning of the university. Historically they have come into deliberative being because universities could not escape them.[1] Discipline, for example, is not a wanted activity. It exists because breaches of good conduct do occur among college youth for which the university necessarily must take responsibility. Moreover, though not a bank or a loan company, the

14

university has also assumed the responsibility of aiding students who lack funds but have the desire and the intellectual potential to continue with their education. A student financial aid program is the response to this need. By and large, student personnel services have come into being and have grown historically because they have been deemed necessary for the achievement of the goals of the university. They have been born as a result of the defensive position of the university; it needed them to protect itself and to maintain its integrity of being.

Insofar as student personnel services have been established on a necessary or defensive basis by universities, they may be termed custodial in their institutional meaning and role. By custodial is meant that these services are organized not so much for the achievement of authentic educational values, but primarily to regulate, control and "care for" students. Take the creation of rooming facilities, for example.[2] Universities previously were geographically dispersed, often distant from urban centers of population, and fewer in number than at present. Traditionally the residence college did not arise out of systematic educational policy so much as it did from the local enthusiasms of religiously minded citizens, state legislatures with limited funds, and similar factors. The basic purpose of residence halls historically was custodial. Students had to be housed and fed under some sort of regimen, and institutional housing facilities seemed to provide the best answer.

More recently, however, student personnel work has sought to be more than custodial in its functions. It has desired and frequently acquired a truly educational function within the university. In some of its aspects it has made significant progress; student activities is an example. In other aspects it has assumed the more highly developed theory and practice of related fields like medicine and clinical psychology. By and large, the amount of educational value implicit in student personnel work has steadily increased, although its proportion of custodial activities also looms large.

Historically, student personnel services are as old as university life itself, if the theory of their necessity is accepted. For as long as students have been selected for admission, have been received into the academic community, have bared their problems to persons employed by universities, have breached rules of conduct, have needed housing and food, have fallen ill — for so long have there been student personnel services, even though these services were not always performed exclusively by personnel of the university. The functions existed and were carried out by persons who by reason of some specialization gained by experience may be termed the forerunners of present-day student personnel workers. From this standpoint, student personnel services are very old.[3]

It is true, however, that the significant growth of these services came with American experience in higher education. Prior to the rise of institutions of higher education in the United States, these functions were conceived of as basically custodial. Within the European universities the notion of responsibility for the total welfare of the individual student was almost unknown. It was the American university which conceived of its responsibilities in other terms. These terms implicitly gave rise to what today is known in higher education as student personnel services, a loosely organized yet coordinated system of non-curricular services to students.

The contrast between European and American ideas of the role of the university has been summarized as follows by Eugenie A. Leonard:

American college life probably differs most from college life in other parts of the world in the existence of a program of student personnel services on all American campuses. While in European colleges all students are presumed to be adults fully capable of meeting their personal, social, vocational, and academic problems without the aid of any university personnel, in the United States students are thought of as immature adolescents requiring personal counsel, social supervision, vocational guidance, and frequently remedial academic classes . . . In the student's personal and social life the institution is held responsible for successful adjustment. Any conduct on the part of a student that is considered a breach of morals reflects as much on the institution as on the student. In Europe, on the other hand, such conduct is not thought to be the concern of the institution, nor does it reflect adversely upon the university's reputation. All conduct outside the classroom is considered to be the responsibility of the student and his family.[4]

Student personnel services in American higher education have undergone several periods of development. In the first, the Colonial years, these services were considered an integral part of the university. Student housing and discipline, and a general concern for the students marked the period. The concern of the educators for the extra-classroom life of their students derived in no small measure from the fact that the early academies and colleges were founded by religiously inspired men and women who saw in them the means of developing personal character as defined by the strict moral tenets of their particular religion. If they were to be true to their convictions, it was necessary for them to be very much concerned about the welfare of their students. That the early colleges were formed with quite definite vocational purposes (training for the ministry and for teaching) meant that a characterological interest was at the core of the institution's values. Colonial colleges were noted for their numerous and detailed rules and regulations, discipline being more prevalent at that time than currently. In every aspect of student life the university officials believed with justification that they were acting *in loco parentis*.

In the Federal period the colleges of the country continued their sense of responsibility for the nonacademic as well as the academic activities of their students. Religious motivation in the founding of colleges tended to be tempered by a growing sense of responsibility toward the whole community, secular as well as sacred, the enlargement of the vocational purposes of the colleges, and the mellowing of some of the ethical strictures of the earlier period. As more young people with more diverse backgrounds of belief and actions came to the colleges it became inappropriate for educators to think of education as a means to personal salvation, although they continued as in the earlier period to consider ethical training and citizenship as fundamental to their total goals.

More careful planning also characterized the Federal period. Originally students were boarded in the homes of the president and the faculty members, sometimes in carefully selected homes in the local community. In time the officials of the universities, faced with enlarged enrollments, found these means inadequate. At this stage dormitories and other physical facilities were created to meet the students' needs. Punishments for breaches of conduct were less often physical than in the Colonial period, although still generously meted out on all campuses.

The Federal period, then, witnessed the establishment of student activities. Confined to their campuses, often in rural areas, under strict behavioral regulations, students turned to the formation of college literary and other societies as a means of self-expression. Collegiate athletics also emerged in this period, approved of largely as a means of ridding students of excess physical energies. Student health became a concern of the college authorities. In other ways the student personnel services begun in the Colonial period blossomed in the Federal period, some new flowers being added to the traditional bouquet.

The distinguishing characteristic of the following period (beginning in the nineteenth century) in the growth of American higher education was the introduction of persons with specifically designated student personnel function and titles. This period was noted for the rapid expansion of higher education, the introduction of a large number of new curricula to meet the demands for a more generally trained citizenry, and the growing complexity of college life and administration. After the Federal period, colleges became more numerous, extending from coast to coast, with those already in existence tending to become much larger. The aims of the universities underwent modification. Previously, higher education had been considered proper only for a select few — those who intended to enter professions such as the ministry and law. Gradually, however, higher education came to be regarded as a necessary background to the many other professions required by a burgeoning economy. Women's colleges were established on the ground that educated men needed educated wives, and that women might make a suitable social contribution, aside from marriage, especially in teaching. Many men's colleges became coeducational, a change introducing a host of new conditions and problems which required a special staff to handle them.

The manner by which specialized personnel came into being to administer the fast-growing student services was neither sudden nor dramatic. As persons were found who could properly relieve college administrators of detailed work with students, the tasks were assigned. As enough tasks were found, they were assigned to people especially skilled in interpersonal relations. Gradually a corps of workers arose who stood in a quasi-administrative position in relation to students, doing what formerly had been done by college administrators:

Trustees could no longer take an active part in campus life. Presidents could no longer personally supervise the study halls, assign students to rooms, or tramp the dormitory halls at midnight. They did not have time to buy the food or teach the students table manners. Disciplinary problems, except for the most serious cases, had to be delegated, along with control of the numerous student activities, to designated personnel in charge of student affairs. Health problems they referred to the physical education departments and medical staffs. Thus all the personnel services started in the Colonial colleges and carried forward through two hundred and fifty years of struggle and experimentation were loosely organized into separate administrative units. These, in turn, became the bases for the present-day unified comprehensive programs of personnel administration in the colleges and universities of the United States.[5]

Student personnel work by the latter half of the nineteenth century had been firmly established, although in primitive fashion by today's standards and organization. Its practitioners were not "professionals" in our sense of the term, since they had undergone no professional training in graduate schools for the work they were called upon to perform, but even now the bulk of student personnel workers in higher education are not specifically trained for the tasks they have assumed.

The twentieth century brought further increases in the number of colleges and students, in the complexity of college administration and specialization, in the proliferation of curricula with its resultant need for interpretation, in the number of student personnel workers, together with the creation of guiding statements for the work, the establishment of professional associations, the beginnings of a professional literature, the development of graduate training programs in the specialty, and the enhancement of the respect with which such workers are regarded in the university and the general community.[6] In spite of all these developments, however, even today student personnel services exist only in embryo form. Student personnel workers lack a serious theoretical basis for their operations; they have only begun to look at themselves through the mirror of research in a critical way; they have hardly learned the full nature of their role in the university.

The rise of student personnel work in higher education has been both the cause and effect of certain other factors operating in American — and indeed Western — society within the last few centuries. The historical presentation given above describes only one dimension of historical reality, that which bears more or less chronological arrangement. But there also have been significant historical changes which, viewed from a more sociological or cultural viewpoint, enable us to secure an even more effective understanding of the current role of student activities in the university. Three significant changes which have occurred outside the university will be discussed as illustrations, as having had serious consequences for the life within the university as well as for society generally.[7]

Quite obviously the functions of the family have undergone significant changes during the past centuries. Directly and indirectly, these changes have encouraged the rise of student personnel work in all of its educational phases. In the main the changes affecting the family may be described as losses in functions. The family had long been the locus for a wide variety of fundamental or "primary group" concerns, as Charles Cooley characterized them. Education, economic activity, religious instruction and worship, political activity to some extent, recreation, and similar pursuits were centered in the family, whether in its nuclear or extended forms. Today, however, in the terminology of two authorities, the family has changed, from "institution to companionship."[8] Signs of the democratization of the family are everywhere present. The older hierarchical formation of the family with the father as the undisputed leader (patriarchal form) has long since given way to a more democratic form in which equality of husband and wife is assumed, maximum freedom of the family members is sought for, and participation of the children in important family decisions is increasingly evident.

In the wake of these changes, here only briefly hinted at, the family has lost much of its behavioral control. The child does not as readily today look to his parents for advice. Parents do not expect their children to turn to them. There is a large degree of individualism apparent in the modern family, so far as the sources of personal guidance are concerned. This relative loss of the guidance function within the family has led to a number of significant consequences, one of which is the rise of specialists whose function it is to advise individuals and families. These experts are participants in what has been termed "the family life movement." They are social workers, clinical psychologists, pastoral counselors, psychiatrists, parent-teacher specialists, group educationists, and others. They employ, in addition to the counseling of individuals, a variety of group and mass forms of education.[9] Student personnel work is one of the elements in the family life movement, broadly conceived. It constitutes a substitute effort at guidance in the light of the changing functions of the family. In many instances, of course, the student personnel worker is a substitute for parents in the sense that the parents are not physically available. But even in nonresidential colleges students often feel more free to discuss their personal problems with a student personnel worker than with their parents. One cannot account for the growth in student personnel work historically without taking into account the relatively rapid and significant changes which have taken place within the family.

Various changes in the occupational structure of society have also influenced the rise of the student personnel work field. With the growth of modern capitalism the varieties of occupation have proliferated. In former times the locality was the center of man's life; the guild and the family were the organizational forms of his economic life. Today, what happens economically in any locality is dependent upon an almost universal interchange of factors, many of which are not clearly economic. Man's work life is no longer centered within the family or simple guilds. It finds its expressions through complex, bureaucratic organizations, whether industry, labor unions, government, or otherwise. The tasks which the individual workman is expected to perform no longer are general. They now call for the highest degree of specialization:[10]

If every worker manufactured a complete car, each would have to be the graduate of an engineering college, and even then he could not do a very good job, since it would be impossible for him to be at once an expert mechanical engineer, electrical engineer, and industrial designer. Besides there would not be enough people with engineering degrees in the country to fill all the positions . . . Moreover, whereas the jack-of-all-trades is necessarily master of none, each employee can become a highly skilled expert in his particular field of specialization.[11]

The development of the division of labor that now characterizes capitalistic economics has had a profound impact upon education in general and higher education specifically. It has meant, first of all, that present-day society demands an almost endless supply of specialists. These require training of some sort or other. The universities as the responsible community institutions for the training of young people have sought to introduce into their curricula the many and various programs needed to give the economy the specialists it requires. It also has meant that the universities, to the degree to which they have been readily responsive to the economic requirements of their communities, have become increasingly large and complex organizationally.[12]

A second consequence of the social division of labor relates to student personnel work. As was indicated earlier in this chapter, the mere fact of the enlargement of American institutions of higher education has encouraged the formation and development of a special corps of workers who within the university's economy are set aside to manage the noncurricular aspects of student life. But other complexities also have been operative. The personnel within universities have been responsive to the same demands of the larger economy for increased specialization. Professors, accordingly, have tended more and more to become specialists — in amino acids, theories of learning, medieval French history, the music of Palestrina, or some other relatively narrow field of interest. One of the most pressing and seemingly unsolvable problems confronting the modern university is the high degree of specialization in the teaching staff. This situation, however, has many ramifications for the curricular and co-curricular life of the student. Increasingly he has difficulty creating a common rationale for his scattered learning. In that sense he is the creature rather than the creator of a fragmentized university. As Sir Walter Moberly has remarked:

> For many years the work of universities has tended to be done in an increasing number of separate water-tight compartments. Both for the students and for staff the attainment of a synoptic view or map of the intellectual world and the relating together of the different disciplines of study, on which Newman laid so much stress, have largely dropped out.[13]

Under these circumstances students are inclined to look to someone or some organization to "make sense" out of their experience, intellectual and otherwise. Since the professor often is concerned with his own specialization to the point of myopia in relation to such practical matters as counseling students and other activities, it is understandable that students look to others for personal and social assistance. This condition has been conducive to the rise of specialized personnel whose function is to interpret the university to the students, to provide opportunities whereby students will have an effective means of discussing their problems and aspirations, and to make it possible for the faculty to be respected in its primary concerns of teaching and research. One may lament the fact that this condition obtains in higher education, and wish that professors were more generalized in their interests and more directly and effectively concerned with students and their problems, but the trends in higher education in the last decades have been arrayed against any other development than that which is current.

In addition to the marked tendency within the university toward professorial specialization there has been a corresponding trend toward the development of a new group of experts — those who are responsible for the noncurricular aspects of students' lives, the student personnel workers. Having been given their responsibilities through the various "defaults" which have been described, student personnel workers quickly saw the need for their own content prerogatives, a sense of being an ingroup (professionalism), and the desirability of instituting training programs for the codification and advancement of the interests and knowledge of the field. These specialists are fast coming into the management of most noncurricular areas within the university, including that of student activities.

The third important change which has affected the rise of student personnel work has taken place in the realm of cultural values. The manner in which cultural values of former times have given way to new beliefs and ideals has been described by many historians, sociologists, and others, even though they seem not to be in detailed agreement amongst themselves. William H. Whyte, Jr., has given one account of these changes.[14] He states that the old Protestant Ethic in which this nation grew great has been replaced by a new Social Ethic.[15] By the Protestant Ethic Mr. Whyte signifies the virtues of self-reliance, thrift, personal ambition, individual independence, and so forth. By Social Ethic he means "that contemporary body of thought which makes morally legitimate the pressures of society against the individual." Its major propositions are three: a belief in the group as the source of creativity; a belief in "belongingness" as the ultimate need of the individual; and a belief in the application of science to achieve this belongingness. This Social Ethic, according to Mr. Whyte, is based on the assumption that there is an intrinsic beneficence in organization life and that the supreme good of the individual is found in identification with social groups. Today it is not the individual hero who is the popular idol; it is the team player.

While it is not necessary to accept every aspect of the system of Mr. Whyte, it is possible to agree readily that there has been a major change or series of changes within the cultural values of Western society. What precise forms these changes have taken may be difficult to describe. But changes everywhere in cultural values have occurred. Barbara Ward says they consist of the division of Christendom, the secularization of living, the rise of despotic governments, and the exaltation of wealth so that avarice and cupidity have ceased to be regarded as vices. She claims that these changes set in about the sixteenth century and are still in progress.[16]

The changes in cultural values, whatever they may be specifically, and however they may have come about historically, have affected the establishment and growth of student personnel services.[17] Secularization, the decline in the authority of religious institutions and precepts, has made possible the rise of the various secular "helping professions" (social work, student personnel work, clinical psychology) as interrelated but culturally identifiable institutions. The decline in the Protestant Ethic loosened the individual's reliance upon himself (*der innere Wert*), and gave impetus to his use of other persons and organizations to solve his life's problems. The growth of leisure-time values, in contrast to the so-called Protestant virtue of hard work, gave the basis for the development of the multiplicity of group activities, including student activities in the university. The rise of strong secular ideologies — communism, scientism, fascism — provided that cultural division which resulted in a value disorientation for many.[18] The growth of sociology and anthropology as charters of the culture of the world in part demonstrated the relativity of all human cultures, making value integration for individuals and groups (including nations) all the more difficult. The growing dependence upon governments and organizations generally for help encouraged the belief that welfare is a good which is extrinsic to the individual and is granted by political — or agency — fiat and effort.

In these and other ways the cultural values have changed so as to affect the whole of life. Student personnel work could not have come into being without these changes. Nor can it long endure without the continuance and acceleration of at least some of them.

Student personnel work, then, limited by the changes which have taken place historically and sociologically, is not a truly autonomous cultural expression. It does not stand independent of the other disciplines and movements within the university. Nor does it in any major way contrast with the role which culture historically and structurally has granted it. It must therefore seek a coherent rationale for itself not simply within the logic of its own dynamics, but in terms of the broader sweeps of culture as they in part play upon it.[19] In this sense it is culture-bound, restricted despite its own "science," to the role assigned it by the larger culture.

These changes have had wide-ranging effects upon personal and social existence generally. It is clear too that the force of their claims has been exerted upon the university. Student personnel work has not failed to feel the impact; to a large extent, it is the expression of that impact. Yet it is possible to discuss the history of student personnel work from a standpoint within the field. Both approaches, it is claimed, are needed for a full understanding of the background of student activities and of student personnel work.

⤨ 3

Shortcomings and Problems

INEVITABLY, in its historical development, the whole field of student activities has suffered from a number of flaws. Indeed, there is every reason to think that higher education itself has failed on innumerable occasions, and in a multiplicity of ways, to meet adequately the changes confronting it in a rapidly growing society. Aside from the downright inadequacies of its individual leaders, a "cultural lag" persists intrinsically within education.[1] Social institutions, of which education is one, are habitually conservative, are themselves great stakes in the existing order of things. Their powers intermingle and dominate society generally. For these and other reasons, then, it is difficult to imagine education as a radical social force.[2] Similarly it is hard to imagine student activities being more advanced than or different from both the total university, which gives it its immediate sustenance, and the other forms of consciously developed group life in society.

So it is, then, that student activities is open to criticism for its historical and institutional limitations, although it may prove more useful to consider the field as in the process of growth. John Dewey laid primary emphasis in his educational philosophy upon the concept of growth, believing it to be the root of all gain in values:

NOTE: This chapter is based in part on my articles, "Three Shortcomings of Student Activities," *Association of American Colleges Bulletin,* 42 (1956), 568–572, and "Some Unexplored Problem Areas in Student Activities," *Teachers College Record,* 57 (1956), 469–474, reproduced here in modified form with the permission of the publishers.

. . . the process of growth, of improvement and progress, rather than the static outcome and result, becomes the significant thing. Not health as an end fixed once and for all, but the needed improvement in health — a continual process — is the end and good . . . Not perfection as a final goal, but the ever-enduring process of perfecting, maturing, refining, is the aim of living . . . Growth itself is the only moral "end." [3]

One need not make growth itself an absolute or final value as did Dewey in order to appreciate its significance in human affairs. Clearly there is no inbred principle within human nature, nor is there any cosmic guarantee that growth will result from human actions, feelings, and thoughts. Growth itself implies value considerations which being comparative protrude beyond the usual connotations of the term. Growth implies an objective standard or standards outside the growth process which stand in judgment over it. Certainly there are moral ends in human experience other than growth.

But growth, interpreted wisely and objectively, is a suitable criterion for viewing the development of a field of human activity. Growth signifies process or even progress as determined by prearranged aims. The element of process indicates the passing from one stage to another, a progression in the attainment of maturity or value. In the previous chapter the development of student personnel work was briefly outlined in order that the various stages which have characterized its history might be perceived. To the extent to which student activities, as a part of student personnel work, has a history it also may be said to have or be a process. It is not clear at this time whether its process can be claimed to be progress, although many would so assert. One can hardly evaluate the nature of its progress if its goals are not precisely known at a prior stage or even at the earliest beginnings of the activity (hylomorphism). Yet, there has been change, change that appears to be relatively patterned. The field has evolved from simple beginnings to the more complex present; from the time of theoryless actionism to that when basic questions are being asked; from the interval when almost any "good" man qualified for leadership to the current period in which professional qualifications are guarded to at least a minimal degree by the requirement of graduate education.

To say that the history of student activities has been one of growth also implies the development from a lower or simpler to a higher or more complex stage in terms of moral evaluation. That which is inferior at an earlier point in time gives way to that which is better. It is inconceivable that growth take place without both the application of criticism to the process and the challenge of prophetic aims to which the growth can be wisely shaped and intelligently encouraged. At every stage in the development of a movement like student activities it is both proper and necessary to bring criticisms to bear upon it, and to describe the areas of its greatest problems.

This fundamentally and briefly is the aim of the present chapter. To begin, three general shortcomings of present-day student activities will be described. Later a series of problem areas will be delineated. It is the purpose of the remainder of the book to explore some tentative "answers" to these shortcomings and problems, although admittedly it does not seem possible within the bounds of current knowledge and university organization to provide prescription-like solutions.

At the present time the three major shortcomings of student activities appear to be (1) its submergence in trivialities; (2) its vapid sentimentality; and (3) its compelling provincialism in ideas.

The submergence of student activities in trivialities is in part a reflection of the general attitude and practice of the modern university.[4] Although the catalogue statements of purposes are lofty indeed and inspire in many laymen a blind trust in the efficacy of higher education, it is well known to those who inhabit the academic community regularly that much that passes for "higher" education is scarcely worthy of the appellation. Higher education not only has become infected with the disease of overspecialization and professionalization to a degree that threatens health; it also has taken on the intellectual fat of a monumental factualism which confuses pedantry with scholarship. This overemphasis upon cold, clear objectivity has led in many instances to an overworked concern with academic trivia. Oftentimes the shuffling and reshuffling of trivialities of knowledge have been termed research, which calls to mind a characterization by the late Carl Becker: "Research, carried on by professors secure in their tenure and under no obligation to concern themselves with the social significance of learning and teaching, tends to run into a barren antiquarianism, as harmless and diverting, and just about as socially useful, as crossword puzzles or contract bridge."[5]

Much of this same concern with trivialities has been cultivated — often proudly — in student activities programs. To the degree to which student activities reflects the curricular concerns of the university it has often simply mirrored the professorial delight with minor details of knowledge. More than ever before in social programs educators are stressing the great values of proper attire, proper speech, tea-cup etiquette, the "successful meeting" (meaning that no profoundly challenging ideas or interests are expressed). All too often it is Dale Carnegie rather than Thoreau who dominates in spirit the most smoothly operating of student activities programs!

Moreover, the organization and conduct of student government regularly reflect an overly conscientious attention to minutiae of rules and regulations. Student government leaders are sometimes more fearful of violating Robert's rules of order than of unleashing a genuinely intellectual idea or program. Devotion to motions, the keeping of the minutes, roll calls, interparliamentary and intraparliamentary relations, and so forth, have tended in many quarters to stultify the formally stated functions of student government, and have made of the high objectives of the student personnel movement a sham and a deception.

But one of the chief aims of the university is to provide students with aid in developing the power to use abstractions in a way that will enable them to meet a variety of conditions and problems. This view has been well stated by Alfred North Whitehead:

For those whose formal education is prolonged beyond the school age, the University course or its equivalent is the great period of generalization. The spirit of generalization should dominate a University . . . A well-planned University course is a wide sweep of generality. I do not mean to say that it should be abstract in the sense of divorce from concrete fact, but that concrete fact should be studied as illustrating the scope of general ideas . . . Whatever be the detail with which you cram the student, the chance of his meeting in after-life exactly that detail is almost infinitesimal; and if he does meet it, he will probably have forgotten what you taught him about it . . . The function of a University is to enable you to shed details in favor of principles.[6]

A fundamental question that must be asked of student activities is: To what extent does student activities assist students in gaining the power of abstraction? Admittedly, at present it contributes relatively little, although its potential is great.

Again, student activities has often been softly sentimental in its organization and implementation. Perhaps this characteristic reflects in part the "finishing school" concept of higher education still predominant even in the curricula of some institutions of higher learning. Under this concept the student is not prepared for participation in the full life of the community, but for some country-club style of life in which the more strenuous, implacable, and imponderable aspects of real life are repressed in favor of a stylized, sophisticated, aristocratic notion of the core of existence. No wonder that some educators speak of real life only when they refer to the tougher, more frustrating, less sentimental phases of the person's role in society! Higher education, including student activities, then, has become to some degree an escape from the full requirements of life, an escape for four years from the sterner demands of a sometimes merciless and impersonal society.[7]

Student activities as presently constituted in most universities also is expressive of an earlier period of American society and higher education. It reflects the values and activities of upper-class, leisure-enjoying young men and women, with fairly adequate family subsidies who fail to find in essentially rural surroundings the kinds of companionship and activities which suit their needs. But the university population of today is a strikingly different group in a largely different environment. The development of mass education on the university plane has inevitably brought into the university a collection of students who represent other than upper-class status. Today's students are in the main from the middle class, and they bring with them the various restraints and aspirations of their class. By and large, they do not possess the leisure time of their scholastic predecessors. Most American college students work regularly to support themselves — some in full, many in part. Faced constantly with bread-and-butter concerns as well as with the desire to secure advanced education, they have less time to give to student activities.

The number of home-resident students in the university creates a condition for university participation unknown to older generations. Today many students must leave the university each day as soon as classes are finished, to work or to assume home responsibilities of one kind or another. The larger number of married students today clearly require a different type of student activities program from the traditional.

Moreover, the fact that a plethora of noncurricular activities engulfs universities in urban areas is seldom viewed in its proper significance for student activities planning and organization. Thus, student activities tends to maintain a genial, historically limited, sentimental conception of its place in the modern university.

Finally, student activities has been surprisingly provincial in its conception of its role in the university and community. It has generally failed to re-evaluate its university and community function adequately in the light of the tremendous changes which have developed in American recreation. The following facts help create the social setting in which student activities must undertake its self-evaluation. Americans spent $4.3 billion for recreation in 1929, and over $12 billion in 1955, according to the National Income Division. About 70 per cent of this latter amount was spent on such "passive" activities as books, magazines, newspapers, admissions to theaters and sports, radio and television purchases and repairs. The remainder bought toys, sports equipment, flowers, memberships in clubs and fraternal organizations, and the like. This total sum does not include the almost $12 billion spent on vacation travel in 1955, nor the $7 billion spent on do-it-yourself hobbies (there were 12 million home workshops in 1955), nor the $28 billion spent in the same year on automobiles and their upkeep. And so it goes. The size of our recreation industry is one of the least recognized, least appreciated aspects of modern American life.

But the fact that the recreational habits of Americans have drastically changed within a few decades has not had a serious impact upon the minds of educators responsible for student activities in the universities. To a striking degree, today's activities programs appear to be much the same as those that grandfather knew. The failure of educators to develop new insights into the field and the means by which it might today serve college students indicates but one of the bases on which the nature and function of student activities must be reconsidered.

The provincialism of student activities and the rapid rise of mass recreation lead one to ask whether the university cannot properly provide for a program that would give intelligently critical students an opportunity to develop new forms of small-group behavior, and thus counteract some of the deleterious effects of mass recreation. Charles Siepmann summarizes these effects as follows:

Mass media inevitably lend themselves to false flattery of the masses, to the excitation of mob emotions and mass hysteria. In a society that cherishes individuality and at the same time when, through lack of educational opportunity, the majority are still intellectually semi-literate, such propaganda can imperil the whole movement toward cultural enlightenment. The virtues of individuality become obscured as suspicion attaches to those insights of the privileged minority that were in many instances defective only in that they were not available at all. The temptation is ever present to treat mass audiences as group entities rather than as individuals, each claiming a respect and due regard for his distinctive and separate personality.[8]

Rather than continue being dominated by the limited views of its function inherited from an earlier period in American history, student activities might well seek to experiment with group forms in which "group entities" and "individuals" are creatively understood and adjusted through the application of intelligence to group designs.

The provincialism of student activities in relation to recreationism is only one illustration of limited outlook and practice. Other examples are the fiercely held arithmetical conception of democracy, the social escapism of the older university orientation, the quick acceptance of the need for rebelliousness on the part of adolescents, the ready antagonism of students toward administrators as a reflection of traditional citizen attitudes toward government, the pettiness of group elections, the lack of institutional loyalty.

The above three major shortcomings illustrate the fact that student activities needs to look at its daily operations critically. In different periods of its growth new problems will arise, requiring enumeration, description, and remedial action. While these shortcomings are related to deficiencies within the field itself, other problems relate mainly to student activities as a phase of the total university and as a cultural expression, and perhaps cannot be categorized so definitively or solved so readily. They generally involve various factors which are outside the province of control by student activities personnel — students and professional workers. But they do invite scrutiny in any survey of the current shortcomings and problems of student activities.

Even though student activities has been so long an established fixture in American higher education, it is still so young as a field for group workers and educational theorists that many problem areas within it still remain to be explored. Of course there always have been programmatic problems: inadequate staffing, fee arrangements, controlling community interferences, seeking out student leadership, establishing appropriate relations with administrators, and the like. Problems of this character —

irritants of the program — will probably never be eliminated. They present a pressing, day-by-day challenge to everyone associated with student activities — students, faculty, professionals, and administrators.

There is still another range of problems around which has developed relatively little information and conviction. These fall in the main into theoretical and institutional categories on which one or another of the "committed" personnel among college populations cannot successfully pose as final authorities. Because these problems are primarily theoretical and institutional, help will be required from a variety of sources and disciplines.

The fact that the main problem areas of student activities today lie within the range of theoretical and institutional categories already points to perhaps the chief deficiency. Student activities possesses neither an adequate general theory nor adequate "intermediate" theories. To put it jocularly, its philosophy is like a pair of steer horns — a point here, a point there, and a lot of bull in between. It is well to note that student activities as a segment of student personnel services and as a professional field is only about a century old, having risen from the necessities of the university situation in the earliest period. Its history has been a compound of sentimental humanitarianism, naive "consciousness of kind," and religiously conceived group ebullitions. As the field developed, layers of professional responsibility from related disciplines were borrowed and shaped according to distinctive needs.

As might be expected, student activities today reflects the general values of past decades — especially those of so-called liberalism — leading to the exaggeration of the nondecisive attributes of human situations, the stress and counterstress upon innocent reason and psychoanalytic subterraneanism, the simple trust in general human goodness, and the exaltation of the expert as the guide of life. Thus, through the contribution of various factors, only some of which have been mentioned, the field of student activities at present rests upon unexamined assumptions which lack profundity, clarity, and cohesiveness. To say this is not to express pity or resentment toward the field; it is said in an effort to describe the situation in which current theoretical effort must find itself and from which it must proceed.[9]

The fundamental need, then, is for a truly comprehensive, interdisciplinary effort to state (or restate) the basis of the existence of student activities in the university. In a sense, our techniques have outstripped our wisdom; we are far more clever in creating methods than in determining the reason for our interest in the first place. Lack of an adequate rationale for student activities in the university makes it all the more difficult to convince administrators and faculty of its cogency and importance.

In addition to the need to know theoretically what the relations are between student activities and the university at large, there is a need for increased understanding of the values by which student activities is conceived and directed. The field is deeply fraught with value options. In other kinds of human pursuits, as in some scientific disciplines, there is no pressing requirement that a valuative position be taken by those engaged in the activity. To a degree all of the sciences, social, physical, biological, and even the disciplines of history and psychology, in their clearly scientific or pure phases require no definite assumption of a value stance.[10] Some would make the same claim for certain aspects of the humanities as well. Not a science in the same sense as those mentioned, in its operations, and based largely on knowledge gained from the several sciences and the humanities, student activities in a sense is an applied science. It is deeply involved with the question of value.

Conceptions of value rest in part upon views of human nature. Workers in student activities always act as if the field had a general theory of human nature in articulate form, and theory of a kind it has, since it is impossible to participate in the human situation without having some notion as to what man is like essentially. In general, student activities has assumed the presuppositions of the so-called liberal estimate of man and his destiny. It is these very assumptions which at present invite analysis in order to determine the degree of their validity.

Another pressing problem area in student activities consists of its relations to the curriculum. If the primary aim of the university is intellectual, as is constantly argued by educators, then an understanding of the relations between that primary purpose and student activities is urgently called for. Instead of conceiving itself to be a self-subsisting, autonomous entity of professional concern within the totality of the university, the field must find its rationale and its justification in relation to the whole purpose of the university. As is apparent everywhere in higher education, it is the curriculum which has been established to fulfill the intellectual aims of the university. Naturally the continuing growth of student activities raises the question of its relations with the curriculum and the goals which the curriculum implies for the university.

The revival of interest among college educators in the fundamental aims of higher education does not generally include sympathy for and understanding of the role of student activities. The report of the Harvard Committee on General Education in a Free Society is clearly unaware of the problem of effecting desirable relations between curriculum and co-curriculum.[11] It can hardly be said to be aware even of the existence of the co-curriculum. Even Huston Smith's exciting book, *The Purposes of Higher Education*, fails to analyze and evaluate the place of student activities in achieving the university's objectives.[12] Even though educators must recognize that the co-curriculum exists, they hardly appear to know what to do about it. They are a long way from formulating an institutional theory regarding its role within the university.

The professionals or virtuosos who supervise student activities have not sufficiently elaborated institutionally sound expositions of the relation of their field to the curriculum purposes of higher education. Any survey of the benefits said to accrue from participating in student activities, such as those constantly reiterated by professional fraternity leaders, will indicate that these activities have value. Usually they are claimed to have instrumental values almost exclusively pertaining to the individual student. By participation the student will gain, we are told, a greater sense of democracy, the social graces, experience in leadership, and knowledge of practical human affairs. We are told that those who participate are more likely to do well academically, to win graduate scholarships, to succeed in later life, and so on. But again these are personal rather than institutional values, and the "causation" arguments themselves leave much to be desired. Of course it may be argued, are not personal values and institutional values identical? In part, they are; again, in part, they are not. That is, institutional values seek to serve the individual student in the final analysis, but through forms which find intellectual and traditional acceptance in the continuing requirements of the university as a social institution. Personal values may be enhanced in a variety of ways by higher education, although they can hardly be said to control in the case of any particular student the aims of the institution.

It is precisely because student activities pretends to have a reasoned existence of its own (i.e., in contributing to personal development) that it lacks a completely adequate and intellectually defensible place in the total college. Should the curriculum and the co-curriculum ideally operate in a parallel fashion within institutions of higher learning? What are the points of relationship? Where do they interpenetrate? What demands does the curriculum make upon the co-curriculum in form, objectives and processes, and vice versa? Such problems of relationship, it is suggested, are genuinely pressing problems, requiring serious and detailed analysis.

The problem of the relationships between curriculum and student activities suggests that there is a growing concern with defining the role of the faculty in co-curricular functions. This question in turn raises others about the nature and the desirability of the rising professionalization within the field of student activities. These questions must be faced in any realistic account of present problems.

Originally faculty members and university administrators were responsible from an institutional point of view for the entire program of student activities, although the students did possess considerable freedom. As specialization of work became a significant bureaucratic feature of the modern university, the faculty became subject-matter specialists with little or no concern for the co-curricular lives of their students. As a result, the noncurricular responsibilities were passed from the faculty first, and later from the administration, to a special corps of workmen. Over the course of years the faculty tended to focus its responsibilities upon the curriculum, and at times became even antagonistic to student activities and other noncurricular aspects of the total university. This condition still holds in many universities.

Yet, the question of the role of the faculty in student activities has not been solved by this withdrawal from responsibility. Can the university afford for the students' sake such high degrees of specialization, both in the curriculum and between the curriculum and the student personnel services? Are there no values which the faculty as faculty possesses to contribute to student activities? Is the faculty helping or hurting its intellectual purposes by assuming little or no responsibility for the co-curriculum? These and other questions deserve to be asked widely in higher education as student activities strives to become an authentic part of the university.

It is true, of course, that in all universities there are faculty members who do take responsibility beyond their curricular duties to participate in student activities. To the extent to which the faculty person is a responsible participant, he is faced with the problem of achieving a more than casual or rotarian concept of his services. As a teacher he must seek for an intellectual explanation of the relations between what he does in the classroom and what he does in student activities. Although faculty members, as the intellectual backbone of the universities, are qualified spokesmen on this theme, they have engaged in too little discussion on a serious plane regarding their dual responsibilities. The problem of relationship remains because faculties apparently lack sufficient impetus to seek solutions on a satisfactory theoretical basis.

That a whole new corps of workers has arisen within universities recently to provide skilled student services also constitutes another phase of the same general problem. On some campuses the faculty appears reluctant to assume responsibility for co-curricular activities. Persistently, faculties have viewed student activities at their best as subintellectual and therefore outside their sphere. The rise of professional workers in the field not only reflects the rise in student enroll ment, but changing concepts of the nature of higher education, failures on the part of existing institutions within the community, and other such factors. It could not have taken place without there having been a change in faculty attitudes and responsibility toward student activities.

That student activities has become more and more the province of specialists merely raises a new problem rather than solves the old. What, we may ask, is the relationship of such professionals to the total staff of the university? How may the curriculum and the co-curriculum become more significantly interrelated if the personnel movement lies in the direction of increasing specialization? What are the implicit values sought by the institution through a program in student activities? On what grounds should a university duplicate social and recreational facilities available within the community? What basis in higher education (meaning the chiefly intellectual concerns of the academic community) does student activities possess? These and other questions regarding the relations between faculty and professionals need to be answered by theoretical constructs which will have institutional perspective.

Universities have been socially set in freedom to pursue the truth. Freedom is their need in order that they, through students, faculty, and administrators, may increasingly apprehend the truth. Yet universities are also socially set to responsibility under authority. In the attainment of truth there must be respect for authority. In fact, truth itself is an authority. Actually, freedom and authority go hand in hand. One cannot be conceived and realized — lived — without the other. This is the dominant outlook of many thoughtful persons in our times. On the other hand, in student activities there persists in pseudoliberal form a view that freedom and authority are not complementary but antithetical. Freedom is what is wanted by the student, both individually and in groups. Authority is what he fears and seeks to avoid. The common student test of successful and democratic campus responsibility is self-government, as though the students had rights and privileges which did not derive from their status as students, from their holding membership in an institutional community in which authority is a foundation stone from the moment of its inception to the present moment of its being. Universities are established through the combination of freedom and authority expressed by the citizenry in part or whole. Boards of trustees possess authority to a degree that in most universities makes the students' cry for freedom sound like a profound arrogation of prerogatives.

In most universities the relation of the faculty to the administration, and their collective relation to the board of trustees and finally to the community (in one form or another) are well recognized in theory and deed. In the student activities area the case is oftentimes different — even the opposite. Students have imbibed a "liberal" culture which has distorted "rights" as opposed to "responsibilities," and have in many instances claimed an autonomy which actually they do not possess. As products of such a culture, they find it difficult to conceive of an authority to which they must ultimately bend their individual preferences and convictions. Part of their disposition may be passed off as "adolescent rebelliousness." But much of it is a result of past and present misconceptions of their role as students in the corporate life of the university.

It is this misconception which presents other theoretical problems in student activities. How to conceive of student activities as providing opportunities for self-expression and development and still maintain the structures of meaning and procedure within the university which are necessary and significant to the education of students? How to educate students into the fuller meaning of freedom as being rooted in responsibility rather than its opposite? How to permit spontaneity and variety based upon individual and small group preferences, and still maintain educational standards of quality and organizational integrity within the academic community? These and similar questions are basic to the need for a reconsideration of the fundamental role of student activities as an educational force in higher education.

Of course the problem is difficult to solve in theory. But it is also increased in perplexity by professional workers in the field who have been educated themselves into accepting a false philosophy of freedom. They too believe, as do the students, that authority is the antithesis of freedom rather than its support. Strangely enough, even administrators have been known to join in the false freedom chorus. In a similar spirit, Mary McCarthy's founder of mythical Jocelyn College upholds permissiveness:

Under his permissive system, the students were free to study or not as they choose; he believed that the healthy organism would elect, like an animal, what was best for it. If the student failed to go in the direction indicated by the results of his testing, or in any direction at all, this was noted down and in time communicated to his parents, merely as a matter of interest — to push him in any way would be a violation of the neutrality of the experiment.[13]

Although this statement describes a fictional situation, actual cases could be quoted from all sections in the country.

The impact of the false theory of freedom as sometimes espoused cannot accurately be assessed. In many universities it is a significantly controlling factor in the operation not only of student activities but the curriculum as well. Its dangers as a public attitude have been forcefully expressed by Walter Lippmann, who says that mass public opinion and legislatures have come to exercise a dominant and dangerous influence over the executive functions of government. The result, he states, is that modern democracies have grown steadily more incapable of ruling wisely in peace and war. The root of the problem lies in the failure to defend and maintain the political faith or "public philosophy" which formed the basis of the convictions of the founding fathers. He calls for restraints upon this generally accepted philosophy and appeals to intellectual and social leaders to find a deeper basis for social responsibility than is current.[14]

If student activities is no more than a reflection and a support for the false philosophy of freedom so often expressed by so-called student leaders and even by professionals in the field, it cannot rightly be claimed that the younger generation is receiving a realistic education — one which would prepare them for the most mature understanding of the local, national, and international communities. Yet, student activities greatly needs a theoretical understanding of this problem, as well as a practical application of the insights gained through theoretical endeavor in order that the next generation of leaders may know both freedom and responsibility.

These, then, are some of the shortcomings and problems with which student activities is faced. Indeed, there are many more. Those chosen for exposition in this chapter to represent some of the smaller and larger deficiencies of the field have been reviewed not in the spirit of rancor, but in the confidence that growth implies criticism; nor have they been criticized without the intention to maintain what is probably the basic requirement of comment in this area: to assert idealism without illusions and to assert realism without cynicism.[15]

The task ahead is sufficiently clear: to tackle some of the problems already indicated and to establish where possible the framework of a philosophy of student activities for the appraisal of others. Where the framework is difficult to perceive, as it often is, it may suffice merely to set up challenges for further thought by those who are engaged in the field.

⤙ 4

Education as a Social Institution

EDUCATION has suffered almost as much as religion from a multiplicity of definitions. Everybody has his own idea as to what education is, and how best it may be described. Most of the definitions offered in the textbooks — and formulated by professional educators — stress one special element at the expense of others. Some identify education with its philosophy, holding that education seeks first of all to achieve certain goals or general values. Others claim that education can be understood only in terms of its long historical course in society. Education is as education does. Still other definitions stress the psychological components, the learning process. Education, it is said, is a highly personal experience, involving a teacher and a student. In addition, other views emphasize the "principles" of education, educational administration, the sociology of education, and so forth. Within each of these approaches to the nature of education various schools of thought contend, differing from one another while accepting certain common standpoints.

Student activities, and student personnel services as well, may be interpreted from almost all of these perspectives.[1] The philosopher of education seeks to understand and justify the nature and existence of student activities by considering its contributions to the over-all purposes of the educational enterprise. What are the philosophical under-

NOTE: This chapter is based in part on my contribution, "Perspectives," in Abraham S. Goodhartz, ed., *A Commitment to Youth* (New York: Bookman Associates, Inc., 1960), pp. 28–48, reproduced here in modified form with the permission of the publisher.

41

pinnings of student activities? What is its view of reality? What values guide it? How does it conceive that students learn about reality? These and other questions are asked by the person whose primary interests in education are philosophic. Again, the historian of education is concerned with the development of student activities. He too will ask questions. What were the circumstances in the past which gave rise to student activities? How has student activities grown and changed with its historical development in many social settings? The person interested in the psychology of learning will make other inquiries. What attitudes and skills are learned in student activities? What are the socio-psychological conditions under which leadership is developed? And so on. Each way of defining education brings a special perspective from which derivative questioning takes place.

It is perhaps impossible for anyone at the present time to construct a theory of higher education that would satisfy everyone. Indeed, such an aim is not mandatory, and if achieved it would deprive educators of opportunities for criticism and for adding to knowledge. Nonetheless, a comprehensive theory of the university is needed to give student activities its rationale and its role. Therefore, it is proposed here to view the university as a social institution — following Malinowski and others.[2] According to this perspective, a university is a system of concerted activities carried on by an organized and specifically designated group of persons who operate under a charter in accordance with definite rules and by means of a material apparatus.

Assuming this conception of the university — as a social institution — does not claim for the university a distinctive role in society insofar as its organization is concerned. Society features other social institutions: Gerard De Gre has described science as a social institution, and Helen Witmer has interpreted social work from this standpoint.[3] James K. Feibleman, who is primarily a philosopher, has recently described the institutions of society in a detailed manner. He considers social institutions not merely as groups of individuals, but as organizations oriented around artifacts. He says that they act as productive units with interacting elements: men manufacture appropriate artifacts, then the artifacts affect the men.[4] His views on social institutions nicely complement those of Malinowski.

The university, first, is a system of concerted, manifold, differentiated, and complex activities. These derive mainly from the formally stated goals of the university.[5] To understand the nature of the university's activities, some investigation is required of the several educational philosophies which currently influence the aims of the university and affect the role of student activities.

One of the widely accepted perspectives on higher education stresses the core principle of the centrality of reason, which holds that the main and even the sole task of the university is intellectual. The argument has been stated in various ways, but the basic assumption is the belief that higher education represents man's organized and persistent search after truth. Truth in this view is generally considered to have no practical or immediate consequences. At least the search for truth is not undertaken in order that practical consequences be achieved. It stresses truth for truth's sake.[6]

Such a perspective on higher education and its main purpose, at least in its most extreme form, tends to oppose student activities as being at worst a type of anti-intellectualism, and at best a worrisome nuisance to the instructor and the student whose full time should be directed toward great, historically derived ideas. The student is thought of as an almost impersonally organized "pure mind" who lives in the unidimensional world of intellectuality. In an extreme form, the instructor is worthy of the bantering attack of W. H. Auden in his decalogue for the "literary intellectual":

> Thou shalt not do as the dean pleases,
> Thou shalt not write thy doctor's thesis
>   On education,
> Thou shalt not worship projects nor
> Shalt thou or thine bow down before
>   Administration.
>
> Thou shalt not answer questionnaires
> Or quizzes upon World-Affairs
>   Nor with compliance
> Take any test. Thou shalt not sit
> With statisticians nor commit
>   A social science.
>
> Thou shalt not be on friendly terms
> With guys in advertising firms,
>   Nor speak with such
> As read the Bible for its prose,
> Nor, above all, make love to those
>   Who wash too much.

> Thou shalt not live within thy means
> Nor on plain water and raw greens.
> If thou must choose
> Between the chances, choose the odd;
> Read *The New Yorker*, trust in God;
> And take short views.[7]

The student personnel work movement in the United States has been largely a nonintellectual effort.[8] At times it has been clearly anti-intellectual. The history of the movement indicates that it arose primarily to answer certain nonintellectual needs of students: housing, student activities, loans, and discipline. In another aspect of its development, student personnel work tended to oppose intellectual values since these were predominantly the prerogatives of the faculty. In opposing intellectual values as the primary and exclusive values, it readily developed a systematic criticism of intellectualism, and a myopic affinity for so-called personal values — as though there were divisions to personality in the fashion of the outdated faculty psychology. Moreover, since student personnel work from its inception was considered to be outside the curriculum, it found it difficult to relate itself directly to the academic side of the university. Even today little in the philosophy of the movement is centered in the academic pursuits of students. The dichotomy and tension which result within the university are surely the responsibility of student personnel workers who have failed to see themselves as university-employed persons who should willingly champion the intellectual basis for the existence of the university as a social institution.

A second perspective on the aims of higher education admits the importance of both intellectual and socio-personal principles. This view lays stress — at times in unequal measure — upon the curriculum and the extra-curriculum, insisting that both are important, though largely for different reasons. One variant of the argument, for example, says the extra-curriculum is simply necessary, that students must have something to do beyond their studying, and that under such circumstances it is institutionally wise to give some recognition to the extra-curriculum. Nonetheless, it is constantly held that the curriculum and the extra-curriculum bear no essential relation to each other; they are run on parallel tracks of interest, standards, and faculty sanctions. Thus, the very term "extra-curriculum" appears when used by some educators to imply a fatal and final divorce between the primarily intellectual task of the university and the ancillary necessity of caring for the "life" of the students. At least, in this view, there is the recognition that something more than the curriculum exists — especially from the standpoint of the students. Within this view a whole range of student personnel services may be offered by the university, with the tolerant concession that the university is probably better with them than without them. In some instances these services are given considerable constructive attention in an effort to make them worthy of the other aspects of the university.

A third perspective on the fundamental philosophy of the university is oriented toward the meeting of student needs. This view does not generally stress the intellectual prerogatives of the university in crystal-clear form, nor does it see education in essentially dualistic terms. Its starting point is the student himself, what he needs. Of course there are several ways by which the needs of students may be defined. The Report of the Harvard Committee on General Education, for example, assumes that it knows what students need, although nowhere within it is the role of student personnel services significantly defined or described.[9] Usually, however, student needs are taken to mean those which students themselves define as important to them. Where this philosophy of higher education has been analyzed and practiced, the student is cast into a variety of roles for which the university provides clarification, knowledge, and skill. So the student is viewed as a person in training to become a citizen, a worker, a family member, a leisure-time person, and an individual soul. Generally speaking, this attitude toward higher education is easily able to recognize the importance of student personnel services. In fact, it cherishes such services, magnifying them into basically important activities of the university. In a few instances these services may tend to take precedence over the other goals a university may set for itself.

Within most universities, however, any one of these philosophies may be found at a given moment. On one occasion the intellectual values of higher education may be stressed, as on Honors Day. On another the ability of the university to meet students' needs may be emphasized, as when a director of admissions is recruiting high school students. Again, annual reports show a noticeable tendency to claim that the university is all things to all men in equal measure of the curriculum and the extra-curriculum. However, not every university represents a mish-mash of educational philosophy.[10] In a noteworthy number of instances, the philosophy of education supported by the institution is made available to all, as set forth in its academic bulletin. Such credos may be the result of intensive and long-termed study by appropriate groups or committees of the institution.

The activities of the university flow from its statement of its goals. Since in all universities there is some emphasis upon higher learning it is clear that the university as a social institution is unique, both by reason of its philosophy and the concrete activities by which that philosophy is put into practice. The degree to which a university establishes and maintains student personnel services depends neither on the cogency or intrinsic quality of these services, nor on any claim to be considered as a professional discipline, but rather on the formulated goals of the institution and its methods of implementing them. As a segment of the total life of the university, student personnel services are subordinate, contingent, correlative.

The university for which only intellectual goals are established is operating under a delusion. Inevitably, there is a place for student personnel services. The intellectual factor in human experience is not compartment-tight. It is not a simple building-block with which a monolithic superstructure of knowledge can be constructed. It is but one variable among many others such as physical and mental health, financial ability, personal maturity, and other facets of the socio-personal individual who finds himself in an institution for higher learning. Even the superior student may be thwarted in his functioning by various aspects of his experience as a complete being. He may be the student who apologizes for his low academic standing in one term by saying: "I guess I did so poorly because I fell out of love last term and that bothered me a great deal." Or, upon graduation his employer may say to a university representative: "He has such a thoroughgoing mind that he hampers his own success by being unable to get along easily and gracefully with his fellow workers." He may be seeking to cope with chronic headaches, a lack of social standing, a deep conflict over career plans, the need to raise money for fees, or some other problem of his daily existence which keeps him from his truest fulfillment not only as a person but as an intellectual.

With such problems the student personnel worker is familiar, and he possesses the necessary training and skill for their alleviation. These services for the entire student body are in a sense "defensively" needed — needed so that the sometimes higher values of the university may be brought to completion and effectiveness. The university, then, does not exist to serve student personnel values. It is the other way around; student personnel services are required to support and realize the full range of activities and goals which the university has chosen for itself and its students.

On the other hand, the role of student personnel services, including student activities, may be put less apologetically. These services may win clear acceptance within the university if they contribute positively to the student's development — personally, socially, and intellectually. The student with a reading disability may be able to graduate from college; he may even be an honor graduate. But it can be argued that he will be a better student if he benefits from the services of a reading clinic. A student may be able to pass an examination in a political science course, but as secretary of a student organization he may gain certain insights into political affairs, insights that could not be transmitted to him within the formal confines of a credit course. Bull sessions with fraternity cohorts may develop his argumentative abilities beyond the practical possibilities of a beginning speech course.

Not merely a repair agency making right what has gone wrong, the student personnel program possesses intrinsic knowledge and skill by which a more complete and effective life may be offered to students. At its best not merely remedial and custodial, the program is a positive contributor to the enrichment of student life. It occupies a legitimate and needful place in the hierarchy of activities and aims of the university.

The constructive character of student personnel services amid the totality of the university and in terms of a clear-cut educational philosophy has been enunciated as follows:

As developments in American life within the past two generations have radically altered the responsibilities of home, church, and other social forces towards the maturing boy and girl, the college has tended to broaden its role considerably. Our democratic society needs men and women who are aware of their cultural heritage, who are trained to think critically, reason logically, act responsibly. At the same time, college students need to discover purposes and values, to feel secure in their relationships with other people, to be accepted by both men and women of their own age group, to become increasingly independent of their parents and other adults. Brooklyn College, therefore, recognizes among its responsibilities the necessity of affording students the best possible intellectual training, and of providing them with a setting in which they may develop socially and emotionally into mature and effective persons. Only as the college, within its setting as an educational institution, meets the demands of both society and the student can it be said to fulfill its obligations.[11]

Such a view, formulated by a leading educator, combines a number of different educational purposes for the university, makes ample room for the full functioning of the curricular and co-curricular aspects of the university, and relates the university as a social institution to the larger values of the community. It is a commendable summary of the goals and the activities of the university.

In accordance with the previously stated conception of the university as a social institution, it is well to note that a social institution consists of a specially designated group of people who conduct the institution's activities. Many and discrete contributions to the total university are made by its personnel — faculty, students, administrators, student personnel workers, and others. These working as a team carry on the activities by which the philosophy of the institution is realized.

In a social institution there are gradations of personnel responsibility. There also is differentiated function. But what marks the effective social institution is the high degree of coordination required so that all persons within the institution harmoniously maintain their assigned duties. From the standpoint of the welfare of the institution all employees are significant in themselves for what they contribute. The man who keeps the buildings warm in wintertime is needed, as is the man who lectures on the art of Georges Rouault. The person who teaches English composition is needed, even as the placement director who helps students gain employment upon graduation.

So far as the university's activities are concerned, the responsibility rests in part upon specialists and in part upon the general activities of the specialists. In a sense everyone in the university is a specialist: professor, business manager, counselor, group leader, and president. Each is valuable to the university because of his specialty. But in another sense, each also is professionally responsible for certain general functions. The counselor must be concerned with and must have knowledge of the work of the professor; otherwise he cannot be an effective counselor. The business manager must have an interest in and knowledge of educational operations. Otherwise, he may hinder rather than help the university in the attainment of its primary goals. The professor, it is further assumed, must have a wide-ranging understanding of and sympathy with the whole set of activities comprised within the university.

Who then has responsibility in the university for student personnel services? A two-fold answer is necessary. To the degree to which personnel is assigned to perform such services, by reason of training, the responsibility rests upon the professional staff. Just as there can be no logic in requiring the professor of geology to teach according to the wishes of another person or group not intimately knowledgeable about the subject, so too for the so-called professional worker in student personnel. He must be respected within the university for his special training. There clearly are student problems concerning which he has the best training available. On these problems the faculty member and others would do well to defer to his knowledge and experience. The student personnel worker, then, like others in the university, is a specialist.

But there are general aspects to student personnel services concerning which all members of the university should be alert, and for which they should take responsibility. Counseling, for example, can scarcely be claimed as the absolute prerogative of the professional student personnel worker. Just about everyone in the university is a counselor — the faculty member when he seeks to answer the student's question about the subjects within the department which are most suitable for him; the business manager when he discusses with the head of the student government the nature of costs in the student cafeteria; the registrar when he explains to a student the requirements for graduation.

By no means, then, do the responsibilities for student personnel work in the university devolve exclusively upon the professional. They rest to a very large degree upon the general personnel of the institution. The professional student personnel worker is regularly involved in only a small number of student relationships compared with the total student body and the number of relations maintained by students with other than student personnel workers. The student personnel worker in many institutions is as limited in his clientele as the instructor of Roman history. Fortunately, however, the health and welfare of the institution are not wholly dependent upon him; rather they rest basically upon the whole membership of the university.

Included within this whole membership of the university, of course, are the students. So far as student personnel work is concerned they too have an important responsibility. The students are not merely persons to whom and for whom things are done by others: faculty, professional workers, and administrators. They are responsible to a large degree for helping themselves to achieve the goals of the institution. To this end, students are seriously and deeply involved in a wide range of activities which concern themselves. In many institutions the students maintain their own government; they manage, at least in part, dormitories, student union buildings, athletic activities, student activities, and other student-centered programs. In some universities the students are assuming major student activities responsibilities, such as the advising of student groups.[12] Students even participate in certain phases of college administration.[13]

According to the definition of a social institution previously supplied, a university consists of a system of concerted activities carried on by an organized and specifically designated group of persons. A social institution also involves a charter and a material apparatus.

The charter by which a university is managed is fairly complex, consisting of several planes of expressed responsibility.[14] On the highest level the laws of the federal, state, and local governments provide the basic sanctioning of the university's operations, including its program of student activities. These laws may be of two general kinds. First are those pertaining to all individuals and organizations regardless of their status as educational institutions. Second are those pertaining directly to the organization and conduct of institutions of education. In addition it is customary for a university to have its own written charter or bylaws by which it specially has declared its intentions to be itself. Such a charter usually defines the auspices of the university, its chosen philosophy, and such matters as the way by which the students and staff are secured, advanced, dismissed, and the like. A charter stands in relation to the university as does a constitution to a republican form of government. It is the "ultimate" basis of appeal. It provides the necessary "law" by which in open fashion every person attached to the university knows the nature of its administration.

In addition there are other rules and regulations comprised under the basic charter of the university. The faculty ordinarily legislates on academic matters: prescribed courses for all students; requirements for departmental majors; residence and citizenship; honors programs. Such legislation becomes an important part of the institution's charter.

Students also may contribute to the charter of the university. The constitutions of student groups, the constitution and bylaws of the student government, informal requirements for social conduct (such as the freshman tipping his hat to a senior), and other "laws" and practices make up a part of the institution's charter. Later in this book a chapter will be devoted to an analysis of the intentions of student activities programs in an effort to show one of the most subtle yet persistent controlling features of the university's charter.

Sometimes the person who cannot easily adapt himself to large-scaled organization speaks of the charter derogatorily as so much red tape. This term may also be used as an instrument of attack by people whose individual preferences run counter to those of the institution. Nonetheless, all social institutions must have a clearly organized set of rules and regulations if institutional coherence is to be preserved. Not everything can be done by anyone at any time. The freedom of all — students, faculty, administration — is enhanced through the intelligent development of an institutional charter, or as Shakespeare put it in *Henry VIII*, "order" gives "each thing view." Without the charter there is no genuine freedom, only unlicensed confusion. The charter at its best provides the tracks upon which the educational train may most easily make its way to its desired destination. At the same time, the charter obviously restricts; the train cannot run in every direction. The authentic need for a carefully worked out charter in a large and complex social institution is hopefully self-evident.[15]

As a social institution, the university also requires and possesses a material apparatus: campus, buildings, classrooms, signs, athletic equipment, stages, blackboards, computing machinery, desks, chalk, interview rooms, test booklets, files, student lounges, and more.[16] These facilities are not distinctive only of higher education. Most large-scaled organizations — industrial, commercial, religious, and governmental — employ much the same sort of apparatus. The university may use electronic computers to analyze the composition of its student body, but such an instrument is also utilized by other kinds of organizations. Although the university possesses no single item of equipment which is distinctively its own, the organization of its material apparatus is distinctive to itself. With all social institutions it is the distinctive patterning of the use of materials which is unique. On the basis of material apparatus alone, it is relatively easy to differentiate, say, between a church and a university.

Student personnel services also share in the institutional requirement of material apparatus, the nature of the equipment usually differing in no way from that found elsewhere within the institution. At one hour an auditorium may be used by students listening to a required lecture in history, at another by those attending a "sing" arranged voluntarily and without formal relation to the curriculum by a group of fraternities.

Yet certain elements in the physical equipment of a university may be more or less distinctive of its student personnel program. The purposeful grouping of fraternity houses, the presence of student lounges for purely social purposes, and the arrangement of interview rooms for counselors may signalize the student activities program. In these and other ways the material apparatus becomes important to realizing the activities and goals by which the institution fulfills itself.

The chief advantage of this approach to the university, considering it primarily as a social institution, is that it does not place sole or primary stress upon a single factor in human experience, nor does it magnify one sort of relationship.[17] The university is a large-scaled, complex, hierarchical enterprise, a system of activities managed by a body of personnel who operate under a charter and through a certain set of physical circumstances.[18] In the context of the university, student personnel services — it is claimed — have no independent or autonomous existence. They exist in order that the basic purpose of the institution be fulfilled. In part the student personnel worker performs specialized responsibilities which other university personnel could not accomplish as effectively. In part, however, his functions are also the responsibility of practically everyone else within the university, since much of what he attempts is by definition also within the province of others. Furthermore, as a feature of student personnel work, student activities is both specialized and nonspecialized. Not existing within the university by any reason of its own choice or demand, but because the university has need of it, it is an auxiliary function within the total social institution of the university. The student activities program secures its rationale only as it supports the chosen goals of the university in the details and general organization of its activities. Theoretically, there can never be a division between the student activities program and the rest of the university, between the curriculum and the noncurriculum. Both are contributors to the achievement of the university's aims. Discriminate cooperation is the methodology by which both make their contributions.

A working conception of human nature is basic to our understanding the nature of student activities. The next chapter is intended to throw light upon the genuinely fundamental question of all education: in what terms shall we conceive of the nature of man? The importance of this question is recognized by Philip H. Phenix in the following words:

The first requirement of any education is that it answer the basic need to be human. In constructing the curriculum the starting point is to make provision for developing those capacities which are fundamental to man as man. Just as reflection on the curriculum raises the central question of values in education, so also does it require a consideration of this other root issue — the nature of man.[19]

The nature of man is currently an important consideration because of the presence, in the student activities field, of certain unanalyzed assumptions about the nature of man, and because of the many conflicting points of view which are honestly held on that subject.

-✕ 5

The Nature of Man

THE student activities worker shares in the current confusions regarding man's nature. This situation is not of his making or choosing; like others, he merely "goes along with it," or perhaps he is held powerless by its tenacity. Certainly the worker is not often prepared to raise questions about the nature of man and the relation of such a conception to his work. His very failure may be taken as an indication of his inability to link his daily activities with the cohering principles of a carefully thought-out theory. As the workers in this field look more penetratingly into the foundations of the work they will come to see that some effort at conceptualization is required, for some idea of man's nature is implied in every phase of student activities, even if it is that man has no knowable nature. Current confusions regarding the nature of man account for much of the misapplication and fruitlessness of endeavor in student activities.

The principal recurrent issue in student personnel work has been appropriately summarized as follows:

Perhaps the most pressing personal issue for every guidance-personnel worker is the determination of what view or combination of views best describes his own concept of his work . . . regardless of the view held, a determination of it requires each worker not only to decide how he regards the individual student but also to consider the society in

NOTE: This chapter is based in part on my article, "Apollo and Dionysius: A View of Student Activities," *Christian Scholar*, 41 (1958), 573–577, reproduced here in modified form with the permission of the publisher.

which the student is to be viewed and how the student's relation to that society is to be taken into account.[1]

Indeed, such is the issue, a recurring issue, for each student personnel worker, and one of the pressing needs of the profession as a whole.

Student activities workers are unfortunately not alone in their inability to relate their work to a theory of the nature of man; practically everyone else faces the same dilemma.[2] As Ernst Cassirer has declared, there is a "crisis in man's knowledge of himself"[3] — a crisis despite the fact that we now possess more empirical information about man than was ever known before. The social sciences and other disciplines which deal with man as man have been rife with conflicting notions about man's ultimate nature. "Nietzsche proclaims the will to power, Freud signalizes the sexual instinct, Marx enthrones the economic instinct. Each theory becomes a Procrustean bed on which the empirical facts are stretched to fit a preconceived pattern."[4] In the face of these growing distortions and oversimplifications in modern society no principle exists by which man's unity and homogeneity may be perceived:

Owing to this development our modern theory of man lost its intellectual center. We acquired instead a complete anarchy of thought. Even in the former times to be sure there was a great discrepancy of opinions and theories relating to this problem. But there remained at least a general orientation, a frame of reference, to which all individual differences might be referred. Metaphysics, theology, mathematics, and biology successively assumed the guidance for thought on the problem of man and determined the line of investigation. The real crisis of this problem manifested itself when such a central power capable of directing all individual efforts ceased to exist. The paramount importance of the problem was still felt in all the different branches of knowledge and inquiry. But an established authority to which one might appeal no longer existed. Theologians, scientists, politicians, sociologists, biologists, psychologists, ethnologists, economists, all approached the problem from their own viewpoints. To combine or unify all these particular aspects and perspectives was impossible. Even within the special fields there was no generally accepted scientific principle. The personal factor became more and more prevalent, and the temperament of the individual writer tended to play a decisive role.[5]

The condition prevailing in the sciences of man is mirrored also in the humanities. Jean Paul Sartre epitomizes the human situation for many in his play *No Exit*, in which three persons find themselves in Hell. Condemned to everlasting wakefulness, the three sit in a furnished living room, where a bright light constantly burns. It is Hell indeed for them since each one is in absolute disagreement with the others. To Sartre there is "no exit" from this tragic situation; man is cut off from his fellow man. No way appears to re-establish the original harmony. This sense of estrangement from that which might give man his sense of balance and meaningfulness is a persistent theme in today's writing. Nathan A. Scott, Jr., has listed such examples as Céline's *Journey to the End of Night*, Djuna Barnes' *Nightwood*, Nathanael West's *Miss Lonelyhearts*, Robert Penn Warren's *World Enough and Time*, André Malraux's *The Walnut Trees of Altenburg*.[6] Undoubtedly there are many more which possess a wistfulness for the authority of certainty which characterized former times.[7]

In strongly critical terms, Charles Glicksberg asserts that current writing is "the literature of absurdity":

Heightened awareness of the meaninglessness of the human situation in a meaningless cosmos has driven modern man into a state of extreme despair . . . this is the crucial problem of the hero in much of contemporary fiction and drama: the man who cannot affirm with conviction, the man who cannot commit himself, the metaphysical "shadow" who has no grasp of reality and no capacity for positive feeling, only a haunting vision of the essential absurdity of his condition.[8]

Into this mold Glicksberg would put such renowned authors as Sartre, Bowles, Malraux, Faulkner, O'Neill, and Camus. W. H. Auden's "age of anxiety" has passed away; it is now the "age of despair." Nihilism, at least in sophisticated circles, is the rusty key to an understanding of man: man not only can no longer believe in anything beyond himself — God, truth, beauty, goodness; he cannot now even believe in himself. Only anarchic "molten gloom" remains.[9]

This brief account of the perspective with which modern literature conceives man, and the cursory review of the situation in the social sciences, are a prelude to an examination of the view of man held by student activities workers. Do they, like their co-workers in other fields, face what Kierkegaard called "sickness unto death"? It is not possible to report accurately upon the views of all workers, although educated guesses are readily available. It seems clear that many workers are glibly unaware of current intellectual and scientific events, so that student activities still seems to be firmly fixed upon the so-called liberal virtues.[10]

The classical lines of the liberal doctrine of man are evident in current student activities thought and practice. Since their sources may not always be known or fully appreciated by the worker, it is well that some account be given of them along with another perspective regarding man, the Judeo-Christian, which has informed the history of the West. The terminology employed here in discussing the sources of these estimates of man will be taken appropriately from the classical literature which invented them. For the sake of brevity they will be described in a simplified form, without reference to the many qualifications which they properly involve.

It was characteristic of Apollonian rationalism to stress the appropriate balance of life, its form and harmony based in reason, "nothing to excess," the efficacy of plain reason. Apollonianism is formalism. On the other hand, Dionysian dynamism, another Greek product, emphasized vitality, movement (both creative and destructive), tragedy, the nonrational. Dionysianism is voluntarism.[11] Apollonianism and Dionysianism each claimed hegemony over man and his world: Reason and process became rival supremacies, yet they were later interpreted as complementaries. Blending in popular thought as extreme and would-be exclusive tendencies in thought and life regularly do, these two philosophies of the nature of man provided an important historical and theoretical setting in which the modern doctrine — the "liberal" doctrine — of man developed.

It is the combination of the Apollonian and the Dionysian views of man that student activities to a significant degree has currently adopted for its own "student personnel point of view." The stress upon reason as the guide to the nature of the satisfying life, the implicit pacifism whereby it is assumed that all human problems (especially those of an interpersonal nature) can be successfully solved through rational applications, the belief that science is the pre-eminent rule of intelligent life and the clue to wisdom, the idea that tradition, race, class, and other ambiguities of social existence are somehow fanciful and transitory — these and other characteristics of the Apollonian view are deeply and simply expressed in student activities within the university.

In accepting the other Greek contribution, however, student activities carefully notes the importance of process, even magnifying it in a few instances into an absolute. For example, it admits the stress and strain of "political" considerations (within the student body, student-faculty relations, and involving students, faculty and administrators). Moreover, it is seriously aware of the need for the voluntaristic character of its enterprise (as divorced from the requirements of the curricular phase of the university). In these and other ways student activities gives expression to the Greek conceptions of the nature of man, conceptions on which the professional worker in student activities, perhaps even unknowingly, has so largely built his theory and practice.

The Judeo-Christian tradition is similar yet dissimilar to the Greek views of man. It rejects the heavy stress of the Apollonians on the cyclic nature of history, and favors a belief in the forward movement of man's development in society. The Judeo-Christian view, while it understands the strong potentials of reason, yet holds reason, like the whole of man, to be tainted with pride, and therefore, with sin. Reason is a wonderful tool when employed within its limitations — the best man has — yet it also stands under God's judgment as being less than God and, thus, a creaturely virtue. Therefore, there are human problems (our time seems to have its full share) to which reason cannot provide a solution. Rather, it may be assumed that reason itself enters into the defect of the situation. But, in the Judeo-Christian view, reason (which calls for justice) may be transformed by grace or love and find its true dimension and function in human affairs. Thus reason, in the Apollonian sense, is redeemed by an extra-rational element, although this element in itself is a fundamental expression of human creatureliness and is clearly not antirational. In this manner the Judeo-Christian view both agrees with and supplements the Apollonian view of man.

Dionysianism never really offered an explanation of human tragedy, in the main seeing tragedy as a function of merciless fate. The Judeo-Christian view knows full well the tragic sense of life conceived in the Dionysian, yet it places intrinsic emphasis not only upon man's rebellion against God, the Fall, and universal guilt, but also upon creation, the incarnation, the Holy Spirit as the guide of life, salvation and the eternal life. The Judeo-Christian conception of man also appreciates the virtue of voluntarism, as did Dionysianism. It understands that freedom is an essential condition to man's moral responsibility, and that creativity itself is rooted in this virtue. In the Protestant formulation, the individual is in one context the supreme criterion of truth, beauty, and goodness. The individual is "saved by faith" but such salvation is an *act* of the individual and not a function simply of his intellectuality. Such acceptance of voluntarism, in contrast to the static rationalism of medieval Thomism and the rationalistic fruits of the Renaissance, tended to produce in its extreme form an anti-Christian arbitrariness. It glorified the "rights" of man, special status derived from wealth, race, and nationality, the "right to be wrong" ideas of growing youth (and of all ages, of course), and the irrational acceptance of the irrational. The hard use of reason in relation to God became the soft use of reason toward man and his goodness. Reason became a tool in Dionysian spirit to justify the essentially nonrational instincts (needs and drives) of man.[12]

The Judeo-Christian tradition accepts the voluntarism of Dionysianism, but with qualification. The core of the restraint which the Judeo-Christian standpoint places upon runaway Dionysianism is that of inclusive and ethical loyalty to traditional values. That is, the Judeo-Christian tradition is troubled with man's disparities and demons. It cannot believe that all human urges are good. There must be hierarchy in values, and a discrimination through reason of standards by which voluntarisms may be judged to be truly human values or disvalues.[13] But, in current Dionysianism the corrosions of skeptical (scientific) thinking have been equated with a decisionless, neutralistic optimism about man's ethical abilities. Uncommittedness and frustration have gone hand in hand. Absolute voluntarism can only bring about absolute chaos, morally and socially. But freedom, says the Judeo-Christian tradition, is preconditioned by order; freedom and order are complementary expressions of the unitary character of the self and of the universe. There is no such thing as freedom standing by itself.[14] It is "freedom under God." The character of the restraint that Dionysian voluntarism seeks to negate is a defensible, ontological, rational ethicism based upon the nature of the Creator. To some degree, then, the structures of reason are applicable to the discovery of this ethicism (natural theology), although ultimately the *mysterium tremendum* of the Source is ever beyond man's grasp, and at times breaks into his ideas and social forms, splitting them open and laying them waste.

The contribution of the Judeo-Christian viewpoint to the understanding and improvement of student activities theory is manifest. The student activities worker assumes that reason and its use are not the final purposes of the student activities program, although reason plays a definite, objective role in it. "Scientific" ways of doing things within the group are to be sought, not as an end in themselves but as means to a final goal—the establishment of a community of justice and love. Although the ethical requirements of both justice and love need the full use of reason, they transcend reason often and at significant points. Without an acceptance of this extra-rational component the worker would seldom if ever attempt the daring, the novel, the hazardous that is implicit in his work as a professional person.

The forms in which student activities programs are organized (reason in application) are not ends in themselves. It is to be assumed that reason cannot of itself provide systematic "answers" to such "questions" as what constitutes the best form of student government, the finest means of sanctioning student groups, the most satisfactory ways of relating the university to fraternities. Reason, of course, must be employed as vigorously as possible in all efforts to provide organization, structure, and form in student activities. Yet reason in itself will not necessarily provide the most defensible form. The role of university tradition, to use only one illustration of the limitation of reason, is apparent in the development of different patterns of practice within different universities. Value may be tied in many instances to the variety of tradition, rather than the unifying force of reason.

The student activities leader also must assume that voluntarism is not a final virtue, although it plays a definite part in student activities. Self-initiated activities are still the best activities, if they in addition meet other qualifications. Like reason, voluntarism is a means to an end—the establishment of a community in which justice and love flourish. It must stand constantly in the university under the judgment of the structures of order—those structures laid down in the university charter and tradition, its stated educational philosophy, the requirements of efficiency, the delineation and goal of community, and in the ethical bases for evaluation by which hierarchical loyalties may be maintained with appropriate commitment.

The thought that students have "self-government" in any autonomous manner is a distortion not only of the condition of university attendance but of the nature of man's freedom. Students find their freedom within the structures of order within the university. Any freedom worth the name is valuable and efficacious only in that it is based on wider and more ethical foundations of loyalty to the whole community. Without a clear recognition of the complementary requirements of the university community as well as the "rights" of students, the freedom desired becomes a rebellious anarchism in which youthfulness may rightfully be discussed with the vocabulary of pathology.[15]

Lest it be said that the previous discussion of reason and voluntarism in the light of the Judeo-Christian faith condemns more than it permits, it is important briefly to view reason and voluntarism in the context of *kairos*. The Greeks with their fine sense of language have given us *kairos*, which means the right time. It is different from *chronos*, the formal time, in that its accent is upon the moment which is heavy with significance and opportunity.[16] Its use in the New Testament has been amply discussed elsewhere and its employment in current philosophy has added it to our vocabulary.[17]

Student activities is both a limited form and a limited process (another way of saying it is based both on reason and voluntarism). Insofar as it is both, it calls for a signal appreciation of the moment, the right time, the moment freighted with meaning and openness. For it is in the moment that decision is required that form and process must find their balance and fruition. It is in the moment of decision that the worker must employ his skill in mustering the most valuable elements in both form and process for the attainment of the human community. In one moment the emphasis may be upon form in the extreme. In other moments it will be upon process in the extreme. Ideally, in practically all moments, both will be related and blended in such a manner as to produce the greatest measure of student freedom within the greatest development of commitment to community.

Because the leader operates in relationships in which *kairos* exists, he can lay claim to being more than an unskilled workman. He can view himself as an artist or a professional. All his knowledge, all the knowledge that science can produce, will not enable him to act intelligently or morally in the *kairos*. Yet he must rest his actions upon the best that science has to offer, and must maintain humility in spirit (the mode of the scientist) to be receptive to advances in knowledge. On the other hand, to say that the leader must be free to act in the *kairos* does not mean that he is at liberty to do as he pleases. His freedom is his opportunity to express responsibility. The student activities leader is free as the artist is free — free to use his colors and canvas in creative ways — but in his use of freedom he expresses also his loyalty to standards and traditions upon which his freedom ultimately rests.

It may seem even after the foregoing discussion of the historical and theoretical aspects of the current doctrine of man in student activities that insufficient account has been taken of the confusion and despair which was outlined in the earlier part of the chapter. Apollonianism and Dionysianism are clearly two current forces in student activities as well as throughout much of life. The Judeo-Christian tradition also has been experiencing a rebirth of intellectual integrity. Edmund Fuller in writing about the West's literary tradition points out that both the Greek and Judeo-Christian strands of thought have been continuously in existence. He is inclined to believe that the Judeo-Christian view has laid the basic philosophy of man for the past and the present. The philosophy of nihilism, he asserts, has secured its strength notably within recent times. Man in the longer tradition is conceived as "individual, responsible, guilty, redeemable." Man in the new nihilism is "biologically accidental, self-sufficient, inherently good, ever-progressing, morally answerable only to his social contracts." Novels which accept the latter conception of man's nature are "the product of despairing self-hatred, extended from the individual self to the whole race of man, with its accompanying will to degradation and humiliation." It is the philosophy of the sub-man.[18]

Another essayist who finds that literature in the American tradition is not exclusively colored by despair is Randall Stewart. His thesis is that the assumption of Christian doctrine regarding man, as formulated by the New England Puritans and carried forward by the conservative wings of both the Protestant and the Roman Catholic churches, is perhaps more American and certainly no less democratic a social tradition than that of the present-day exponents of nihilism. He believes that such writers as Hawthorne, Melville, Henry James, T. S. Eliot, and William Faulkner stand in that primary tradition. Although this tradition was in part neglected and in part fell afoul of the radical thought of the nineteen twenties and thirties, it is now undergoing a process of restatement and reinstatement. He thinks that without the formulation of the Judeo-Christian doctrine of man and the divine tragedy of the eternal war between good and evil much of the cultural heritage of the West is meaningless and that our own despairing days rightly fall into the abyss of nothingness.[19]

Stephen Spender, also in the historical vein, puts the two traditions of literature into a somewhat different perspective, although he seems at many points to be in agreement with both Stewart and Fuller. Spender sees the rise and fall of a succession of literary efforts within the last decades.[20] In the middle thirties appeared those who sought to reconstruct the world, in the terms of their own "personified ideal." With the onrush of events these writers, often Marxists, have met a predictable fate. Those who remained behind their iron curtain of Marxist doctrine have continued to express their versions of idealism. Those who allied themselves spiritually with the West's free societies have formed another stage or tradition, that of "anti-vision and despair." But there were others, non-Marxists, who also belonged to the first group. Individualists mainly, holding no common view of man and society, although in agreement upon the need for radical change, they reflected the influence of Rimbaud, Rilke, Yeats, and D. H. Lawrence.

The second stage or period in the literary development of recent years, characterized by anti-vision and despair, has taken, says Spender, Orwell as its saint and leading example. Here opposition to the grand visions of life of the earlier period is almost absolute. Being is swallowed up by nonbeing. Art becomes merely the recounting of the process by which despair becomes all-encompassing.

Today, however, the third stage has been reached, and is characterized by three orthodoxies. The first of these is prevenient Marxism, although the number of its adherents is very small. The second is that form of literary effort which is supported by the foundations, universities, and mass media of communication. This literature suffers from a lack of imaginative boldness, from an overintellectualization. The third orthodoxy is that of the "religious and Christian." Although Spender finds himself uneasy in his own attitudes toward the current kinds of religious writing, he is able to discuss it with some clarity, at least recognizing that religion is playing an increasingly significant role in literature today.[21]

Although Spender's analysis is fraught with serious oversimplification and his own values do not always suit his readers, he has provided another indication that the "wasteland" characteristic of so much modern literary effort may well be ephemeral, and that the rebirth of an authentic tradition of Judeo-Christian understanding may be dawning.

Nathan M. Pusey, president of Harvard University, told his students that the glimmering of renewed religious interest is a part of the broader dissatisfaction "with what has come to seem an exclusive, arid and unpromising secular approach to life":

But whatever its source, it seems to me, one should recognize and be thankful for the fact and encourage it where one may . . . And we can do this without subtracting from, but indeed in fuller recognition of, the indispensable requirement within the university, which remains, as it has been first and always, to seek to know . . . The fruits of intellect unsupported by faith are not necessarily a richer life, but more often superciliousness, fastidiousness, or even lackluster and despair . . . Somehow the full experience of liberal learning must miss these pitfalls . . . And it is because of this that its concern is not only for widened knowledge but also for deepened faith. Beyond the intellectual quest there is another, where one steps out on the venture of faith.[22]

That President Pusey can accurately point to a quest beyond the intellectual is indicative of a profound stirring within modern man's estimate of himself and his predicament. The crisis in which man stands in his self-evaluation is not merely literary. Novels and others forms of expression are simply extensions of the problem.

The problem in the evaluation of man derives from older times, older than the scholasticism of the medieval period, although this philosophy was decisive for the staging of the present. In scholasticism, both in its Platonic and Aristotelian forms, the contrast between the existence and essence of the world was accepted. Existence was the world of imperfect reality. The essential realm was that of true being. Above both was God, holding them together in unity. The rationalism of the scholastic philosophy is a form of Apollonianism. In contrast to its dominance in the teaching of the period was the outlook of Augustine and Scotus, who believed that both existence and essence were a part of the ultimate reality. Accepting the unifying role of God, they thought that God was more than the unity between the realms of existence and essence. He was also will, and as such played an active role in the transformation of existence into essence. God was the power in being which actualized the potential in existence. The groundwork for the efforts of men had been laid.

Later, during the Renaissance and the Reformation, the role of man in the achievement of the divine unity of things came strongly to the forefront. Man was the measure of the universe, the partner of God in the actualization of existence. For man to assert his constructive efforts was not taken to be an expression of his demonism, the fall of man, but of his redemption and his divine character. Man, having become a part of God, viewed himself as an intrinsic part of the essential realm of being.

The widest acceptance of the Renaissance viewpoint in philosophy occurred in Georg Hegel. Although Hegel recognized the existential elements in man's experience, the antithesis, he regularly contrasted it with what amounted to the essential, the thesis. In the tension between the existential and the essential some modification of both took place, but finally synthesis resulted. This synthesis, it appears, of necessity is a clearer expression of the thesis than it is of the antithesis. In a sense the synthesis has been providentially preordained to be more of an essential nature than either of its ingredients. If it were not there would be no progress, and progress certainly is of the nature of essence rather than existence.

This idea in the philosophy of Hegel pertained to a variety of problems, including the historical. In the historical process the record is clear. Essence, now synthesis, is constantly triumphing over existence. The gap between man and God is regularly narrowing. The humanity of God is ever being expressed and the divinity of man is ever being achieved. Finally, both man and God become in some sense one; the Kingdom of God is a practical possibility on earth. Although men are not always happy and reasonable at any one point of their existence, they ultimately will be proven to be happy and reasonable since the idea of progress necessarily requires it. Thus reason tied to progress inevitably leads to perfection.

The romantic belief in man's efficacy and goodness in the eighteenth century was protested by other estimates of man's nature in the nineteenth and twentieth. Criticism of progressivism occurred as early as the nineteenth century, even though the gospel of Hegelianism popularly dominated. Our current philosophies which assert the constructive goodness of man are rooted in the prevailing systems of the much earlier centuries. The revolt against Hegelianism took place largely within the first half of the nineteenth century, although many are only now feeling the truth and full impact of the antiromantic view of man.

The basic point of criticism brought against Hegelian progressivism emphasized the estrangement between man and his essential nature, between man and society, between man and life itself. Instead of being a co-realizer with God of the final realm of essence, man was conceived to be truly and profoundly established as unchanging existence. As some like to say, a deep abyss lies between existential and essential man.[23]

The outlook of Kierkegaard is a striking illustration of an anti-Hegelian philosophy or theology which teaches that man is estranged from himself. In his *Concept of Dread* Kierkegaard pointed out that man is not only haunted by a failure to maintain himself in perfect harmony with himself. He is not only a creature of imperfect dimensions and capacities (including his reason). He is ever haunted and frustrated by a pervading concept of dread which is more horrible and profound than the psychologists' notion of anxiety. Despite the several partially efficacious means of self-improvement available to him, including psychiatry, religion, and education, man is powerless to realize his full potentiality. Indeed, he is powerless to maintain himself against the forces of despair and negation.

Again, the outlook of Marx is a primary illustration of man's estrangement from society.[24] The specific economic theories of Marx, as is well known by now, are clearly discreditable on scientific grounds. The manner in which Marxism has been perverted politically in the Soviet Union is also a sadly known fact. In a sense, Marx is more significant for his moral or spiritual prophetism. He saw clearly that the society of his time, whether capitalistic or not, failed to provide men with a sense of fundamental belongingness. They were cut off from the centers of self-management. They were antagonists of the social order. They were estranged. This is man's existential condition socially. One may disagree with Marx's economic and political conclusions, but one cannot disagree with his feelings about the nature of man and society. Men, despite the social sciences and all manner of popular education, have not been able to overcome the essential conflict (abyss) between the welfare of the individual and the society which at many points seems to stand against him.

Capitalism is not the ogre, though it may accentuate the individualistic and competitive features of society in its relation to the individual. Communism seeks to overcome individualism by stressing community. But the community of the communistic world is not true community. It is a perversion of the community in that the individual is swallowed up within a collectivity. His individualism is denied. The benefits of the freedom taken for granted in Hegelianism, by which the actualization of the potential is achieved, are denied in communism. The individual depends not on his own valorous efforts in cooperation with a self-actualizing God; he depends upon a transcendent historical process (dialectical materialism) for the achievement of the final stage in man's historical quest. The goal will be achieved without man and even despite him. This distortion of freedom, of the nature of the individual, of the character of the historical process, and, of other values and truths, makes the Marxists' teachings, both in their original form and in the Soviet version, clearly inadequate and demonic.[25]

Man in all historical conditions of advanced societies feels estranged from society. Society, by reason of its lack of cohesion, its ambiguities, and its open conflicts, regularly presents a challenge to man as individual man. Moreover, there appears to be no possible means, including that of reason, by which man can transcend this limitation. If self-actualization takes place historically it must be the result of the will of God and not that of the creative efforts of the individual, since the individual is estranged from the essential sources of power by which being itself is realized.

There also has been a revolt against Hegelian optimism in connection with man's view of life itself. Nietzsche may be taken as an illustration of the stance. The accepted orders of personal and social existence, according to Nietzsche, are those which lead to the progressive dehumanization and devitalization of man. No positive gain can be achieved in their continuance. The course of life historically is not from existence to essence; rather, it is the other way around. Life is bound by false values. There is need for a "transvaluation of values," that is, those values which dominate life today — esthetic, ethical, and religious — need to be overthrown. Only their opposites have the power of restoring the essential harmony between man and life.

In the critical viewpoint which has provided the current estimate of man, the concept of estrangement is dominant. The older masters may not be eagerly read: Pascal, Kierkegaard, Marx, Schopenhauer, Nietzsche. The newer and more derivative writers, however, form a considerable part of the reading of the intellectual of the times: Sartre, Camus, Heidegger, Marcel, Jaspers.[26] All are in agreement on at least one point, the estrangement of man.

The request that President Pusey makes, therefore, is one not easily answered. It is true that he is fully aware that the breezy, optimistic, secular or liberal estimate of man which predominated in its original and vital form prior to the nineteenth century still has great power in the university. He also appears to see that the critical view of man's essential nature and powers, largely a result of nineteenth-century experience, has value as a corrective. Not even the life of reason can save man from his estrangement. "Stepping out on the venture of faith" is the summary of his prescription. The nature of this venture and of the faith involved requires masterful and profound explanation. Student activities workers can share in this explanation, but surely they cannot be its sole dictators.

Student activities, working as it does with human beings in action situations, cannot long forego the opportunity of examining its own presuppositions regarding the nature of man. It will proceed hopefully from the desultory, accepting, derived, disjointed and unexamined position it presently holds to one which is more systematic, comprehensive, defensible, and constructive.[27] It is not necessary that student activities be the passive recipient of theories developed in other disciplines. Because of the nature of its own experience with human beings it stands in a singularly advantageous position to formulate its own viewpoint and make a contribution to those disciplines from which historically it has borrowed so much. The task will not be completed by one person, one graduate school, or one movement within the field. If it is true to the creative tensions of the historical process it will never find its end. Yet it must be begun with openmindedness, sympathy for differences, and resoluteness to achieve the goal.[28]

The nature of man is but one of many theoretical problems which confront student activities. Another is the problem of determining what theoretical generalizations are available to student personnel service, which calls for the systematization of viewpoints already in use, whether they are widely recognized or not. Unless student personnel work is able to achieve an understanding of its theoretical possibilities there can be no meaningful research. Without research the critical self-growth of the field will be retarded.

✦ 6

Theoretical Constructs

ALFRED NORTH WHITEHEAD once observed that "we are entering upon an age of reconstruction, in religion, in science, and in political thought. Such ages, if they are to avoid mere ignorant oscillation between extremes, must seek truth in its ultimate depths."[1] Since 1925, when Whitehead made his comment, there have been striking reconstructions in religion, science, and political thought. Sometimes this movement has oscillated; sometimes it has lacked an appreciation of ultimate depths. All the same, there have been seriously productive efforts which have sought both to avoid extremes and to develop profound understanding.

In religion, for example, a wide-scaled reorientation among distinguished minds (the Niebuhrs, Maritain, Herberg) as well as among the laity has taken place. The easy-going, activistically inclined, socially concerned, reason-dependent kind of American Christianity, after dominating a whole era, has gradually given way to a religious consciousness which stresses transcendent virtues, deep theological grounding, complicated social reasoning regarding the "new creation," and a clear distinction between time and eternity. The reconstruction Whitehead anticipated has measurably been achieved in the religious sphere. Similarly, scientific and political thought have undergone reconstruction.

NOTE: This chapter is based in part on my article, "Theoretical Constructs in Student Personnel Work," *Journal of Higher Education*, 28 (1957), 319–325, reproduced here in modified form with the permission of the publisher.

During the past decades, however, student personnel work has been relatively unconcerned and inactive in formulating and extending theory. First among the reasons for this condition has been the tremendous pressure of wholly practical concerns. The job at hand has hardly allowed student activities the "ivory tower" solitude and objectivity necessary for the development of high theory. Its custodial function has been accepted by many as its principal reason for being. Busy in supervising the laboratory, student personnel work has had scarcely the time and energy to return to the lecture in order to discover why the laboratory is operated in the first place.

Student personnel work has been content in the main to borrow its theories from other disciplines.[2] Analytic counselors have taken large chunks of Freudian or modified Freudian theory and have adapted them — oftentimes artfully — to the counseling function. Rogersian counselors have depended deeply upon the views of a man who learned the fundamentals of nondirective psychology in the Pennsylvania School of Social Work (chiefly under Taft and Robinson), which borrowed its theory from the functionalism of Otto Rank. Similarly, student activities workers only recently have been reading and using the materials developed in the "group dynamics" literature in which sociologists, social group workers, and social psychologists have been notably productive. There is certainly no harm in borrowing; in many ways it is a genuine virtue. Yet sooner or later (preferably sooner) it is obligatory upon a mature profession and discipline to promulgate its own theoretical constructs.

As an applied discipline, student personnel work necessarily must borrow from the theoretical sciences, the findings of the biological and social sciences being particularly relevant. Philosophy, moreover, assists student activities by its insistence upon ultimate coherence and meaningfulness. Classifying student personnel work as an applied science, however, does not relieve it of its own theoretical task, because the various contributing pure disciplines do not agree in all particulars regarding man and his social experience. Student personnel work therefore must fashion its own theory in relation to the whole of the pertinent knowledge available to it.

Student personnel work also has its own contribution to make to theory. In this connection it is significant to note that David Riesman recently substituted the terms "old" and "new" for "pure" and "applied," so far as the several disciplines are concerned. That is, he believes that to a considerable extent those disciplines which are old are characterized as pure, and that those which appeared only recently upon the academic scene are classified as applied. Such a distinction, if true, does not distinguish between basic entities, but reflects biased attitudes. He also shows that the new disciplines evince greater vitality and imaginativeness in interpreting factual materials than do the old.[3] If this is true, student personnel work as a new discipline possesses a genuine opportunity to make important theoretical contributions.

There is, too, an active distaste for theoretical activity among some student personnel workers. Perhaps this is in part a result of the selective process in the staffing of student personnel operations — those with a "practical" bent are preferred over those who by undergraduate education and personal organization are inclined to ask about the "ultimate depths." In part, the distaste for theory may be laid at the door of the professional schools in which workers are trained; courses may be too heavily biased in favor of technique rather than theory. Surely, it is also held by those of a neo-positivistic persuasion who feel that research enables them to forego asking the deeper questions. Whatever the basis for distaste, it exists to some extent, for Charles Wesley Cannom can say: "That philosophy has any relation to the theory and practice of personnel work will doubtless surprise some readers."[4] That such surprise exists has fostered the belief that student personnel work still awaits its period of reconstruction, and the hope that the next significant developments in the field will lie in the theoretical or philosophical spheres.

To an impressive extent the task of theory is answered quickly by many student personnel workers with the phrase "the student personnel point of view." This baneful rejoinder means that the field is not seriously in need of theoretical advancement because its theoretical needs have been met with a philosophy or a point of view. This stance or faith has been embodied in books, conferences, and articles with uncritical regularity. Its fountainhead is the well-known booklet, originally a product of a two-day conference, published in 1937 by the American Council on Education,[5] and republished in 1949. The main thesis is stated as follows: "The student personnel point of view encompasses the student as a whole." Clearly this finding is not new in the thought and practice of institutions of higher learning in America, although the university constantly needs to be reminded that it is an institutional goal and not merely the function of a corps of specialized workers. Considered as a philosophy or theory of student personnel work, it is decidedly vapid and sentimental rather than precisely theoretical in its intention and analysis.

As a relative newcomer to the academic scene, student personnel work has perhaps fallen into the "whole man" notion as a pious means to asserting its purity and acceptability. Surely few can quarrel with the point of view, although Robert Hutchins has consistently maintained that education of the whole man is one of the most meaningless phrases in educational discussion. To him "the task of education is to make rational animals more perfectly rational."[6] Aside from Hutchins and others, however, acceptance of the slogan of the whole man is widespread. In terms of the power politics of the university, the espousal by student personnel work of the archetypal idea of the whole man has given it a selling point which far outreaches any intellectual worth the term may possess.

That student personnel workers are in a special situation relative to their training, the number and nature of their student relations, and their over-all ability and perceptiveness to contribute massively to the whole man is a common but erroneous assertion. Many have been trained in as narrow a set of graduate school requirements as any other academician. They usually have fewer contact hours with students than do classroom teachers, and then only with a small fraction of the total body of students, and in specialized ways. There is little reason to think of student personnel workers as having greater ability than their colleagues on the faculty of the university. In many instances less formal training is required of them. Also it is difficult to see whether any special virtue lies either in the technique or philosophy of the worker. His techniques in one degree or another are widely practiced by others, and his philosophy, to be defensible, must transcend his own private preference in supporting the university's general goals. These goals, presumably accepted by everyone employed by the university, must be viewed as in process, and therefore liable to modification by the university's personnel.

So far as the goals of higher education are concerned generally, it is not to student personnel workers traditionally that thinking men have looked. Rather it is to members of traditional disciplines within the university which have developed greater depth of analysis and perception. The academic community listens with respect to persons like the philosopher Theodore M. Greene when he writes: "The final test of our efforts *must* be the deepest convictions, the actual behavior, the character and lives of our students after they leave our sheltered campuses. Have we really helped them to become more alive and sensitive, better husbands, better citizens, more humble and resolute and tolerant as human beings?" [7] This statement of educational perspective, of course, is very close to that traditionally advanced by student personnel workers.

Granted that student personnel workers are willing to construct a theory, what requirements must be met? A theory, to merit attention, must possess the following attributes: (1) its propositions must be stated as rigorously defined concepts; (2) concepts must be consistent with one another; (3) concepts must be such that generalizations can be deductively derived from them and given illuminating relevance and support; and (4) concepts must prepare the way for further observation and verification that will increase man's comprehension of the fullest reality. Thus evaluated a point of view is no enduring substitute for theory, and well may confuse the essential issues.

These ingredients of a satisfactory theory are in themselves "ideal types," as Max Weber might have termed them, abstracted from a large number of instances without implying that any one instance carries all of the attributes. However, even diverse formulations in theory have an efficacy which is beneficial. Although the psychologies of John B. Watson and Sigmund Freud are in sharp disagreement on the nature of man, both have been productive of serious human gains, each in its own way. So it is with differing schools of education, physical therapy, medicine, and social work. Although disparities exist and are even helpful in certain contexts, the theoretician still should strive for absolute objectivity. He must not be content with contradictions and half-truths. He must search for that which is the ultimate truth, even though in fact he may not reach it completely.

The reconstruction of an adequate theory of student personnel services is a challenge not easily met. Its realization presents difficulties which are not exclusive to the discipline but are found in other fields. Three difficulties may be mentioned (necessarily with marked superficiality) to illustrate the variety and complexity of the problem.

The first is linguistic. Every developed discipline rests ultimately upon common linguistic observances, which enable meaning to be widely and quickly shared. Student personnel work at present suffers from a hodgepodge of terms, many of which have been taken from other disciplines. It is not uncommon to find in some writing a single paragraph employing word and phrase categories which in another discipline carry different and even opposing theoretical meanings. The problem of the translatability of categories from one field to another has been given insufficient attention.

Again, the substitution of scientific terms for equivalents in everyday use raises problems which often invite evasiveness or arouse defensiveness. The degree to which professional terms have a shared and accepted meaning to some, and an indeterminate and questionable meaning to others, also bears consideration.[8]

Second, the work of reconstruction also requires serious attention to the relationships between research and theory. It is easy to say that no significant research can be conducted without significant theory, yet researchers all too commonly proceed as though genuine theoretical effort is somehow opposed to their activity. On the other hand, theorists also go their merry way without appreciating the fact that their efforts do not generate an autonomous truth, but are productive at best of constructs which require verification through scientific means.[9]

Third, while a theory in a given discipline ideally should be characteristic of that discipline and reflect its special needs and procedures, it must be distinguished by a high degree of relatedness to the theories in other disciplines. An adequate theory in student personnel work should find appropriate counterparts in a wide range of other disciplines — in philosophy, sociology, theology, social psychology, cultural anthropology, and the humanities. Paul Tillich, a foremost leader in contemporary reconstructionist movements, having described his life as one lived on the boundaries of some twelve contrasting interests and disciplines, says: "It is the dialectical character of existence, that each of its possibilities drives on its own accord to its border line and to the limiting power beyond the boundary."[10]

As student personnel work enters its age of reconstruction and develops theories of "ultimate depth" it will need to fulfill the drives within it to meet its own boundary, and will be compelled to cross that boundary. But to cross the boundaries of knowledge and experience intelligently, signifies both a willingness to face outwards and to be richly conversant with that which lies beyond the boundary.

The efforts to delineate a general theory for student personnel services have fallen into a number of categories of preference. Each category possesses meaning and has contributed to the development of the discipline. Furthermore, the efforts reflect and illustrate theories which are even more comprehensive and abstractive. A listing of these categories with brief comments may indicate the main possible courses of theory development within student personnel work.[11] References also will be made to people who have made significant contributions to the category.

The first type of theory looks to the community for the ultimate source and validity of its meaning. It enjoys using political concepts which involve some notion of power to resolve human differences of belief and action. Its historical hero is Plato, who sought the ideal community in which human variations and strivings would find a collective balance and order not possible to the natural man and his unrestrained impulses. Social order, a feature of such theory, continually asks: Will the proposed construct aid equilibrium or disequilibrium in society? Further, the theory is tinged with deep respect for the law, with a genuine belief that persons can be controlled and even beneficially developed through the enjoinment of legal methods. Its mode of operation is rational in that it asserts that all actions must be resolved in terms of the total community and its values, and in that it believes that reason possesses the necessary virtue to achieve the establishment and maintenance of social order.

The second type, ontological theory, looks to the nature of things — to reality or being — as the ultimate justification and verification of its meaning. It too is an accepter of the basic harmony between man and his fellow men, and seeks to show in studies of cooperation that peace and harmony are natural requirements without which man is untrue to his essential selfhood. It too is rational in that it believes that man can properly exploit reason and nature for the discovery of the nature of things. Science is its hero, and Aristotle, Plotinus, and Spinoza are some of its prophets. It is impressed with the harmony between physical nature and man, and seeks to employ analogies between the two as proof of the harmony of existence.[12] It is gnostic in its pretensions. Mathematical substitutes for reality (statistical correlations) are often taken for reality itself. Its concern is with proof rather than community feeling or achievement.

The third, mystic theory, is established on the basis of intuitions and visions. It talks about the various ways of knowing, as though the universe of meaning were a house to which there are different doors, some easier to open than others. Some people wish, we are told, to take the more laborious way of probing the nature of being. The mystical theory claims a constant and ready access to the deeper centers of meaning. The goal of such theories is the enjoyment of a relationship, the full glow of disclosed values and possibilities, and the status which derives from being on intimate terms with the heart of reality. It possesses what has been called for student personnel workers a "deontologic" efficacy.[13] Its heroes are Philo, Augustine, the Stoics, and the mystics of all ages. Mystic theories tend to be self-validating.

The fourth, anthropologic theory, is concerned with man as man, man the social animal, man the source and goal of humane values. It conceives of man — its constant reference — as intrinsically nonabsolute or uniform in composition, capable of study and varying conclusions. It is interested in concrete sociological and anthropologic investigations as means of throwing light upon man's complexity. Historically anthropologic theorists have been Pascal, Kierkegaard, and Dostoevski, among others. Not denying that man possesses an inward life, they have asserted the complexity of establishing at any point the final nature of man and his experience. They have not been too impressed with analogies to physical nature, but believe that man constitutes his own special problem — nature can wait.

The fifth, historical theory, finds its justification in events. It seeks to provide constructs which essentially involve historical reality. It is tradition-minded. It seeks new meanings, but these are largely developments, not new intuitions. New values are not created so much by rigorous scientific (gnostic) investigations as by getting close to historical happenings and meanings on which can be built present-day constructs.[14] Epistemologically it is a kind of theory which accepts and uses revelation. It often talks about a sharp break between man and nature; man is transnatural at least in certain aspects of his being. It is the theory of the Hebrew prophets, Judeo-Christian eschatology, Hegel in his theory of history, Reinhold Niebuhr, Martin Buber, Robert Nisbet, and others. In this view reason is helpful but defective or incomplete in its

methodology, science an instrument which runs the temptation of becoming scientism. Truth is disclosed through acts (or series of acts)
within a general, time-bound continuum.

These five types of theoretical constructs are suggestions for the reconstruction of theory in student personnel work. One or more may be
used for further and more specific elaboration of theories pertaining to
the discipline, yet with relevance "across the boundaries." Some may
be more appropriate to certain kinds of service operations which are a
part of the discipline than to other kinds. For example, student activities
workers may find the historical construct more productive of meaning
and value than any of the others. Yet student activities workers generally
have been seeking to understand their work by considering other approaches to theory.

The words of Mary Parker Follett, written almost fifty years ago,
have special relevance today to student personnel workers: "Never
settle down within the theory you have chosen, the cause you have
embraced; know that another theory, another cause exists, and seek
that. The enhancement of life is not for the comfort-lover. As soon as
you succeed — real success means something arising to overthrow your
security."[15]

The five categories of general theory are sufficiently generalized to
be applicable to many areas of inquiry and analysis. Undoubtedly, they
will undergo modification as they are applied to concrete situations
under investigation. In effect they represent stances from which the
same human experience may be viewed variably. As a means of making
their application more concrete, the following "event" is presented as
a situation to which the five categories can be applied in a preliminary
and suggestive way:

At an Eastern college, the student literary journal was impounded by
the Dean because it contained materials which were clearly obscene.
The journal is guided by a faculty adviser personally, and is responsible
to the faculty through a faculty-student committee. Later the journal
was published. Almost immediately, sharp criticisms of the college were
raised for its having allowed the publication. One group within the
faculty and the community resented an "off color" presentation of the
activities of a priest of the Roman Catholic Church. Another group
within the faculty and the community was offended by an article which
ridiculed Orthodox Judaism. Another group was critical because they

thought that censorship had been practiced by the Dean prior to the journal's publication.

If a researcher wishing to understand the event were to apply the five categories as a guide to his investigation, what differences in the kinds of questions he would ask of himself and the situation would these categories create? How would his practical efforts be influenced by the stance which he assumed in relation to the problem?

The community-minded theoretician might ask: What effect did the event have upon the sense of campus cohesion? What effect was made upon the college's standing in the community? By the application of power from which source (mayor, college president, or board) was the situation resolved?

The ontologically minded theoretician might ask: What is the size of the problem? How many people are involved and with what quantitative results? How can the reality of the event be described in objective (mathematical) terms? What essentially and descriptively happened in the situation?

The mystically minded theoretician might ask: Out of which motives did the actions arise, and for which goals not superficially discernible? What was the qualitative effect of the event upon values in general? What can and should one learn from this event?

The anthropologically minded theoretician might ask: How is this event related structurally (human organization of persons and groups) to similar and dissimilar situations in other settings? In what manner does this event illustrate conclusions generally demonstrable concerning man and his behavior? In what sense may the event be considered a social process with analyzable parts?

The historically minded theoretician might ask: How has this particular event developed in the light of the past within the college and the community? In what way does this situation secure its specific meaning from understanding the past occurrences of this sort in higher education? What does the concrete act disclose of the nature of human behavior?

Obviously these questions are not exhaustive of the meanings behind the five categories of theory; they are intended merely to be illustrative. Despite an evident overlap among the questions, there also is a distinctiveness which is often only assumed to be present in empirical studies employing such theoretical constructs.

Admittedly, what has been said here about the nature and types of theoretical constructs currently available to student personnel workers is only a beginning. On the basis of criticism and other independent investigation the field may in time develop a substantial and dependable body of general theory.

-≮ 7

Values

TO A large degree the form of student activities is shaped by the kinds of interests brought to bear upon it. These many types of interests have combined to produce a large, complex, scattered pattern of activities in American universities and colleges, a configuration molded over decades by the diverse and even conflicting attitudes of students, faculties, administrators, and communities. To make sense of this scattered pattern of activities is one of the principal tasks facing the university today. What is needed is an adequate phenomenology of student activities. Phenomenological achievements, it is hoped, will lead eventually to ontological clarity.

Present interests affecting the form of student activities may be classified roughly under five categories:

First is personal interest. The living, naive, continuing involvement of young men and women in initiating and maintaining student activities groups and programs transcends all other interests. On the basis of the personal interest of students in student activities all other interests have been built.

The second, the pragmatic interest, accepts the personal interest of students in activities programs, and seeks to create practical means by which personal interest may be satisfied in a healthy, normal, and flour-

NOTE: This chapter is based in part on my article, "Values and Student Activities," *Teachers College Record*, 58 (1957), 316–322, reproduced here in modified form with the permission of the publisher.

80

ishing manner. The common concern of university administrators and student personnel workers is mainly devoted to the pragmatic interest.

The third, therapeutic interest, is based upon the well-known fact that not all individual students and groups of students (established through personal interest and sustained in part through pragmatic efforts) are able to maintain a perfect and harmonious existence. At least a segment of student activities interest must be constantly devoted by all personnel of the university to the development of a "clinical" attitude and methodology by which students in need may be restored to their intended felicity.

Fourth is research. In recent years especially, research activities have become increasingly important among workers in the human disciplines who are concerned with the phenomenon of student activities. The various studies, many of a statistical nature, are quite well known to professional student personnel workers, but much less well known popularly, and much less influential in shaping behavior than might be guessed. Research — through the statistical method, anthropological and cultural studies, case analyses, and other means — has assembled a greater mass of stubborn fact than has ever been available.

Fifth is theory. Interest in the theory of student activities has been much less pronounced, productive, and promising than other interests, in part because the behavioral sciences have had little time in which to develop genuine basic theories. The social sciences are in their infancy, and often, unfortunately, they are infantile in their expressions.

Confused over "measurement" and "evaluation," student personnel workers at times have thought mistakenly that it is possible to measure the delicate, complex relations which exist within their programs in the university. In relying too readily upon mathematical symbols of reality, they have failed to understand the serious limitations in method that the behavioral sciences present at this time.

Evaluation is a broader term than "measurement," and is not antithetical to it. One may evaluate a student activities program by employing a wide variety of techniques which do not pretend to measure. The case conference method surely is a highly constructive way in which to evaluate the effectiveness of a student activities program. Yet, at most points the case cannot be judged to be objective fact; it is a congeries of objective and subjective factors to which are brought the varying backgrounds and attitudes of the conference participants: ". . . it is possible to *measure* fields of physical force and energy. But personnel work deals with the intangibles — with human relations, with human programs and activities, with development itself, and with personality. Here measurement, in the strict sense of the term, is not possible . . . Thus, *evaluation*, rather than quantitative measurement, must be the basis for the assessment of personnel work."[1]

Serious theories of student activities, moreover, have been lacking because so many workers, in striving to break away from their historic orientations in theology and philosophy, have not yet recovered a taste for theoretical considerations. Having sadly split theory from research, they have been content merely to amass facts. They may be charged, in the poetry of Leonard Bacon, with

> Interpreting the simplest symbol wrong,
> Missing the gold and treasuring the tin,
> Dwelling on the trivial so long,
> And spinning allegory out so thin
> That the line parts, and neither brawn or brain
> Can splice the mainbrace of the mind again.[2]

With the severing of the umbilical cord between theory and research the study of student activities has lost the source of its nourishment and in some quarters has frittered away its energies in dwelling on the trivial. Of the many varying attitudes toward the separation of theory and research, three principal ones will be discussed briefly.

The first is stolid empiricism. The stolid empiricist insists that meanings and values have no place in scientific activity. Because theoretical analyses always appear to be rooted inescapably in cultural or personal biases of one sort or another, they cannot be taken seriously, it is said. Thus, the "true scientist" must abjure all subjective factors. He must study student activities with the cold calculations which the astronomer supposedly brings to his survey of the planets in their courses. Edward B. Titchener clearly supports this attitude:

Meanings must be stripped away before his [the scientist's] work can begin, and meanings must be kept away while his work proceeds. Disinterested and impersonal, he makes himself one with the facts of nature; he moves in the domain of bare existence; and his intercourse with the facts is both observation and observance.[3]

It was in this spirit of extreme empiricism that the late Alfred C. Kinsey and his researchers deplored the existence of the normative concepts of normal and abnormal. These concepts and others, Kinsey claimed, have seriously retarded our understanding of sexuality. In the same vein, advocates of a strictly empirical approach to student activities firmly believe that it is or will become possible to account for complex human activities on the basis of mathematical symbols reflecting quantitative reality. The result, it is claimed, will enable student activities workers both to predict student behavior and to control it for beneficial ends.

Such antipathy toward reason only leads to the glorification of methodology and the ultimate denial of research progress. This fact has been pointed out for the field of family research by Ruth Nanda Anshen in a form which creates analogous insights for the field of student activities:

The denial or neglect of objective reason, and consequently of logic and meaning, was symptomatic of — as it was the condition antecedent to — the historical fact that neither philosophy nor sociology has presented to the culture of the world a penetrating causal analysis of the transitional aspects of the human family. We search in vain for a comprehensive analysis of the family structure in terms of cause and law. Yet it is not astonishing that none is to be found, since, in the absence of logic and meaning, causality and jurisprudence cease to possess any relevancy. Thus man submits himself to an implacable empiricism, oblivious of the fact that empiricism itself annuls those very principles by which science and finally even empiricism may be vindicated.[4]

Not only does rigorous empiricism annul itself in the final analysis by denying the reality and potency of objective reason; it fails to face empirically the fact of value. The element of normativeness is certainly a most apparent factor in human experience without which human behavior cannot justifiably be explained or understood. For the social sciences and student activities simply to rule value out of existence while preferring to investigate exclusively the quantitative aspects of behavior is not scientific and surely is not helpful. While student activities will need to employ some empirical methods in its task of self-understanding, it will also need to develop the use of reason and to analyze the problems attendant upon the assertion of value preferences by the full use of reason.

The second view may be termed positivistic reductionism. Ernest Mach was probably its leading scientific exponent. His work, however, was anticipated to some extent by David Hume's *Treatise of Human*

Nature in 1739 and by the substance-sensation concepts of Thomas Hobbes in 1665. According to Mach, science consists in a continually progressing adaptation of ideas to facts: science does not disregard theory; it purifies it and modifies it. Facts reign supreme; theories are pre-scientific ways by which men express their desires. Science clarifies desires and valuatively is a distinctly progressive enterprise leading to the fulfillment of man's real desires. By his "doctrine of elements," Mach asserted the propriety of "reducing" complex ideas to "simple sentences." These simple sentences become the building blocks out of which the whole structure and process of reality are to be ultimately known and controlled.[5]

This view of the role of theory in science, maintained also by Rudolf Carnap in his discussions of the significance of "syntactical sentences,"[6] is persuasively argued by Richard von Mises:

The construction of a general scientific theory, i.e., of a system of mutually connectible statements about the world of observation is possible only if we start with the simplest sentences, the meanings of which are, so to speak, self-evident. On the basis of such sentences we have to develop a language, gradually advancing by testing each newly incorporated sentence to determine whether it is connectible with the previous ones. The ultimate goal of the theory is clear. It attempts to embrace everything that is open to our experience and observation, i.e., the phenomena of "nature" outside of us as well as those within ourselves, along with the actions of our fellow men which intrude upon us with their various reverberations in the past and present — in short, everything that can be meant by the terms natural and cultural sciences.[7]

Although the development of positivistic reductionism in the social sciences has not been without its benefits, even as Mach's notions have been constructively felt in physics, it also has its serious limitations. Does it genuinely help to reduce complex concepts into simple sentences? Are not the same perplexing elements we find in our analyses of complex sentences again encountered in our analyses of simple sentences? Does not the whole notion of positivistic reductionism comprise in itself a complicated and intriguing theory of human knowledge which can never be adequately evaluated on the basis of simple sentences? May it not be, as empirically minded William James said in his *Meaning of Truth*, that truth itself may elude any clever verbal formulation of it? Or, as Morris Cohen asserted: "I am a mystic in holding that all words point to a realm of being deeper and wider than the words themselves."[8] And again, if we accept the dictum of Nietzsche that "it is originally language which works at the formation of concepts, at later times it is science," how can nonscientific language form the basis for scientific endeavor?[9]

The main virtue of logical positivism, so far as student activities is concerned, would seem to be its deep and fierce concern with the use of concepts, words, sentences. It can help student activities workers to purify their fundamental language of aims and methods. In this limited sense positivism can readily be employed, since obviously so much of the terminology of the field rests upon relatively uncritical premises even so far as language is involved.

But positivistic reductionism probably will not provide a complete method for student activities. Other approaches to student group behavior will necessarily have to be used. The chief failure of positivism appears at the point where nonquantitative matters are being discussed.[10] How can positivism determine the rightness of a student court as a disciplinary agency of the university? How can positivism correctly conclude that one play production is esthetically successful and another a failure? How can positivism evaluate intrinsically the justness of rules regulating an athletic contest? How can positivism determine what the in-hour of a dormitory should be? It would seem that the more important the questions in student activities, the more readily the elements of value apply. Student activities needs indeed to understand the logic of its processes, but more significantly it needs to understand the value basis on which actions are taken. Positivism offers little help on value questions; its "sensation research" cannot subsume theory. Student activities cannot be understood in terms of simple sentences.

The third effort may be described as value theory. The presumed simple accumulation of facts is usually not so simple, for every accumulation assumes some sort of theoretical underpinning, if only that there is no theoretical underpinning. Those who take part in building up what the Germans call *Materialhuberei* reveal an insufficient grasp of the complexities of the human situation. But not all social scientists share in what Eric Voegelin has called "the perversion of relevance." Some, and perhaps their number is increasing, are openly aware of the interdependence of research and theory. The next great developments in the social sciences will come with the creation of ever more coherent and efficacious mediate and ultimate theories. Student activities research, moreover, is sorely in need of such advances in theory.

Alfred North Whitehead said: "It requires a very unusual mind to undertake the analysis of the obvious." Max Weber's was such a mind. His importance primarily derives from his creation of an *episteme* in contrast to the familiar *doxa*. Weber surpassed most social scientists in his willingness to recognize values as an intrinsic part of every social situation. By this acknowledgment, he opened the door to a thoroughgoing consideration of the role of theory in social and political action.[11]

Science, according to Weber, cannot determine what the range of worth might be within a set of contrasting values or theories. Science in this sense is value-free. It cannot tell men how to live. It can, on the other hand, tell them what the consequences will be if they base their actions upon particular values or theories. The origin of values and their choice are for Weber an expression of "demonism," that is, they are rooted in trans-scientific reality and cannot be accurately weighed or evaluated by science itself. Unfortunately, Weber's doctrine of demonism provides no ultimate basis for help on the most perplexing problems with which men are confronted — problems in the realm of final human commitment.

In contrast, men cannot be unconcerned about the application of whatever values they choose to follow. Weber's "ethics of responsibility" make clear the need for persons to act responsibly in conformance with their consciously elaborated values. Science can aid values by asking that men act responsibly. Weber's thought as thus developed stands rather close to certain brands of modern existentialism.

The function of social science, if Weber left the matter here, would be open to sharp criticism. He seems until now to be making science simply the handmaiden of pragmatic actors in the social scene. Science can interpret after the fact: but can it also validate? This question persists in his work and finds its answer in the concept of "ethics of intention" or *Gesinnungsethik*. By his ethics of intention Weber asserts that every system of action has its own inherent justification. No ultimate validation is ever possible, by this view; one can only ask if the result achieves what is desired. If it does, the social act is validated.

On this point Weber seems to be standing in a quagmire. Intention may be satisfactory to one who views the action from "within." But what about the person who stands "outside" a particular system of meaning, as everyone stands to some degree? Can one rationally justify inconsistencies and systematic contradictions within the general value realm?[12] Perhaps the "practical" scientist can, though surely this lack of an over-all ethics of responsibility will not impress most favorably. Would Weber not have to agree with the Marxist who had accepted his particular social theory as well as with his own interpretation of the Capitalism-Protestantism development? That Weber was not thoroughly value-free is shown in his selection of religions for inclusion in his three-volume study of the sociology of religion. Is there no standard of objectivity in science itself?

It would seem that Max Weber's contribution to the understanding of the role of theory in social science is ambiguous. It is promising in that it is willing to accede to the recognition of theory and its importance in understanding every human situation. It is open to criticism in that it fails to face fully the trans-scientific outreach of social science theory. He makes theory relevant to research, but he lacks a theological and philosophical rigor in approaching the ultimate aspects of his views. A similar evaluation could be made in detail, if space permitted, of his analysis of cause and effect, and his effort to construct "ideal types." In both instances Weber provides excellent tools for social analysis. He fortunately applies objective reason to the causality of action, but unfortunately not to the basic principles of order underlying social phenomena. He fortunately sees the validity of employing objective reason in synthesizing and interpreting scattered social events, but unfortunately fails to see that the attainment of such a degree of responsibility leads further to decisions regarding the value hierarchy of ideal types. Weber considered his work a process of disenchantment (*Entzauberung*), perhaps because he was unable to formulate an adequate philosophy of ultimate concern.[13]

The study of student activities needs persons like Weber who are faithful both to the requirements of research and the fructifying influence of sound theories. But it also needs persons who are able to work with patience in creating theories which will not renege on the ultimate factors involved in an ethics of responsibility.

To the degree to which stolid empiricism, positivistic reductionism, and value theory in the social sciences have been unable to penetrate to the core of the problem confronting the student activities worker in the university — the source and validation of value — it remains for philosophy and theology (or philosophical theology) to take up the task. This, of course, is another way of saying that no one should expect science to solve the problem of value, since in itself value rests upon trans-scientific grounds. Or, to express it another way, science is pertinent to one range of experience within the totality of reality, and philosophy and theology are appropriate disciplines for another range. Both ranges, it may be assumed, are overlapping, rationally harmonious, and comprise the fullness of being.

It would be impractical at this point to attempt to delineate the many ways in which the problem of value has been approached in the past and at present by philosophers and theologians. Education itself has provided its own philosophers who have established at least a point of departure. Although differing on many details among themselves, the following have tried to elaborate educational philosophies of values based upon reason: William C. Bagley, Herman H. Horne, Robert Ulich, Frederick S. Breed, Ross L. Finney, Gordon Chalmers, J. Donald Butler, Michael Demiashkevich, Robert M. Hutchins. Others like Jacques Maritain, Bernard I. Bell, Aldous Huxley, T. S. Eliot, and Mortimer Adler also have written on the subject. As yet, however, there has been no systematic or noteworthy effort by student activities workers to develop sturdy theories for their field based upon the work of these and other theorists and critics who in some respects run against the dominant stream of educational thought. Two illustrations at this point may prove suggestive.

Robert Ulich has written a number of books which set forth his theoretical views.[14] In sum, he is not unsympathetic to certain aspects of the more empirically oriented schools of educational thought. Nevertheless, he stresses the importance of "transpersonal" planes of reality, certain generalizations regarding the nature of being itself, and the universality of law within the universe. He asserts the validity and significance of objective reason as the participant in the order "which represents the unity of principles and laws." He also speaks of "the All-Embracing," and of "the divine ground" of human experience, although these terms may prove to be less than illuminating to some of his readers. To Ulich, then, there is no need to view reality in truncated terms, the empirical and the theoretical. He is willing to recognize

both in a continuum which comprises man's personal and social experience.

A more orthodox Christian standpoint is espoused by J. Donald
Butler. He finds in the concept of God a satisfactory support and answer
to the perplexities of value inquiries:

> Viewed from the standpoint of fact and value, God is the actuality
> of all value. In Him there is nothing which is only possible or potential;
> all value which is ultimately good is actual in Him. Within Him no
> growth or development or realization is needed. In the order which
> he has created and to which he gives present existence, there is a kind
> of openness, freedom, indeterminacy, absence of value, contradiction of
> value, and such which make room for the kind of growth and develop-
> ment by which individual souls may come into existence. Here there
> is necessarily a separation and distinction between what is actual and
> what is potential . . . He is all value, the infinity of value which is
> yet undreamed of in the created order.[15]

Although Butler's language is expressive of a former period of theological thought, its intrinsic meaning is not foreign to the theological
formulations of recent decades, which have employed a different terminology.[16] The chief dangers apparent in Butler's approach are the
tendency to terminological obscurantism, the recession to the former
sentimental period in student personnel service of soul-saving under
the guise of promoting religion, and the vacuity of certain elements.
Even so, Butler clearly recognizes that the quantitative orders of human experience do not fully account for man and that — for education
generally and for student activities particularly — those value conceptions not totally bound by a strict empiricism may nonetheless possess
validity.

Aside from "final" solutions to the problem of values, it is possible
for student activities to make progress inductively in understanding
its place in discussions of value. Student activities workers do have a
part to play even though it may be limited.

Student activities workers can rightly claim competency regarding
mediate theories of value that relate to their particular functions. In
constructing these theories, in deriving them from the discrete experiences of their professional activities, they have used a specialized language. It is becoming increasingly apparent, however, that such workers
need to relate their mediate theories of value to the more ultimate
theories of philosophers and theologians.[17] Because of their concentra-

tion on formal training and experience, workers are often incompetent to deal with the ultimate theories, at least until they have studied them in detail. As a start they might welcome the active participation of minds more philosophically and theologically competent, in the determination of student activities theory. Of course it is entirely possible that philosophers and theologians too would benefit from this relationship.

It is interesting to note that at present some theologians are open to considering the information made available to them by the applied sciences. One of the most notable, Paul Tillich, discusses theology's dependence upon existential formulations of the nature of man as follows:

> The systematic theologian cannot do this alone; he needs the help of the creative representatives of existentialism in all realms of culture. He needs the support of the practical explorers of man's predicament, such as ministers, educators, psychoanalysts, and counselors. The theologian must reinterpret the traditional religious symbols and theological concepts in the light of the material he receives from these people. He must be aware of the fact that terms like "sin" and "judgment" have lost not their truth but rather an expressive power which can be regained only if they are filled with the insights into human nature which existentialism (including depth psychology) has given to us.[18]

If theologians are able to learn in openminded spirit from those who maintain direct and practical relations with people, is it not reasonable to suppose that student personnel workers and others should be open to the findings of the theologians?

In this connection it is helpful to note that the Massachusetts Institute of Technology during the academic year 1955–1956 appointed Professor Robert S. Hartman, "a pioneer in value theory," to a visiting professorship in the humanities and as a consultant to the Dean of Students. His appointment was financed by the Ford Foundation Fund for the Advancement of Education. The memorandum submitted to the Foundation preparatory to the appointment stated that "in the current evolution of undergraduate education at M.I.T. there has been increasing concern with values — in curriculum planning, improvement of teaching, and the development of residential facilities; in all levels of administration; in faculty committees; in admissions; in scholarships and student aid; in public relations."[19] While the responsibilities of the dean of students do not include all of these phases of university activity, they do involve several. In describing the scope of his duties at M.I.T., Professor Hartman says: "To mention three kinds of problems in which I am engaged, one refers to the exact formulations of value, the second to seemingly small problems with large theoretical implica- tions, and the third to very large problems, which demand value- theoretical explications."[20]

As an example of the first type of problem, Professor Hartman asks the following question: "How seriously can and should M.I.T. take its commitment to moral and spiritual values?" This problem, of course, exceeds the exact limits of student activities and pertains to the whole of the university. Student activities, obviously having an important role in the education of technologists as well as others, necessarily comprises a part of the total study.

The second problem is translated into the terminology of student personnel service as counseling. On this score, Professor Hartman says perhaps too little:

Thus, in the usual two categories of student problems, personal and academic ones, my counseling activity is not too different from any other counseling; except that I try to make clear to the student the background of my advice and its implications. This has led, in some cases, to a student's self analysis and thus the solution of his problem by making clear to himself the nature and significance of the values involved. Here the knowledge of value theory proved practically helpful.[21]

From this brief description it is difficult to discern how Professor Hartman's counseling differs, if at all, from that offered by other faculty members and professional counselors on the staff of the uni- versity. If it is not substantially different from counseling as offered by others, it would prove instructive to know to what degree the others are as carefully aware of the genuinely theoretical aspects of student counseling.

The third kind of problem, according to Professor Hartman, is one of definition, of clarifying "the meaning of the much used — and abused — term 'the whole man' in the M.I.T. educational vocabulary":

I have found some confusion as to what this term means. For example, a faculty member said that "the whole man" was "he who does everything well but nothing very well," a graduate student said that he was "not the one to get into graduate school," and an editorial in *The Tech* jokingly referred to the whole man as the one Wellesley girls liked.[22]

Without tracing out in detail Professor Hartman's reasoning in attacking the problem of defining the "whole man," it is easy to see the special relevance of the question to student activities and to the whole of the student personnel movement. Unfortunately, the literature offers little more than facile definitions and descriptions; there is hardly in existence a thoroughgoing exposition of its meaning for student activities. Moreover — and this is the point for its present consideration — it is difficult to assume that student personnel workers are competent to evaluate the fullest meaning and impact of the term without the aid of others, philosophers and theologians, who have made a special interest of the conception of the "whole man" which undergirds serious discussion of the problem.

Although Professor Hartman's work at M.I.T. is not completely summarized above, it is clear that the role of the philosopher (and the theologian) has a place in the development of a more adequate theory, especially value theory, in student activities. The "answers" to the "questions" which might well be raised through interdisciplinary discussions of the theoretical underpinning of student activities in the university have scarcely been formulated, let alone solved. It is to be hoped that through cooperative efforts within the university the task may begin, and that in time through patient and thoughtful collaboration the field of student activities may secure a more comprehensive, coherent, and effective theory by which to guide its programs.

The discussion in this chapter shows, if nothing else, that student activities has a long way to go in reaching thoughtful theoretical positions regarding values basic to its practice. While the task of drawing firm conclusions is admittedly difficult, it is also fundamental to the further maturing of the field. Student activities cannot long endure with prestige and effectiveness without facing this problem.

The scope of values in student activities, however, is not determined exclusively by rational or logical factors. Empirical accounts can describe the nonlogical elements which compose the traditional values held by various universities. They cannot validate them, nor can they create a hierarchical interpretation among university heritages of the ultimate values which higher education might support. In the next chapter an attempt will be made to outline some of the "intentions" of

student activities systems. Not totally rational, these intentions themselves are the cultural expression of particular values which seem to
dominate and characterize certain universities. Although the discussion may appear on the surface to make the problem of values even
more complicated and frustrating, the conscious purpose is quite different. It is to show that the empirical study of campus behavior
necessarily must take into account certain "styles" or intentions of the
university community.

⤝ 8

Intentions

PERHAPS the two most frequently advocated aims of student activities have become all too familiar: the development of personal maturity, and the growth of responsible, democratic citizenship among students.[1] The professional workers have elaborated these two themes with manifold variations. Even the nonprofessionals concerned with student life (students, administrators, laymen in the community) have taken up the jargon and have raised these goals into guarantees of "democratic" student personnel practice within the university.

These *raisons d'être* for student activities, however, are not complete or final any more than are the keywords "liberty, equality, and fraternity" a full and cogent explanation of the French Revolution. In studying either student activities, the French Revolution, or any other historical and group pattern, one must look for more complex rationales as well as causes. Individual maturity and democratic citizenship are obviously not causative explanations, but rather "intentions" (*der Zweck*) for a current group fact. As such, they are incomplete and fragmentary. Lacking a proper group perspective, these concepts smack of a biased outlook formed by a preoccupation with psychology and political science. Admittedly, they represent the *idée fixe* of a large corps of professional workers presently engaged in student activities.

NOTE: This chapter is based in part on my article, "The Intentions of Student-Activities Systems," *Journal of Higher Education*, 27 (1956), 256–263, 290, reproduced here in modified form with the permission of the publisher.

Other ways of expressing the intentions of student activities programs may be conceived.[2] Other constructs may produce even greater understanding of the role of student activities in the university. Without pretending to suggest a final rationale, the following intentions may be discussed as indicating other ways of interpreting student activities systems within the university: conformism, anarchism, and ritualism.

The conformist philosophy intends to maintain student activities in accord with accepted standards and practices of proper function. Success is measured by the extent to which accepted standards are assumed or acted upon in the field. That standards may be questionable or even unavailable is not considered. It is believed that an "open system" of student activities is undesirable, although the subterfuge of openness may be employed to achieve and maintain the standards. The conformism may be of the left or right, socially, politically, educationally, or religiously; adherence to the stance is deemed more important than the substance. The accepted is the "faked absolute," in the terms of Max Ascoli, the value one does not question. It is "the given."

What, then, are some of the "givens" of current student activities practice? One has already been mentioned — the intention of many professional leaders of student activities: personal maturity and democratic leadership. Although this view enjoys wide currency among the leaders, its acceptance within the university suffers both from neglect and disbelief. Despite the literature, it is not clearly apparent that student activities programs achieve in reality what the professional workers think they are abstractly achieving. To apply the accepted professional standard to the day-by-day operations of student activities in specific universities would show partial achievements, areas of neglect, and even denial of the formal standard. As the professional workers well understand, the assumption cannot be made that even a majority of the administrators, faculty, and students accept as realistic the standard of the professional workers. Other and usually more mundanely reasoned expositions are widely held in the university at large.

College tradition itself represents another conformist intention. It need not be illustrated in detail the extent to which the spirit of Alma Mater, the reverence for past ways of doing things, the inherited rigidities of administrative practice, the shared values of a long history, and other such factors constitute a predominant intention of a large number of universities.[3] The high school personality of the entering freshman is deliberately "matured," so that by the time of college graduation he becomes a stereotyped replica, recognizable as a typical graduate from his institution, shaped by a tradition of bygone days.[4] Such character organization becomes the union card for many college graduates in the employment world. While student activities leaders may speak long and loud about the development of individual personality as one of their principal objectives, too often they really have in mind a particular type of personality — the personality sanctioned by the traditions of the university.[5]

Obviously conformism to community standards is another significant student activities intention. No one would claim in the face of the present uneasy era of university-community relations on such matters as political radicalism that student activities is not directed in part toward community conformity. The fact is that such activities have always been guided by what was accepted by the general community. Indeed, insofar as universities have educated for economic and social success they have had to insist upon an education of conformism. The universities have produced far more community priests than prophets.

The idea that student activities helps train the student to meet his citizenship requirements and opportunities is part and parcel of the conformistic intention of community standards. As much sentimentalism has been spoken, written, and practiced in universities on this subject as any other. The idea that the university community rather precisely parallels the general political society is at the base of much of the misunderstanding and malpractice. The notion that campus activities are somehow more realistic or provide better training grounds for later democratic participation when infused with the pettiness, contention, and lack of ethics of political society surely contributes heavily to the apathy and weariness of the mass of students in their post-graduation activities as members of local communities. The simulation within the university of the community's full range of political reality, especially with most of the weaknesses and evils of off-campus politics, is a major blind spot in many current student activities systems. Community conformism is surely a significant intention implicit in many of these programs.

Conformist intentions, tending to be acted upon as absolutes, imply directive authority. Where universities are clear about their intentions, they not only offer their values to their students but work both directly and indirectly to achieve and maintain them. Almost any catalogue (especially student handbooks) contains the codified tenets by which the conformist intention is declared and enforced. Disciplinary officers and agencies must have a close understanding of the intention and work with its spirit.

Conformist intentions are also achieved and maintained by indirection. In our time, "indirection" has become almost synonymous with "professionalism" in student activities, and a flow of reports in recent years has analyzed the various and refined methods of employing indirection. The usual method is to provide groups with whatever freedom they desire as long as they arrive at the same conformistic values held by those who bear final responsibility:

With the proper use of group decisions, one can attain far greater control of a group of people than can be achieved by the use of fear . . . One of the effective motivation factors in influencing behavior is that of social pressure, as utilized under Lewin's type of democratic leadership. In attempting to obtain unanimous group solutions and in protecting minorities the leader is able to harness social pressure for constructive ends.[6]

Shades of George Orwell's *1984!*

Very often indirection merely assumes that the group decision will meet the intention of the student activities program. But what, may we ask, does the leader do when the group decision widely fails to approximate the declared intention of the university? What does the leader do when the group decision is openly, deeply, and hostilely at variance with the values of the university? Is the answer simply more manipulation — more clever indirection? Surely, the rationalist fallacies undergirding so much of group work on the campus cry for a vigorous rational response.

The anarchist philosophy of student activities asserts that conforming values are either not available upon objective consideration or that they are not to be applied, if available, because of certain ultimate and procedural dispositions. A correlative of the philosophy suggests that each person or group seeks and acts upon its own values through the use of whatever experience is available — thus anarchism as a description of this intention.

Obviously the impact of the absolutist-relativist position, as developed in a score of disciplines in the last century, has had its effect upon student personnel work. Briefly, this view holds that all values are situationally relative, that universals cannot be constructed from partial experience, and that ultimately the individual and his preferences are the final criteria of selection and action. One may speak of it as "absolutist-relativist" because it turns the relativity which practically all would recognize to one degree or another into an absolute. William Graham Sumner defined the absolutist-relativist position succinctly: "The goodness or badness of mores consists entirely in their adjustment to the life conditions and the interests of the time and place."[7] Anthropologists, such as Ruth Benedict in her *Patterns of Culture*, and more recently Melville Herskovits in *Man and His Works*, have elaborated this theme in scholarly detail.[8] Institutional economists have also tended to favor a similar outlook; Adam Smith's idea of *laissez-faire* was actually a forerunner of latter-day views in economics. Psychology also has developed a similar bias. The school of Carl Rogers, even with its recent amendments, has not been able to extricate itself from the dilemmas raised by assuming the correctness of the absolutist-relativist position.

These fragmentary comments on the absolutist-relativist position in several disciplines are certainly not meant to be exhaustive. They hopefully indicate the positivistic temper so widely characteristic of our times, among intellectuals. Their counterparts in the literature of the student personnel movement are quite familiar to workers within and to teachers and others outside the field. So many student activities leaders assume that their basic contribution to the group work process on the campus is that of facilitator, arbiter, encourager rather than that of teacher, administrator, or directive guide. The quickness with which counselors of individual students and student activities leaders are prone to differentiate themselves sharply from teachers and administrators represents not only a factually significant area of university tension and conflict, but the dogmatic maintenance of professional shibboleths about the intentions of counseling and student activities systems in the university.

Skepticism and neutrality are two of the most frequently nurtured values of the anarchist intention. The skepticism is based upon the assumption that conforming values cannot be objectively apprehended and that, therefore, the search for them is unintelligent and wasteful.

In value-decision situations in which students participate, the skeptical attitude says in effect "hands-off" on questions concerning the ultimate validity of value preferences. In fact, the skeptical attitude may go further to disillusion students and discourage them from asking such questions. Student groups, from this point of view, are told that the fundamental gains in student activities are individualistic — development of personality. To the extent that group goals are entertained, aside from citizenship, it is claimed that the group process itself is its own sanction. Participationism, an instrumental value, often becomes the chief value of campus group activities.

Neutrality toward values is another attitude possible to the absolutist-relativist worker in student activities.[9] The worker, uncertain of his own or his institution's values, or, if certain, of their relation to the activities of student groups, may claim that the leader's basic contribution is that of facilitating the growth of the values of each and every individual and group according to the personal preferences of the individuals and groups. Neutrality in this sense is probably more widely practiced than skepticism, although there is a relationship between them. Indeed, from the point of tolerating variety there has grown in many universities the attitude that variety, even conflicting variety, should be actively supported and extended in the student activities program. This attitude is commonly bolstered with a pseudoliberal, democratic, humanitarian, collegiate metaphysics.

One of the patent results of neutralism in student activities is the practice of an exaggerated egalitarianism. Everyone must be represented, for example, in so-called student government. According to one widely used booklet on student government, a school council "must include everybody, students, teachers, engineers, janitors, principal, counselors. It must give everybody a feeling of partnership." Within many student governments there is a constant debate regarding equal representation. By this is meant an arithmetically formulated democracy so calculated that the various factions within the university are reduced to wholes and fractions of wholes. The problem becomes: what is the relative representative value of the college president versus a student or a collection of students in a fraternity, club, or other organization? Unless everyone is everyone's equal in the vote, it is assumed, there is no vital democracy.

The manner in which universities have virtually abdicated responsibility for student political groups (those with only campus interests and those with broader purposes) reveals how far neutralism has advanced in student activities. An instructional department or a special office of student activities may sponsor a variety of paralleling and even conflicting political groups without feeling responsibility toward ultimate political issues. Prejudices of knowledge are quickly corrected in the classroom, but prejudices of personal values are considered to be outside the province of professionally trained student personnel workers. The bias of neutralism toward athletics in the university passed from the scene some years ago, although carryovers of the past remain, but neutralism toward student activities values continues with wide-scaled support. It is interesting to note that when fraternities speak of their autonomy from the university, some administrators are quick and appreciative to accept their claim.

Obviously the intention of anarchism in student activities can become a conformist value, as it has in many universities. Anarchism, in such situations, is the accepted value, and anyone who wishes to modify it, even in the name of reason, is looked upon as a maladjusted obstructionist.

Student activities systems with an anarchist bent have had the support of leading relativist educators, especially in the past. For example, the educational philosophy which supports the "free-election" curriculum has rested to a notable degree upon a relativist base. Prior to his election to the presidency of Harvard University in 1869, Charles William Eliot expounded this philosophy in the *Atlantic Monthly*, and said in one of his articles: "The natural bent and peculiar quality of every boy's mind should be sacredly regarded in his education . . ."[10] The extension of this view from the organization of the curriculum to the supervision of student activities was a relatively easy matter. The more recent modification of the elective philosophy at a variety of universities interestingly has not brought an accompanying or paralleling change in student activities philosophy or practice.

Arthur H. Compton, former chancellor of Washington University has observed that the higher education of the past was mainly concerned with the transmission of the cultural heritage and that since the Second World War higher education has been called upon to train youth for the making of important decisions regarding "the rapid change of our social order, with special relation to the rising importance of technology, our increasing interdependence and our inescapable involvement in the world's affairs . . . The fact is that the higher education which we inherited from the prewar era was not designed for preparing students to make such decisions."[11] Unfortunately, what the appropriate role of student activities might be in educating for decision was not suggested.

Ritualism as an intention of student activities systems is based upon the value of regularized customs and procedures, the acceptance of symbols as a means of creating cooperation, and the use of campus rituals for the achievement and maintenance of status. Though usually not consciously considered as a basis for behavior by most students and their student activities leaders, in a significant sense ritualism is a secondary layer of university experience in student activities, but important because it does not always possess deliberative awareness. Its symbolic character indicates its emotional rather than its rational appeal — thus there is not always a conscious awareness of ritualism and its role.

In the past, psychoanalysts, anthropologists, and others (sometimes each posing as the other) have tried to describe the role of ritual in human affairs. In psychology, Freud combined a systematic psychology with a questionable anthropology in *Totem and Taboo*[12] to arrive at certain conclusions regarding ritual. Theodore Reik's *Ritual: Psychoanalytic Studies*[13] provides further information on the subject. Erich Fromm has also attempted to analyze this theme in *The Forgotten Language*,[14] although he, like Freud, Reik, and others, confines his labors to ritual's sub-themes of dreams, fairy tales, and myths. The role of ritual in man's wakeful social experience has not been as adequately studied.

Universities contain vast riches of ritual experience. Hastings Rashdall, especially in the second half of his third volume on *The Universities of Europe in the Middle Ages*,[15] has sought to delineate the content of university ritual by discussing the origins of the peculiar dress of university personnel, town-gown relations, problems of social status groups, student behavior and discipline, and the like. Ernest Earnest, in *Academic Procession*,[16] has achieved sharp understanding of what he calls "informal" aspects of collegiate history in the United States. Unfortunately, both studies, and the few others like them, fail to develop a systematic view of the role of ritual.

Edward Y. Hartshorne, however, has provided an unusually perceptive analysis of "undergraduate society and the college culture" which
includes some discussion of the role of ritual.[17] He outlines "three
stages of analysis: (1) on the demographic processes involved — selection, training, and subsequent disposition of personnel; (2) on the
formal organization and material equipment of the college, which may
be called its 'official culture'; and (3) on the informal 'unofficial culture'
of the students, developed by them in their process of adjusting to the
official culture."

While Hartshorne's materials do not formally distinguish between
the curricular and co-curricular aspects of the university, it may be
assumed that much the same kinds of ritual behavior surround both
aspects. The content of the curricular ritual may differ from that of
the co-curricular, but the form and function probably remain much the
same for both. Certainly, in Hartshorne's terms, ritualism in student
activities is a part of the official and unofficial cultures.[18]

Participation in ritualized behavior by college students may be more
educative (changing the person's character) in student activities than
in curricular studies. In student activities such behavior truly constitutes
the university's culture, and adjustment to it by students is taken as an
important — sometimes controlling — requirement of the university. The
claim is not usually made that the ritual behavior is ultimately valuable.
Conformity to the developed ritual patterns may be expected or not.
More likely they will be viewed as tradition, that is, simply to be accepted without rational justification, but on grounds of emotional
appeal and history. Hartshorne says:

The "Harvard" accent . . . may be modified slightly by each generation of students, but it is not created by them; it lives through them,
but also existed before their appearance on the scene and endures after
their departure . . . What is true of speech is also true of norms governing dress, study, humor, sportsmanship, recreation, dating, eating,
and the like.[19]

What person who has lived on a university campus for a decade or two
has not been impressed with the ritualized response of students, mainly
females, to changing patterns of dress! Writ large, this imitative,
security-finding-in-conformity acknowledgment of the importance of
symbols to campus success is a kind of behavior which is the root of
the ritualistic intention in student activities.

Apparently the maintenance of striving and achieving behavior among students is based in part upon the use and abuse of appropriate symbols. The use of Greek letters as titles for social organizations, the meaning in student affairs of athletic letters, the location of eating cliques in the common dining room, the listing of offices in the year-book, the wearing of keys and pins which portray a mysterious symbology to the uninitiated — these and other symbols found in student activities systems are related to problems of the student's social status. While his position in the campus status scale may be measured to an extent by the quantitative analysis of such symbols, the whole story is not told by them. Superficially and officially the securing of status symbols provides an apt clue to the position of the student in the social organization of the university, but care must be taken to note where possession of such paraphernalia and honors reflects an inverted (is it here that the importance of Hartshorne's "unofficial" and Cohen's "subculture" are relevant?) scale of values: the female winner of a beauty contest may be popular with the males and unpopular with the females. Or, in the illustration of Hartshorne:

Concealment of honorific *Symbols* occurs with respect to "social" distinction. Members of exclusive social clubs are often under oath never to tell an outsider that they are club members. If there are insignia of membership, such as watch charms or neck-ties, it is considered bad taste to wear them — although "social climbers" are expected to display imitations of the real thing.[20]

So it is that Phi Beta Kappa keys are kept hidden in situations where intelligence is not a high value!

Although Hartshorne is able to distinguish between the official and unofficial culture of the whole university, it seems possible to suggest that a variety of cultures vie for acceptance, some official, others not. Among the faculty, student personnel workers, and administrators can usually be found the so-called official representations of campus culture. The differences and even conflicts among these representations are well known to the officialdom as well as to the more perceptive students. Again, a variety of campus cultures, characterized by wide range and deep antagonisms (as between fraternity and nonfraternity students), exists among the students. At certain points in theory and practice the cultures of officials and of students may meet in strong agreement. At other points disagreement may be found.

Because of the variety of campus cultures, the task of coordination and synthesis is of particular delicacy and importance. What the role of the professional student activities worker should be in this situation is not easy to prescribe, especially since by one intention or another the worker usually has assumed a value position which is simply one among the many in need of synthesizing. Surely one of the requirements for the worker is that he attain a genuine understanding of the complexity of the ritual situation confronting him. That in itself may take considerable time, uncommon talent, and personality.

The emotionally derived preconceptions of the workers themselves need to be recognized and overcome. One authoritative text speaks of fraternities and sororities in their concern for status achievement as offending "the listener who believes in the innate dignity and value of every individual and who abhors the philosophy of special privilege for a few." This judgment which obviously identified the writers with the culture of the nonfraternity students, is an example of a ritualistic response to a huge and complex social problem both on and off the campus. Judging the values and disvalues of fraternity and sorority culture requires an objectivity and skill in the formulation of such judgments for which the training of most student personnel workers hardly provides competency.

The university has often been called an academic community.[21] The term as commonly used is most vague in meaning. At times it seems to connote a group of individuals — students and faculty — who busy themselves simply with reading scholarly books. At other times it seems to suggest that the university community has a claim upon the totality of the experience of those who make it up. It describes a way of life.

The university will be viewed as a community in more precise terms when analyses have been made of the role of symbols in its daily activities. A symbol differs from a sign in depth and range of content. An expressive mechanism, a sign becomes a communicative channel only after a slow process of standardization. Limited to meanings contained within itself, a sign does not point beyond itself to a transcendent meaning. A symbol, on the other hand, does point beyond itself to a meaning which can be appreciated but cannot be appropriated to lesser purposes. The sign is a tool of exact communication; the symbol is an instrument of social cohesion. A sign is appropriate to a community; a symbol is appropriate to a communion.[22]

When signs are transformed into symbols as a result of constant communication and the building up of values which surpass the everyday bonds between people, a marked change occurs in the growth of a community. A sign enables members to communicate with each other, but in time a sign may become a symbol, a basic form of common property evoking communal values. Animals can make gestures and signs, they can communicate, but only members of a human community can share the full appreciation of lives lived in reference to meaningful and power-laden symbols. Symbols, because of the implied and actual social agreement on values, become authoritative controlling agents in the life of the community and form the first line of community responsibility for individuals. In accepting the common symbol system of the community we acknowledge its totality and its claim upon our private actions.

It appears that two regular social developments are involved when a highly ordered system of symbols occurs within a community. First is the growth of what may be called the juridical community, based upon symbols which have been translated into law. The common values of the persons composing the community pass beyond individualistic acceptance to become systematized as fundamental bylaws of social action. The perfection of the symbol system of the community, therefore, serves as the foundation for the government. Government, whether on the campus or off, employs the commonly accepted symbols to maintain certain social efficiencies and communal requirements. A tension constantly exists in juridical communities between the power of symbols as controlling agents over conduct and the need for practical means of enforcement (police, courts, the military). It is the task of political administration to seek creative compromises whereby the intelligent use of appeal and force will create the most advantages for the community.

The second form of community derived from symbols is the charismatic community, or the communion.[23] Here the same symbol system runs a very different course. The product, too, differs from the juridical community. The juridical community is bound by common law; the charismatic community, by common expressions of trust and faith. The object of the common faith is not as clearly defined as in juridical, since in the charismatic form the symbol most clearly is a symbol — that is, it points far beyond itself to a meaning which is not easily comprehended. The faith which binds its members may be likened to religious faith, and in some instances it may be religious faith. The members of the encompassing juridical community may also be members of the charismatic community, although fewer persons tend to be caught up by the extreme devotion required by the latter. A person may be said to have two memberships open to him, although he may resign himself with belonging to only one, the juridical.

To paraphrase Max Weber, where there is double membership there is a "church." Single membership in the charismatic community is that of the "sect." In campus terms, the student body may feel itself to be a part of the juridical community, but the student government leaders may consider themselves members of both communities and more expressly members of the charismatic community. They may feel the community's symbol system more acutely, and possess a more devoted sense of mission toward the university than do the members of the student body. The same may be true of the faculty, and perhaps even of the administration.

In the charismatic community the members may claim to be motivated in their actions by ideals of service to their fellow members. In part this is true. But they must find the wellspring of their motivation in some other source in order that it be nurtured and sustained, especially in times of frustration and despair. The members, then, derive their highest inspiration, not from their fellow members, but from the hierarchy of overriding symbols which binds the members in the first place. The object of devotion is not service to fellow members but observance of the symbols, an acknowledgment of the transcendent meaning to which the symbols point.

The official meetings of the charismatic community are not social occasions characterized by the informal give and take of debate and discussion. They are more akin to the religious communion service: private uniquenesses are submerged and an emotionally pervading sense of seriousness dominates. By virtue of his office the presiding leader at the meetings is not considered merely as one of the members. He is the object of extreme courtesy, obedience, petition, and ritual. Meetings may be convened to discuss or devise means of stimulating devotion to the heritage of the community and appreciation of its leadership, its present accomplishments and future plans. The member who receives emotional satisfaction from the proceedings and says that he "got something out of the meeting" is not referring to any one event or statement but is simply expressing his over-all emotional response to the fellowship of the group. Not so much a characteristic of the juridical community, fellowship is a more fundamental, more intensely realized quality of the charismatic experience.

The place where the meetings are held, a particular room or building set aside for this one purpose, may have special attributes that are conducive to the group's aims and aspirations. Members of the juridical community can never quite understand why special space should be required by their charismatic counterparts, space that is used infrequently. The members of the charismatic community, however, do understand. To them, the meeting place expresses the sanctification of their status and purposes. It imparts feelings of reverence, of being within hallowed walls. The area itself may be decorated with appropriate material symbols. The gavel, for example, may be an instrument not only of calling to order but a constant reminder of the flow of authority from one officeholder to another. Drapes, special chairs, candelabra, and customary procedures (rituals) may help enforce the idea of the meeting as an expression of the charismatic community.

Men participate in a large number of juridical and charismatic communities. Every campus involves more than one, and the campus as a whole is constantly seeking to realize itself in one form or another of the community. But a word of warning may be appropriate, too. The pretensions of student activities workers, student leaders, other student personnel workers, administration, faculty, and others should never be encouraged to entertain the belief that the ultimate community for all members of the university is the university. It is a peculiarly questionable form of idolatry that would make of the university that community (of a charismatic nature, of course) which is the final and chief security and hope of men. Such a position in human affairs is not given to the university. While its goals are lofty indeed, and its realization of community is often notable, the university is not the *sangha* for the Buddhist, the sacred community for the Jew, or the church for the Christian.

It is in the church or its equivalents that men's ultimate security and stimulation in community are met. The church is the focal point in human motivation at its highest. Around the church cluster the most exalted symbols given to men. The university may approximate in some of its aspects the community which is the church, but it cannot supplant the church in the minds and affections of persons. Not being the only social institution, the university is less than universal in its claim upon individuals. Other institutions, familial, economic, political, and social, have similar claims to make. Yet all, both individually and collectively, only partially appeal to men's final loyalties. When any one of the social institutions is magnified distortedly in its scope, it becomes idolatrous. The magnification of the state as the ultimate community is tragically evident in Nazism and in Soviet Communism.[24] For the university to make a similar appeal is unthinkable.

It is probably on this very point that the old "whole man" theory of student personnel work is found most wanting. The belief that student personnel work can meet the needs of the whole man is incongruous and fatuous within the practical reality of the university and indicative of a secularized religious hope unrealistically founded. Student personnel work need not seek to carry this impossible burden. It can neither create whole men nor establish the ultimate community in student activities. Its role both in the university and in society generally is much more severely limited.

One of the most important functions of the universalizing church is to criticize prophetically any social institution which seeks to supplant it. Other institutions have particularistic functions, and are limited by their own logic to meet particular human needs. Yet within them also are the seeds of illogical development by which they, one or all, assert themselves as the final good. The task of the church, when this occurs, is to expose their pretensions and arrogance. The fact that student personnel work at many points is divorced from the social sciences, theology, philosophy, and other disciplines has misled many workers into viewing the field as independent, as an autonomous "queen of the sciences."

From this brief description it may be seen that the nature of the university community from the standpoint of symbolization requires more extensive study. The term "university community" may be employed in at least two ways: as signifying the juridical and as signifying the charismatic. These forms of the community exist side by side, and in many phases overlap. In many universities they are in constant tension, the tension between those people with minimal yet real concern and respect for the community, and those who have intense devotion and willingness to sacrifice themselves for the benefit of a reality whose beneficence can only be pointed to through the employment of symbols. The application of the idea of the two communities to other facets of university life is also apparent.

This analysis of the conformist, anarchist, and ritualistic intentions in student activities has been attempted to show in a tentative and hopefully suggestive manner how the various aims and intentions of student activities are understood. Other possible intentions also readily come to mind: retreatism (a form of collective asceticism), and innovationism (the ultimate value of encouraging change, change, change). Moreover, as theoretical means of understanding student activities, all of these intentions and purposes have both strengths and weaknesses; some combination would enhance the final truth of the matter. Further study, bolstered by empirical investigation, is required to establish the validity of such constructs, and to determine their mode in concrete situations. Further study of the nature of the university as a community is also indicated.

As a professional responsibility student activities not only involves communities but concrete small groups. Content merely to accept the fact that these groups are multifarious in type, workers have made no attempt to systematically classify them. In part, this failure is a result of unfamiliarity with social science efforts in past decades to categorize groups; and in part, a result of a tendency among student activities workers to be overcome by their pragmatic interests — they have "better" things to do with their time. Furthermore, some say that the task of classifying groups is merely theoretical — presumably, theoretical activities have no practical consequences.

Yet, the development of general procedures is based upon a knowledge of the divisions and subdivisions of a subject or activity to which the general laws are supposedly to be applied. Conversely, it is scientifically impossible to arrive at generalizing principles unless the cases on which the principles are drawn can be adequately classified. Disparate cases can never be made to yield a single conclusion. Therefore the work of classifying groups is not only one of significant interest and speculative satisfaction, but is absolutely necessary for the further growth of the field.

✈ 9

Group Classification

LUDWIG GUMPLOWICZ in 1899 prophetically declared that it is possible to formulate laws governing the behavior of groups, although he wrongly thought that group behavior was neither determined nor influenced by the behavior of individuals within the group.[1] Since his time considerable effort to determine these laws has been deployed by sociologists, social psychologists, student activities leaders, and others.[2] Attention also has been given, especially more recently, to the internal structure of groups and the interpersonal relations of the members. This latter effort perhaps dominates the field of "group dynamics" today, and comprises a most fascinating phase of man's concern with his behavior. The present special interest in small groups is viewed by Robert Faris as a revelatory source of information on individual personality, and as a logical meeting place for sociology and social psychology as related disciplines.[3] From all sides, as interest grows in the nature of group life, new insights have been gained for student activities.

The interest of student activities workers is directed more toward investigating the internal structures of groups and the interpersonal relations of group members than toward the establishment of suitable categories of group classification. This bias on the part of the workers

NOTE: This chapter is based in part on my article, "Group Classification in Student Activities," *Peabody Journal of Education*, 34 (1957), 195–204, reproduced here in modified form with the permission of the publisher.

110

is largely to be expected, in view of the interests of investigators in other disciplines.

Student activities has suffered low status in the university in part from not having been clearly defined. University administrators and faculties usually possess no comprehensive awareness of the variety and complexity of the groups that exist under the general banner of student activities. Too often university policies are formulated with a particular segment of student activities in mind and without a sufficiently detailed knowledge of the manifold nature of the group life of the campus. For these and other reasons, student activities needs to study not only the internal structures of student activities groups and the interpersonal relations among their members; it also needs to exert serious efforts at group classification.

It would not be wise, however, to assume that the problem of group classification can be easily solved. Apparently, the present energies of researchers in group dynamics are being spent in studying the present concerns because of past failures to solve the general problem of group classification. The failures of the past seem to fall into two categories. First, those who have been at work to define the nature of and differences between groups (mainly sociologists and social psychologists) have failed to develop thoroughly consistent and inclusive systems of classification. This failure may be owing to the bewildering variety of groups. A group by definition is an aggregate of individuals which endures for a period of time, which has one or more interests and activities in common to bind it together, and which possesses some kind of organization (leaders and followers, rules for operation). Special descriptions of groups have been formulated which discuss only one or two aspects of a group and fail to establish systematic accounts of all groups. Thus such descriptions as "primary versus secondary groups," "in versus out groups," and "ethnocentric groups" have been devised. In themselves they create worthwhile understandings of group life, yet they fail to fit into a pattern of analysis in which all groups might find a logical place. Not all groups fit into any one of the descriptions offered.

Sociologists and others have tried to create classificatory systems by which groups generally may be understood. Edward A. Ross, early in this century, devised a general system containing the following categories: (1) fortuitous groups (crowds); (2) natural groups (families, clans); (3) interest groups (states, confederacies, guilds); and (4) likeness groups (professions, classes).[4] Others, such as John L. Gillen and John P. Gillen, have adopted similar classifications with some modifications peculiar to their own formulation.[5]

These paradigms provide a convenient and illuminating account of the nature of group life, although on certain specifics they may be found wanting. Ross's system, for example, being highly rationalistic, largely fails to recognize that the interrelations among the four kinds of groups are at times and places more significant than the simple and isolated category. The relationship of the Prussian military group (category four) to the organization and operation of the Bismarckian German state (group three) is of more than incidental importance. Moreover, the similarity of certain groups which for Ross are subsumed under a particular category may be questioned. Professions and classes may be bound by "likeness," yet likeness can never account satisfactorily for the gross existential differences between professions and classes. It is for reasons such as these that sociologists, social psychologists, and others have recently shied away from taking classificatory systems of groups too seriously.

Yet, there is a second basis on which to establish systems of group classification, to which those who currently investigate group life have shown a reluctance to give thought and energy. Such systems commonly fail to appreciate sufficiently the nonlogical aspects of group life. They are too eager to press groups into an overly simplified structural analysis. Or, in Raymond B. Cattell's language, "even when sociologists . . . have recognized that a group exists only because and so long as it satisfies psychological needs, they have failed to appreciate the nature of the ergic and the metanergic needs that are involved in its support."[6] In some instances, as in "ethnocentric groups" and "primary and secondary groups," the ultimate psychological dynamic involved in group formation and, therefore, of classification, is that of threat to group security. This singling out of a special factor of motivation as an explanation of the totality of group life (or at least a most significant phase of it) unfortunately indicates a monofactored social psychology.

The group theory of Ludwig von Wiese is a good example of the oversimplification of group syntality. Although von Wiese was greatly interested in group process, and interpreted the development of particular group forms as a result of psychological factors, he employed categories (such as associative and dissociative, integrated and differentiated, constructive and destructive) which fundamentally revolve around the notion of threat. Amalgamation and conflict are the key terms in his classification of groups. While one could hardly deny that von Wiese's contribution was important, one would also have to note its severe limitations from a social-psychological viewpoint.[7] The distinction of "systems" and "congeries" employed by Pitirim Sorokin, Carle Zimmerman, and Charles Galpin appears to be more comprehensive and defensible.[8]

Although the foregoing offers at least two reasons for giving up any effort to suggest a fundamental system of group classification for student activities and for concentrating on internal structure and interpersonal relations, the effort cannot stop at this point. For one thing, it can be assumed that some system of group classification is either tacit or explicit in all discussions of group behavior. A review of the research at present accomplished will quickly demonstrate that no researcher can begin his activities without a conception not only of the group or groups with which he wishes to deal, but a conception of groups in general. Kenneth D. Benne and Grace Levit show this to be true in their analysis of nine approaches in research on the nature of groups.[9]

Analysis of particular groups or constellations of groups is generally undertaken with two purposes — these purposes being intrinsic in scientific method. First, science seeks to gain understanding of particular and unique phases of human and natural reality. Second, and of cardinal significance, science seeks to gain understanding of general reality through comparative and abstractive efforts. Whenever the second aim of inquiry into the nature of group life is entertained, a theory of the group must be held which in itself comprises an acceptance of the possibility of group classification. The researcher who seeks to make a logical system of the kinds of groups that exist can hardly be thought by that effort to be illogical, unpsychological, or unscientific. Christoph Heinicke and Robert F. Bales in their efforts to discover the developmental trends in the structure of small groups use a device termed "status consensus" in order to dichotomize the groups used in their experiment.[10] So, also, David G. Hays and Robert R. Bush, studying status reactions in informal groups, establish a "voting model" and a "group actor model" in order to analyze their problem.[11] These researchers are not unusual in distinguishing among groups under observation; they are maintaining a basic requirement of the scientific method. Like others, they are to some degree discriminating rationally among groups. Group classification, whether to include all groups or merely some, is essentially such an operation.[12]

The student activities program of a university is notably characterized by variety — of leadership, size of groups, group organization, group programs and activities, age and sex of members, social views toward group process (authoritarianism, conservatism, and the like), roles of members, physical conditionings, abilities of the individual members, group statuses, methods of communication. Is it at all possible to construct a system of classification which will impose meaning on this variety? Do any "common denominator" elements within the variety fall into significant patterns that will further one's understanding of student activities?

As with previous efforts to classify groups, the classification of student activities groups appears to be amenable to two general divisions: (1) noninclusive classifications, and (2) inclusive classifications. To some extent the noninclusive classifications which have been developed in disciplines other than student activities are also meaningful within the field. It is possible to speak of "in versus out groups," "ethnocentric groups," and so forth, in some phases of student activities. In this sense a partial system of classification already is available and in use within student activities.

But is it possible to establish other categories of a noninclusive nature by which student activities might be interpreted more precisely, and, therefore, more meaningfully? Perhaps it is possible. The following noninclusive patterns may prove helpful, especially if viewed as "ideal types" or polar expressions of what in most instances occurs not in "versus" form but as "both . . . and."

The first pattern is that of audience-focused groups versus self-focused groups. In student activities some groups exist to satisfy the interests of audiences as well as those of the members of the group. A varsity players group, for example, secures significant pleasure and training from its activities. The members may bring different motivations to bear upon their individual performances. But basically the activity cannot be understood properly without taking account of its relationship to a factor outside the group, namely, the audience. The activity can never be for the group alone what it is for the group and the audience.

Many student activities groups function with little or no relation to an audience. A hiking club exists not because it wishes to demonstrate the benefits of hiking to an audience. It may on rare occasions engage in such a demonstration, perhaps as part of a student activities "day" on the campus, but the group does not exist primarily for such activities. It was formed to provide its members with association and activity in hiking.

In this manner, then, it is possible to conceive of groups on the campus which may be classified according to the audience factor alone.

The second pattern is that of curricularly oriented groups versus noncurricularly oriented groups. Certain student activities groups seem to be more directly related to the university curriculum than others. Others seem to bear little or no relation to the curriculum. The home economics group, for example, which has grown out of a department of home economics sponsorship and the needs of the students within that specialization for noncurricular association in order to further their interests, may well reflect in many aspects of its life its basic tie to an academic content provided by the university in a particular department of instruction. The group may practice a number of activities, such as trips to factories, "socials," and job placement, but fundamentally it is oriented toward home economics, a curricular program.

On the other hand, a group of bridge-playing students may engage in a recognized part of a student activities program, but it cannot be claimed that its presence on the campus is directly related to any phase of the curriculum. It exists for non-curricular purposes: for the pleasure of the members, to develop the skill of the players, to advance the "cause" on the campus and elsewhere (there are intercollegiate contests). It is true that the members may call upon knowledge learned in the curricular aspects of university life to improve their playing, and their motives in joining the group may be personal, but essentially the group is noncurricularly oriented.

The third pattern is that of institutionally led groups versus membership led groups. It is evident that some student activities groups require for their success the supervision and control of institutional personnel. It is difficult to imagine a debate group being able to manage their interests effectively without a faculty member who coaches or supervises. A debate group may be able to establish its success by permitting many of its activities to be managed and decided by the student members, either individually, in committees, or as a total membership. But at some point the group relies upon the training, skill, and experience of the faculty leader.

Certain student groups on the campus may be permitted a large degree of self-control and self-supervision. Social organizations, for example, usually come under this heading. The social organization requires some degree of supervision by the university (at times a great deal), but generally the organization and execution of the group's purposes can be accomplished without the overly close attention of a trained, skilled, and experienced faculty member or a professional student activities leader.[13] In some universities a student adviser system takes the place of a faculty adviser arrangement for social groups. Special education in leadership may be afforded the student advisers by the faculty or others to whom the task has been delegated.

The fourth pattern is that of heterogeneous groups versus homogeneous groups. Certain student activities groups are, as the sociologists say, unenacted groups, with a low degree of social cohesion, the members never being called upon for a decision regarding their membership. The group formed by the diners in a student cafeteria is an example. Usually no one calls them together; they have no officers or stated constitution. Eating is the chief interest which brings them together, although other motives may enter into the situation.

In contrast, an art group may be highly homogeneous, by definition excluding those students who lack an interest, and by prescription excluding those without talent in the medium. Students who join generally make a definite decision to participate and are highly conscious of the fundamental purpose of the group. The members are likely to feel that they need each other for mutual comparison and stimulation.[14]

The fifth pattern is that of large groups versus small groups. Student activities groups vary considerably in size of memberships. The senior class which meets to plan a prom is a group decidedly different from a student society which meets to discuss Chinese classics.

These five noninclusive ways of classifying student activities groups are not meant to be exhaustive. Nor is it intended that they should be considered mutually exclusive; a particular group may fit into more than one of the five categories. The categories do not in themselves represent an attempt to uncover and systematize the psychological factors which are operative in the initiation and maintenance of student activities groups. It is hoped that these categories may be employed in conducting practical, psychological, experimental analyses of the nature of group life in student activities.

The formulation of a general classification of student activities groups is more difficult than the establishment of noninclusive group categories principally because of the sheer number and variety of groups under consideration. Though efforts made in the past have been inadequate, recent advances in the study and understanding of groups have opened the way to more effective attacks on this logically rigorous task.[15] The following five-fold classification is suggested as a beginning effort.

Heterogeneous groups include those groups whose membership is not asked to make decisions regarding the group, and whose composition is highly varied so far as sex, intensity of interest, and sense of commitment are concerned.

Status groups include honor societies, university-wide policy making committees, faculty-student groups, in which, regardless of the specific responsibility of the group, a notable measure of prestige accrues to the members.[16]

Interest groups are composed of those students who possess a problem or skill concerning which a specific kind of activity acts as a satisfaction. Such interests may not relate to career choice but rather to curiosity and pleasure needs.

Social groups are formed for the chief purpose of enabling students to associate with each other in a pleasurable activity, and with a relatively "low" form of organization and directiveness. Usually their programs do not capitalize on specific and well-developed skills on the part of their members.

Students with a clearly defined vocational objective, such as teaching, medicine, the ministry, or social work, may form and maintain groups to exploit their career needs. Closely attached to departments of instruction, these groups represent to some degree an extension of the curriculum of the university.

The five suggested categories of student activities groups, again, are not meant to be final. Nor is it intended that each student group can be catalogued into only one of the types. Problems of motivation of the individual members and the internal structures of student groups remain to be examined in a separate context. The group classification is established as a means of clarifying the nature of group life in student activities, and as a means of supplying points for investigation and comparison of research findings.

The nature of the groups which engage the attention and skill of student activities workers provides a basic subject for investigation. The investigation of such groups will depend upon the possibilities of conceptual organization coupled with specific research activities to test their validity.

Basic to the whole organization of student groups in the university, however, stands the problem of freedom. Traditionally there has been an almost rebellious demand on the part of students for freedom. Often not caring to understand what they wanted, they have sought to be freed of restrictions imposed by the university upon their persons or their groups. Universities, on the other hand, having been traditionally impressed with the need for the maintenance of order, have logically been unable to afford every freedom demanded by students; anarchy would result and the necessary coherence by which the university maintains itself as a social institution would be destroyed. As a result of these two ideas of the role of freedom, especially in student activities, tensions and conflicts have characterized student-university relations. The problem of freedom, then, is basic to an understanding of the nature of student activities and its place within the university.

⤏≮ 10

Freedom

ON EVERY side the health of freedom on the university campus is an object of concern. Conservatives claim that nearly everywhere freedom is on the run before the avalanche-like movements of collectivism. To the conservative, collectivism means a freedom-denying condition in society, which in these latter days has infected the American campus. Take for example the views of E. Merrill Root, professor of English at Earlham College, when he speaks openly of "collectivism on the campus." By this he means that the "collectivist Left" has seized control of the university by intimidating those who believe in traditional values (especially of free enterprise) and has indoctrinated a whole generation into the supposed benefits of societal collectivism. Professor Root apparently believes that only the student wishes for true freedom of expression. Faculties are cowed into collectivistic conformity insofar as they do not willingly favor it. Even boards of trustees lean over backwards to protect the leftists, including communists and fellow-travelers. To such an extent does he wish the university to accept his brand of freedom that he is willing to go to authoritarian lengths to guarantee it, asserting that parents, alumni, and educators should demand that "50 per cent of the faculty passionately and articulately uphold free enterprise."[1]

NOTE: This chapter is based in part on my article, "Freedom in Student Activities," *Educational Theory*, 8 (1958), 213–225, reproduced here in modified form with the permission of the publisher.

Of course it is easy to point out that Professor Root thoroughly misunderstands the nature of the university. The university does not exist to insure a percentage of advocacy of anything, unless it be such values as personal integrity and acknowledgment of truth. The task of the university is to maintain free inquiry, to enable faculty and students to teach and learn according to the principles of the uncontrolled although informed mind. By lumping liberals with communists and fellow-travelers Root is doing his own cause a disservice, since so many liberals are fiercely anti-communist. By attaching his doctrine to the primacy of economic determinacy he himself misreads history and even economics, and falls rather deeply into the Marxian fallacy. Nevertheless, he is sure that the university does not have true freedom and he sincerely wants it to change its ways in order to attain it.

On the other extreme stands Robert M. MacIver, professor emeritus of political philosophy and sociology at Columbia University. His position is most clearly revealed in a book written for the American Academic Freedom Project, sponsored by the Louis M. Rabinowitz Foundation.[2] The book, however, does not represent the views either of the Foundation or of Columbia University, but rather the results of study by its author and his own convictions.

Professor MacIver believes that the social climate in America today reflects the conservatism that Professor Root advocates. To the "liberal" MacIver that climate is decidedly reactionary, and he spends considerable energy in exposing the "pseudo-educational" associations of Allen Zoll and Merwin Hart as though these were truly dominant groups with significant influence on the American campus: "These are the forces that in our time most seriously threaten not only academic freedom but the whole broad freedom of thought." In addition to such associations, Professor MacIver outlines threats from individual writers like William F. Buckley, Jr., special interest organizations, fanatically patriotic groups, and congressional committees.[3] In all, the picture Professor MacIver paints is black, almost pitch black. True freedom, he tells us, is almost nonexistent on the university campus.

Like Professor Root, MacIver misreads the current community and university scene. He magnifies the thought and actions of small, generally unrecognized groups, as if these organizations were on the same footing as the large, well-accepted educational associations (such as the National Education Association and the American Association of

University Professors). In an unscientific manner, he cites isolated instances in which academic freedom has been violated to make a case for its almost total absence in the university. He overlooks the fact that, with the exception of some denominational colleges, universities everywhere have placed responsibility as to what shall be taught, and how, upon faculties. In the main it is the faculty of the university which not only believes in but practices academic freedom.[4]

Both from the right and the left, then, the fate of freedom on the university campus has been sharply questioned. Although the health of freedom has been consistently diagnosed as poor, disagreement on the pathology persists.[5]

It can hardly be maintained that most students have a sophisticated understanding of the theoretical implications of the present disagreement over freedom in the university. Many students, nevertheless, firmly believe in freedom — their freedom in the university community. Their belief may be attributed to many diverse factors.

First is political involvement. Some students, probably a small minority on any campus, hold membership in social and political groups (either on or off the campus or both) which possess a relatively well-developed doctrine of freedom. Young Republicans and Young Democrats may disagree as to what freedom means on the campus, but they have their views on it and eagerly discuss it. Such opinions are usually doctrinaire rather than objective.

Second is self-interest. Many students and their groups assert a belief in freedom largely because that belief is related to certain goals they wish to achieve.[6] Student governments traditionally have wanted to be "self-governments" in the conviction that they thereby would withstand encroachments from faculty or administration. It is to their interest, they reason, to assert their need for a nearly absolute freedom. Again, fraternities and sororities have regularly claimed independence from university controls in the name of freedom — the freedom of the student to associate with whom he pleases and to organize his life according to the principles he recognizes.

The demand for freedom as a stratagem for the attainment of personal and group power is not described here in moralistic terms. Rather it is accepted as a basic principle of human existence even as the unpopular Thomas Hobbes recognized it:

I put for a general inclination of all mankind, a perpetual and restless desire of power after power, that ceaseth only in death. And the cause of this is not always that a man hopes for a more intensive delight than he has already attained to, or that he cannot be content with a moderate power; but because he cannot assure the power and means to live well which he hath present, without the acquisition of more.[7]

Basically the same desire for absolute and absolutely self-corrupting power marked the life of Caius Marius, the first man to be made Consul of Rome seven times, who, according to Plutarch, ended his life in a feverish madness because his thirst for adulation had not been fully quenched.

Third is educational growth. Students claim the freedom to make mistakes because by so doing they undergo genuine growth. Faculty and administrators frequently agree with students on this point and sometimes appear to glory in the ability of the students to make mistakes in conducting their activities. Sympathizers with this viewpoint are reluctant to assert the inevitability that everybody will make a mistake now and then — "to err is human"; they turn fallibility into a "right" as though the ability to err would be atrophied if not practiced constantly. Yet it is mainly on the grounds of high educational theory that the claim to freedom is made in many cases.

Fourth is adolescent rebelliousness. Students find unwelcome the suggestion that the freedom they demand is related to a need to rebel against the traditional standards and activities of their homes and community. More often it is the faculty and administration who elaborate this notion, excusing students who misuse their freedom or who cry for more as simply creatures who are bound by unconsciously directed urges given to a particular period of their development.

Fifth is institutional permissiveness, freedom (meaning permissiveness as a doctrine) for students being written into the institutional framework as a basic conviction of those responsible for the university over the years: faculty, administration, and trustees. The philosophy of permissiveness in some universities, despite the changes which have occurred in the direction of "general education," is featured both in the curricular as well as the co-curricular aspects of the institution's corporate life, reminding one of the Verdurin household in Proust's *Swann's Way*: "The Verdurins never invited you to dinner; you had your 'place laid' there. There was never any programme for the evening's entertainment. The young pianist would play, but only if he felt inclined, for no one was forced to do anything, and, as M. Verdurin used to say: 'We're all friends here. Liberty Hall, you know!'"[8]

The idea that freedom means the absence of all restraint is apparent in much of the discussion of freedom in our time. It is a veiled postulate underlying much of the commentary by students on their relations to the university. To be free, they say, is to be unhampered in their choice of courses and in the exercise of their interests in the co-curricular life of the university. Such a conception of freedom, however, is absolutely unhistorical and impossible in the experience of men. Franz Boas, the noted anthropologist, made this point upon reflecting on the place of freedom in primitive societies (where one might suspect there is perfect freedom):

Interference with the freedom of action or the personal comfort of an individual by fellow-tribesmen may occur even in the simplest societies. Such interference is generally based on personal conflicts. Two individuals may strive for possession of the same object. If the customs of the community permit, the conflict may be decided by combat between the antagonists and may also involve their friends. Unfriendly gossip may create a condition against which the individual cannot successfully contend and which limits his freedom of action within the social group . . . Such conflicts between individuals, or between individuals and society as a whole, or between groups unfriendly to each other, may encroach seriously upon the freedom of the individual.[9]

Moreover, absolute freedom from restraint would make of freedom an evil force in human relations. Lincoln's adversaries based their slavery arguments upon this absolute doctrine of freedom. Freedom, they said, permitted a man to buy and sell slaves. In his notable debate with Douglas, Lincoln summarized this conception for his opposition in the following words: "It is, as a principle, no other than that if one man chooses to make a slave of another man, neither that other man nor anybody else has a right to object."[10]

In limited degree, however, freedom from restraint is possible, in that every person possesses spheres within his experience in which he acknowledges greater and lesser external restraint. One is more free to choose a movie than to self-determine the basis on which admission to a university can be secured. One is less free to drive on the highway than to garden on one's own property. So it goes. Even within the university the variety of situations in which freedom from restraint exists is striking. A student may not be entirely free in his freshman and sophomore years to elect courses, but he enjoys greater freedom as a junior and senior. In general the student has less freedom within the classroom than in student activities. Again, one may have more freedom within a hiking club than within a debate team.

It is well to note the situational limitations to the pure expression of freedom. The student who fails to acknowledge and act upon the requirements of freedom appropriate to each situation within the university (especially in student activities) is not a heroic reformer, but a maladjusted person who has still to develop a mature understanding of himself, of the intellectual basis for his actions, and of the requirements of social living.[11]

Behind the practice of situational freedom in the university lies an all-important assumption: the student may be granted increased freedom from restraint to the degree that he is able to match the situation with personal maturity. The university does not in our day permit the student to choose any course program from his freshman to his senior year on the theory that he is sufficiently mature to take such decisions. But the university may well believe that as a student progresses in maturity he may develop the judgment to make intelligent decisions regarding his academic choices. Some such philosophy of personal maturity, if consistently held, should be apparent also in student activities, although it must be quickly admitted that all too often it is not.

A further difficulty in interpreting freedom as the absence of restraint lies in its often taking the form of a mechanistic, power-driven need system, in the university as well as in the community generally. That is to say that students who look upon freedom in these terms may conclude that the only freedom they are able to possess and exercise is that which they have won from reluctant and even opposed faculties and administrations. In this spirit, students may keep a mental tally sheet of the present stock of freedom and wage campaigns to increase that stock. Such an attitude toward freedom encourages the lowest forms of cheap political activity; if this attitude prevails, the very meaning of freedom in the university suffers.

Apparently this sort of belief in freedom molds some of the efforts of students to secure "student rights." Obviously the mere assertion of rights does not validate them. Usually the listing of rights by students mirrors the claim of rights in the political community. Students (even national associations of student groups) sometimes claim that there are certain inalienable rights accorded them in their status as students. These rights, students say, are supported by "natural law." Their rights to self-government, to freedom of the press, and to equal representation in the determination of certain university policies, they say, are based upon the achievements of rational democracy, and that anyone who denies these rights is not an educator but an outdated tyrant.

Students who make these assertions, however, fail to understand their academic instruction adequately. They would be hard put in the light of present scholarship to defend their views successfully on the grounds of natural law, for as Leo Strauss has pointed out, the distinction between *physis* and *nomos* in the history of the idea of natural law has consistently involved a transnatural basis for the belief in man's rights.[12]

There is little reason to assume that the rights accorded man in the political community are automatically those granted by nature to students in the university.[13] Students are nowhere more weak and illogical in arguing for rights than when they claim an extension of their rights in society into the university. In conceiving the essential character of the university as a special political community within the larger community, they perform a distinct disservice to the university. This conclusion is rightly affirmed in a recent report of the United States Student Association, which points out that this claim

. . . overlooks the fact that the student is not in the same position as the adult citizen. In the political community, anyone who is twenty-one has the right to participate in determining the way the community is run, but the college is a bureaucratic organization, an institution rather than a political community, and in the college the student is not only in the sociological position of a client, but as well is in the legal position of a child.[14]

If freedom, then, cannot fully be understood to mean the absence of restraint, what is it intrinsically, and how does it relate to the field of student activities in particular? Freedom is not a right of man, but an essential condition of human existence. Freedom is not an attribute of any other reality, but a unique reality in itself.[15] All other realities are confined and defined by their own natures. They are what they are. But freedom, although its course is harmonious with its nature, must of necessity determine itself. As Paul Tillich puts it: "Freedom is the possibility of transcending its nature."[16]

It is difficult to know just why freedom is its own special reality, separate from others and distinguished by potentiality and actualization beyond human prediction and comprehension. On this score some insights have been offered historically, although they lack a convincingness which is completely satisfying. Perhaps Alfred North Whitehead has said the best that can be said about this aspect of freedom:

> The peculiarity of the course of history illustrates the joint relevance of the "ontological principle" and of this categorial obligation. The evolution of history can be rationalized by the consideration of the determination of successors by antecedents. But, on the other hand, the evolution of history is incapable of rationalization because it exhibits a selected flux of participating forms. No reason, internal to history, can be assigned why that flux of forms, rather than another flux, should have been illustrated. It is true that any flux must exhibit the character of internal determination. So much follows from the ontological principle. But every instance of internal determination assumes *that* flux up to *that* point. There is no reason why there could be no alternative flux exhibiting that principle of internal determination. The actual flux presents itself with the character of being merely "given." It does not disclose any peculiar character of "perfection" . . . Further, in the case of those actualities whose immediate experience is most completely open to us, namely, human beings, the final decision of the immediate subject-superject, constituting the ultimate modification of subjective aim, is the foundation of our experience of responsibility, of approbation or of disapprobation, of self-approval or of self-reproach, of freedom, of emphasis. This element in experience is too large to be put aside merely as misconstruction.[17]

One might wish that Whitehead had amplified his remarks on the fundamental fact of freedom in human experience, yet what he has said is as apt a description as any.[18] Possibly only a theological metaphysics can ultimately provide a satisfying understanding of the constitution of human freedom. Nonhistorical explanations, however, tend to deny man his true freedom, for that is dependent in part upon his ability in history to determine his own nature and history, and indeed to become something new in the processes of history. So, history and freedom are dialectically related complementaries whose dependence upon each other gives each its distinctive meaning.

The character of freedom is existential rather than merely political. From the political standpoint, the slave in the Greek and Roman societies was not a free being because he lacked significantly the possibility of self-fulfillment in society. Nor, according to the Greeks, were the

barbarians fully free men, because they lacked the humanizing opportunities given to the Greeks. Yet when the Greeks' capacity for political
self-determination was shattered by the Romans, the Epicureans and
Stoics realized other aspects of freedom. For the Epicureans, freedom
in its totality constituted what Michael Polanyi in this latter day has
termed "private freedom": "There are many things an individual can
do . . . the social effects of which are considered negligible by the
authorities as well as by the consensus of opinion throughout society."[19]
That is private freedom, and the Epicureans took refuge in it as the
whole substance of freedom.

The Stoics, on the other hand, influenced as they were by the almost universal extension of Roman citizenship, were inclined to find
their definition of freedom in Roman citizenship. Roman citizenship
gave men the opportunity to participate thoroughly in history, and
therefore find their full freedom.

Less political than the Stoic was the Christian view of freedom.
Through the grace of God the Christian was liberated from the hold
of sin, guilt, and the evil powers. This freedom was not dependent
upon the political community, but rather upon the church, that is,
an assembly of those called out of society in their new freedom. The
Christian, as Paul noted, gained a new citizenship, universal in scope,
historical in implication, and transcendent in its ground. Especially in
the Protestant view of Christian freedom were freedom and equality
conjoined, since all believers were equal in status before God, and in
the responsibilities of their new citizenship.

In these various historical contexts, freedom has been conceived
from dissimilar points of view, yet with the general agreement that
freedom pertains intrinsically to man as man and to man as historical
actor.

For student activities this conception of freedom has many implications. Surely, this idea of freedom is more comprehensive, profound,
and basic to behavior, whether individual or group, than that espoused
under the idea of freedom as the absence of restraint. Freedom in student activities is not freedom *from;* it is freedom *for.* An inevitable consequence of selfhood and institutional participation, it is not a petty
gain requiring petty means of attainment. Freedom is not an aspect of
the human self, such as the mind, nor is it a socially compartmentalized
function, such as political freedom. Freedom involves the total person.

It exists for the person throughout his participation in life, although its dynamic quality requires that it either be fulfilled or risk losing its meaning.

Freedom in this sense bespeaks the creative utilization of the student's potentialities. These potentialities are able to fulfill themselves because of freedom, but freedom in itself is not the essential goal. In his whole university experience, the student is faced constantly with the task of self-fulfillment in freedom, and in devotion to the social context in which his freedom historically must be expressed. In fact the student, like all others, exercises his freedom through three kinds of creative expression.

First is meaningful creativity. The expression of freedom must be meaningful for the student. He must have a share in deciding how he can make his commitment to action meaningful; the meaning cannot be given to him by the faculty or by administrators. Of course it is not necessary that the student always initiate his own meaningfulness, but whatever purposes he gives himself to must have a meaning he cannot deny for himself. If the student acts upon the purposes not indicated by his own conviction, he is in effect being enslaved and denied the meaningful use of his freedom. The student and the student group must intrinsically believe in the worthwhileness or meaningfulness of their activities. The student group must permit the development of sincere and meaningful acceptance of the group's purposes by the individual member, allowing him a share in the decisions necessary for the full exercise of his individual freedom and the fulfillment of the group's purposes.

Freedom, then, must be rooted in meaningfulness rather than in sheer opportunity for self-expression.[20] This fact has been made clear for college instructors by Professor Sidney Hook, who criticizes the statement of Robert Hutchins that "everywhere in the U.S. university professors, whether or not they have tenure, are silenced by the general atmosphere of repression." Professor Hook says that professors are not silent, that there is no conspiracy against free discussion in the university. Then he goes on to say:

It may be that we educators do not talk as much as we should, but we have talked more than we ever have in the past. The question is: What do we have to say? My point is that we do not talk enough about problems, and the little we do talk is ineffectual. As a kind of compensation for this ineffectuality, there is often heard in educational quarters a new slogan — the importance of nonconformism. It requires only a moment's reflection to see that the terms "conformity" and "nonconformity" are relational and that, unless one knows the what, why, and how of conformity or nonconformity, the terms are meaningless, more accurately emotive symbols communicating at best a mood. In a sense, the greatest nonconformist in modern times was Adolf Hitler. He even refused to conform to the traditionally despotic ways of degrading man but strove to carve out new worlds of infamy for himself.[21]

Students likewise need not glory in either conformity or nonconformity. They have no quarrel with any person or group within the university or the community over their need for self-expression. First of all they need to achieve meaningfulness by the creative use of freedom, and that meaningfulness is not an automatic concomitant or product of their freedom.

The second kind of creative expression is autonomous creativity, the freedom to act within the laws inherent in the situation in which the individual or the group finds itself without the employment by the members of influence extrinsic to the situation. (This view makes use of the traditional meaning of autonomous.) Such freedom recognizes the student's obligation to express his freedom within the objective structure of the group or situation in which he participates. For the student to act in a manner which denies the intrinsic importance of the social form granted to him for his expression is for him to pervert his freedom. He may be more or less adept in various group situations, but he must follow the basic requirements of the given situation if he expects to find self-fulfillment and to contribute to the progress of the group.[22]

In a parallel sense, the judge must perform his function in relation to the law. The teacher must find his freedom within the areas of knowledge in which he possesses competency. The racer can excel only by staying on the course. So, too, the student must find his freedom in creative involvement in the social forms at hand. The student who fails to act within the objective structure of the given social situation denies his historical freedom. He misuses himself and denies himself his true fulfillment.[23]

Accordingly, the so-called pranks of students must be considered inappropriate and immoral not simply because they cause the university embarrassment, nor because they violate community standards, but because they are abuses of man's nature as a freedom-possessing creature. Unrealized and unfulfilled in self-negating, self-destructive behavior, his true expression must be sought creatively in activities which are meaningful and appropriate within the social medium.

Recently a number of universities and educators have shown a change in attitude toward misconduct. Burton P. Fowler, principal of the Germantown Friends School in Philadelphia, in a letter to *The New York Times*, has questioned the propriety of certain prankish activities:

Following the recent riots staged at several of our leading colleges, the one characteristic comment of the college authorities as well as that of the press seems to be that "boys will be boys." It is true that boys will be boys until they are expected to be men.

Is it not possible that too many bright boys who have not grown up are being admitted to college, and after they get there are having their intellects cultivated at the expense of their behavior . . .

Hazing, fraternity rushing, excessive drinking, commercialized athletics and other campus mores that long ago should have been outmoded are not reassuring to the citizen who looks at the high cost of a college education. When college boys engage in battles with the police, destroy property, and behave insultingly toward girls, or vice versa, it is dismissed as "a combination of youth and spring," while in the slums of our great cities we call similar behavior delinquency, or in prison riots we call it insurrection . . .

There is a real danger, I believe, that this careless freedom from the responsibility of college life, a kind of perpetual Halloween atmosphere, will persist until, like the athletic scandals of last year, it may threaten public respect for the whole of higher education.[24]

Although Dr. Fowler's tone may seem too moralistic to allow any parallel with the idea that freedom imposes its own restraints appropriate to the situation in which it is being expressed, his standpoint reveals his awareness of the objective conditions in which university students should act.

On May 21, 1956, between 80 and 100 students of the University of Kansas paid a visit to the campus of Baker University (twelve miles away) and conducted a "panty raid" at Alpha Chi Omega sorority. On May 31, 1956, the administration of the University of Kansas dismissed fifty-eight of the participants in the riot. Discussion for some time was held among educators as to whether the University of Kansas acted wisely, with many diverse views being expressed. The editor of *School and Society*, however, pointed out the improper use of freedom by the students in the following manner:

News of "panty raids" and similar incidents do much to lower the prestige of higher education at home and abroad. By putting a strong foot down on such nonsense, the colleges can convince young men — and young women, for that matter, too — that the high jinks do not mix with higher education. With enrollment expected to mount skyward and with faculties and facilities increasing at more modest rates, there should be no room in the college and university for the so-called student who is whiling away his time amid indifferent academic and behavioral standards. What is needed is the *real* student whose main interest is learning.[25]

As previously stated, the student cannot divorce himself in his use of freedom from the situation in which he finds himself. He is bone of the bone and flesh of the flesh of the social group or institution in which he acts.[26] It is proper, then, that he be asked to possess and express personal maturity (internalized control) in autonomously relating his use of freedom to the objective structure of the social situation.

The third kind of creative expression is self-fulfilling creativity. If freedom is to be meaningful in its expression and appropriate to its surroundings, it should lead to the self-fulfillment of the individual. As the personal aim of the possession of freedom, self-fulfillment entails belief in the fundamental ability of persons to change, develop, or mature. Man is a self-fulfilling creature. It is this feature of his nature which in degree marks him from nature. Man, in other words, is able to transcend himself. He can become that which he is not. But his self-fulfillment is rooted in his freedom, for without freedom man would be forced to remain at a given stage of maturity for an indefinite period of time. Because man is free, he is able to change.

Self-fulfillment has its sterner aspects in which the principal concern is not the feeling of the person but his objective attainment.[27] The student who claims that he is fulfilling himself through a given activity needs to be reminded of the variety of criteria by which fulfillment may be evaluated. In the sphere of freedom not all roads lead to Rome. The student group which asserts an independence regardless of its university relationship is violating the autonomous requirements of freedom and perverting the proper sort of fulfillment which is open to it — a fulfillment which stresses community and cooperation rather than factionalism and disorder.

It can be assumed that students as individuals and in groups do not necessarily have the maturity to judge the entire content of their self-fulfillment. Like any person, the student finds his criteria of evaluation through his association with others. The university, somewhat like the churches, is in part a community of grace in which the members help each other to the fullest maturity. The student editor, for example, who resists the suggestions or instructions of the faculty adviser is failing to maintain that openness toward the objective evaluation of his self-fulfillment which is proper to the possession of freedom. The student government which seeks to maintain a severe independence from faculty and administrators, and views every suggestion with pained and troubled reaction, is operating under a false philosophy of freedom, and in the process shutting itself off from the community of suggestion and criticism by which students are able to judge their own progress in self-fulfillment. Freedom is not a right to do as one pleases; it is the condition of creative self-fulfillment in which the self and others participate within the contexts of autonomy and meaningfulness.

Yet the sterner, contentful aspects of self-fulfilling creativity must find a balance with the sense of joy and happiness resulting from partial self-fulfillment. Much of student activities exists to provide forms of happiness to students and a sense on their part of mastering new content and skills. It is entirely proper that such enthusiasm be a complement to student activities, both for individuals and groups. But the happiness to be sought is that of *eudaimonia* rather than *hedone*. *Hedone* expresses the "pleasure principle." Happiness, in the sense of *eudaimonia*, is accompanied by pleasure, but happiness is also attainable in which little or no pleasure is present. *Eudaimonia* expresses the actualization of the student's potential self-fulfillment. It is a condition of exultation and joy — the joy of accomplishment, the joy resulting from the true use of freedom.

Ideally, individual student achievement should be characterized by *eudaimonia*. Although this happiness cannot be given to the student, he can be sympathetically helped to achieve it, and its attainment can be noted and shared by others — students, family, faculty, and administrators.

On the other hand, the possibility of achieving happiness in student activities should not be too easily conceived. The student is prone to the same need for "the courage to be" that all men experience. Like others, he is threatened by the anxieties of fate and death, of emptiness and loss of meaning, and of guilt and condemnation.[28] All three threats are endemic to human experience, and are therefore present in the activities of the student in all phases of his life. A student activities philosophy which presents nothing but a breezy optimism regarding students' possibilities for achievement is basically unrealistic. In the long run such a philosophy may well be harmful to the welfare of the students.

The achievement of a philosophy of student activities which fully recognizes the total dimensions of man as a historically founded creature capable of freedom is one of the pressing and current needs of the university. The comments of David Riesman on the desirability of "inner direction" make a popular beginning, although Riesman is hardly aware of the profound problem of the sources of inner directedness in an industrial society.[29] Persons usually are not argued into accepting a new stance of life; and if they could be, the question still would remain of the sources of the dynamism or power necessary for the fulfillment of the rational ideal. Such an existential question seems ultimately to require a religious answer.

Walter Lippmann also has tackled much the same problem in the arena of public action and thought, contending that mass public opinion and legislatures have come to exercise a dominant and dangerous influence over the executive functions of government. The result, he states, is that modern democracies have grown more and more incapable of ruling wisely in peace and war. The root of the problem lies in the failure to maintain and defend the political faith of "public philosophy" which formed the basis of the convictions of the founding fathers. He calls for restraints upon the popularly accepted philosophy, and appeals to intellectual and social leaders to find a deeper basis for social responsibility than is current.[30]

In addition to Riesman and Lippmann many others are at work seeking answers to the perplexities which confront man in this period. Their efforts may not be easily translatable into the language and practice of student activities workers, who in turn may well have important contributions to make in the current dialogue concerning man, his nature and destiny. For in the final analysis the dialogue must be faced by student activities workers, and its implications must be accepted if the workers themselves are to enjoy that freedom for growth which is their condition by reason of their human existence.

-≮ 11

The Curriculum and the Co-curriculum

AS A social institution, the university consists of a variety of activities related to a hierarchy of purposes. Although it is possible to differentiate among the activities as to quality and value to the university, it is unwise to establish categoric antitheses among them under the mistaken notion that only the "best" activities contribute to the ultimate aims of the university. All have their role to play; each should lend support to the other. Even so, this view of the unity within diversity of the institution's activities and purposes is not readily accepted in some thoughtful quarters within the university. The tendency to see two main sets of activities with divergent purposes, the curriculum versus the co-curriculum, is still widely prevalent.

On one extreme the university is defined as a place where young people may sternly exercise their minds and achieve a massive accumulation of knowledge. Facts, many people say, are supreme, so the university is the place to get factual knowledge. This conception of higher education caricatures the student much in the manner of the perceptive American novelist Thomas Wolfe, one of whose characters prowls "the stacks of the library at night, pulling books out of a thousand shelves and reading them like a madman." This is the philosophy of "red-eyed education," which asserts the primacy of facts gained

NOTE: This chapter is based in part on my article, "Red-Eyed vs. Muscular Education," *motive magazine* (The Division of Higher Education of the Methodist Church), 18 (1956), 8–10, reproduced here in modified form with the permission of the publisher.

134

through reading books, and of "notebook education," derived from scribbling in a notebook what some professor got firsthand from a book.

While one may despair at the extreme form which this educational philosophy may take, it is not possible or desirable to scoff at it com-pletely, for, indeed, there is a genuine and wide-scaled need for greater thoughtfulness on the part of students. The democratization of higher education, though highly desirable and almost inevitable in a society such as our own, has not always meant that scholarly standards have been maintained or heightened. To some degree, it has encouraged universities to take refuge in merely factual education. In spite of mis-interpretations of the role of the intellect in higher education, however, there is a continuing need to stress the importance of high level cerebration.

One need only look at our popular culture to understand that a detached and profound view of life is required by the times. The prevalence of comic-book culture, ranging from "All Western" to "Dick Tracy," reveals how dependent many are upon these superficial anal-yses of human foibles, how they seek to escape responsibility through identification with a superman stereotype. The dominance of western movies and science-fantasy fiction, moreover, surely has meaning in much the same sense. Again, the success books, found in almost every drug store today, tell how human failure, combined with the innocent belief founded often on strange counterparts of the Christian message or on an outworn humanism which stresses perfectibility in this life, has responded to commercial exploitation. How many people willingly turn away from the sterner and more intellectually demanding aspects of high religion to take their ethics from these palatable paper-covered books! Was not Bruce Barton's *The Man Nobody Knows* written in anticipation of this trend, even in a most sacred area of faith?[1]

Cannot sophistication also be superficial? The man who laughs life off in a constant repetition of ancient jokes, who employs humor as a defense against reality, and who reads *The New Yorker* as his bible of cocktail party conversation, surely misses out on the plainer and saner aspects of life.

Unfortunately, many Americans today view life as amounting to little more ideally than having wrought-iron dining room furniture, the latest Book-of-the-Month selection, a twenty-three-inch television screen, aluminum storm windows and doors, and this year's Cadillac in the garage, all being paid for on the installment plan.

So, too, with other aspects of our popular culture. Advertising, with its vulgar treatment of the intimate aspects of marriage and family life and its delineation of the public as morons unable to distinguish between "better" and "best," deceives many into accepting a jazzed-up conception of even the simple necessities of life.

Our culture, fortunately, has its deeper and more respectable features, and one should never assume naively that popular culture is the total culture of a society. But there is constant need for those who are engaged in higher education not to be satisfied with the grosser elements of the popular culture. Higher education makes a greater pretense in aiming at more than simply the transmission of popular culture. It is engaged in a strenuous struggle with reality itself in all its phases. It seeks to rest life on first principles, not on third or fourth. Its call is to responsibility, not merely to pleasure.

In recent years, moreover, there has developed a greater appreciation of the practicality of the impractical. A generation ago, universities were much more concerned with applied science both in the laboratory and social science sense. Higher education was conceived sometimes as being an adjunct to efforts, for example, to improve the refrigerator. Today, however, in the atomic age, relatively lighter stress is given to simple and immediate application. Now, more and more, the most abstruse factors in our human and physical experience are recognized as the most relevant to our pressing problems. The delicate interrelations between mathematics and physics on the higher planes have been impressed upon even the layman, who sometimes talks the language of the expert without fully realizing its scientific import. Today, with governments and private organizations spending millions of dollars on so-called pure or theoretical research, the intellectual quest of the student has assumed a new — and practical — value.

Aside from scientific needs there are other reasons for the importance of intellectual pursuits in the university. The democratic heritage requires considerable and constant attention to humane and social values. It is trite to say that it will profit us nothing if we gain the whole world through atomic struggle and lose our souls in the gaining. A strong America, a phrase often heard these days, must mean an America which upholds firm convictions and practices regarding justice and righteousness. The sources of these values need to be explored more often than once each generation. They need to be seen in their historic perspective. Their relevance to ever changing social situations requires expert, informed leaders and followers. The social sciences and the humanities provide the student with the opportunity of formulating and testing his values in the light of the thought of the past and present. In these areas of knowledge, too, there is need for strenuous and careful thought.

Although the student might well consider his intellectual development as one of the legitimate expectancies to pursue as he makes his way through the university, higher education should mean more than intellectual preparation alone, important as that training may be. The development of other aspects of the personality also enters into higher education. A keen mind unable to communicate effectively what it knows to others is of little social value. The bright student who neglects to develop through his university experience the ability of later participating in groups, such as a staff meeting of his work organization, his church's congregational meeting, or the local PTA, has not really achieved a full education. He carries with him everywhere a serious social handicap.

The dangers of oversocialization at the university have long been a favorite subject of caricature. "Joe College" is a popular stereotype of the college student, unfortunately emulated by students whose values are superficial, whose expectations of what higher education has to offer them are poorly developed and sadly limited. Put into music by Count Basie, the student is conceived as one who "wears Brooks clothes and white shoes all the time; gets three C's, a D, and thinks checks from home sublime." This is the philosophy of "muscular education" — an education which looks to the physical and social movement of the student. It is "fraternity-tea education," as though through socializing influences alone the student will win an education adequate for himself and for his future service to the community.

Despite the caricatures, however, the social education of the college student persists as an important consideration in his total development. It is significant in part because there is good reason to believe that unless the student matures socially as he learns intellectually, his intellectual growth will be stunted. In other words, a socially mature person is able to learn abstract and factual matter at least as readily as the less mature. In another sense, learning cannot be achieved unless it involves the whole person, there is no dichotomized individuality for the college student or anyone else. We learn with our full beings. Therefore, it is well to think of an education as involving all factors in the person's makeup.

Social education, or education for citizenship, is sorely needed today, not alone because of the vast complications of America's international posture, but because of the complexity of living in local communities. America's international requirements call for persons in nonprofessional capacities — as well as in specialized activities such as foreign service — who have a mature understanding of the needs and aspirations of the many and varied peoples of the world, and for persons who are able to relate themselves effectively in the social sphere to the meeting of manifold tensions and conflicts.

In our local communities, too, there is need for further applications of democracy — the rule of justice and opportunity by the people. Ferdinand Lundberg, who in the past has tackled the shortcomings of the rich, has stressed our lack of vigorous democratic responsibility in *The Treason of the People*.[2] Actually the theme is older than he thinks, although his emotion and current data give the idea new force for our time. The book has its technical and logical inadequacies, but among its strengths is the clear assertion that while the people pay lip service to the high ideals of pure democracy, they very often decline to work for such a democracy and, indeed, at times willfully seek to sabotage it. Democracy cannot long survive a lethargic or apathetic people. It requires the highest degree of alert understanding among the people, plus a resolute will on their part to strive constantly to increase their democratic achievements.

Higher education should provide students with the understanding they need to work toward a more effective democracy. But something more than simple understanding is required. Democracy requires persons who are skilled in human relations, widely experienced in working toward democratic ideals, and able to combine realistically their intellectualized solutions to social problems with the actual social situations in which they are seeking improvement. Through participation in student activities beyond the classroom, in which democratic cooperation is enjoined, the student places himself in a convenient and often effective environment in which he can learn how to use all his resources for the enrichment of democratic living, both within the university, and upon graduation, in the local community and in the world.

Recent studies of the college graduate as a type in American culture have tended to stress the cash value of a college education. A case in point is *They Went to College: The College Graduate of Today* by Ernest Havemann and Patricia Salter West.[3] In this book, the result of a careful study sponsored by *Time* magazine of 9064 college graduates of more than 1000 American colleges, the inquiry touches on practically all aspects of the value of a college education, but seems to stress in particular the economic, pointing out to what degree higher education will help line the pockets of youth. While all such topics need investigation they may lead to a serious misunderstanding of the deeper potentials of higher education. They may tend to suggest that the primary or even the only reason for attendance at college is the possibility of increasing one's later income.[4]

Fortunately, the very studies which stress the economic advantages of a college education also often bring their readers face to face with the fact that not all graduates earn more money than nongraduates. The Havemann and West study, for example, notes that a Phi Beta Kappa key and student government officership do not commonly bring advanced earnings upon graduation. At several points their study seems to show the opposite.

Increased personal earnings may be a principal motivation of many students in seeking a university education. But clearly, students who attend institutions of higher education have other reasons, among which are intellectual curiosity and social contribution. Probably these and other motives are to be found for everyone within the university, including the faculty and the administration.

The foregoing account of the traditional manner in which the activities and purposes of the university have been viewed shows that from the standpoint of social utility and personal motivation the division is unnecessary, oversimplified, and a distortion of the realities of the university and the community. But it admittedly is not a sufficiently sturdy philosophy of higher education to overcome the traditional division of the activities of the university into the curriculum and the noncurriculum. It has been expressed, moreover, primarily in apologetic terms. Another effort is required by which student activities in particular is related positively and comprehensively to the total university and its most serious pursuits. This statement should draw upon an apologetics, but its substance should be defensible from the standpoint of objective reason.

In contrast to the personal and social utilitarian views of education which often are presented and which have their rightful role in certain levels of discussion, it is possible to assert that the university exists for a fundamental reason which at its core is not utilitarian at all. In fact, all utilitarian values are derivative; they cannot in themselves maintain their efficacy without being related to more basic planes of meaning and reality.

Although the university exists to fulfill a number of different goals, all of them worthy and desirable in university life, they exist in relation to each other, not on an even plane of value, but in relation to some standard of normative concern. What, then, aside from the multiplicity of worthy purposes attributed to the university, is the prime goal of higher education? It is the apprehension of reality.

Reality consists of many features. It may be described in terms of the actual and the potential. In part the university is devoted to the understanding of that which exists — in the sense that it observably was and is. In another part the university reaches beyond itself to apprehend factual and value elements which at a given moment are not known. In other words, the university is concerned both with the conditions under which the Roman civilization disintegrated, and with the possibilities of further reduction of nuclear particles.

Reality also consists of existence and essence. That which exists expresses a power to be. Its nature always takes a concrete form which reminds the observer that it represents another aspect of reality, the essential. Man feels this about himself, too. He seeks actualization through concrete experiences; yet every stage of his development from childhood to old age is necessarily less satisfying in achievement than it might be. This sense of estrangement in man regarding himself and his actualization points to an essential nature of man which existential man is ever striving to realize, but which in the nature of things he only achieves imperfectly. Reality, thus, is existence and essence.

Although reality has other attributes than those which have been mentioned, the apprehension of reality is no mean purpose for the university. It is a goal which calls for the fullest devotion of the many disciplines into which the university intellectually or scientifically is organized. Certain aspects of the university's responsibility toward the apprehension of reality necessarily transcend the functions of the university, as, for example, the quest for the nature of the ground of reality. But the university has a sufficiently burdensome and attractive goal to maintain its activities and enthusiasms for the indefinite future.

In its fundamental task then, of apprehending reality, the university may relate reality once found to specialized functions, such as the improvement of critical thinking, the enrichment of the esthetic sense, or the development of practical skills in social work, medicine, or engineering; but its basic reason for existence is none of these applications. Rather the university seeks to grasp reality in greater and greater degrees.

José Ortega y Gasset asks, "What is the mission of the university?" Unfortunately, he is satisfied with approximate goals: the transmission of culture, the teaching of the professions, and scientific research and the training of new scientists.[5] Perhaps the greatest popular danger in lay and professional interpretations of the role of the university in the present time is that which fails to see in the university anything more than a mediate device for personal and cultural advances. This general view in the long run is in itself self-defeating.

The question rightfully may be asked, however, as to what means are available to the university for the apprehension of reality. Although there are almost as many answers to this question as there are teachers and students, the answer perhaps most productive for the present purpose is: the means of pure and practical reason. Some may prefer to these Kantian phrases the more common terms "curriculum" and "extra-curriculum." Other terms which might be used are: "reflection" and "action," "analysis" and "synthesis," "intellection" and "practice."

To relate student activities thus to the basic task of the university is to claim that it is a part of the essential problem of living itself, for life is concerned with the grasping of reality through both reflection and action. Pure and practical reason — or the curriculum and the co-curriculum — are fundamental requirements in the fulfillment of any search for a deeper understanding of reality. The university, then, does well in combining consciously and devotedly these two paramount elements in its essential burden.

It is clear, however, that there are many university administrators, faculty members, and students who do not view courses and student activities as comprising two aspects of the primary function of the university, but who adamantly claim that student activities is *extra-curricular*, that is, something beyond and aside from the curriculum. They condescendingly tolerate student activities as a sometimes nasty, sometimes amusing area of university life. This myopic curricular bias Woodrow Wilson expressed very clearly:

Life at college is one thing, the *work* of the college another, entirely separate and distinct. The *life* is the field that is left free for athletics not only, but also for every other amusement and diversion. Studies are no part of that *life*, and there is no competition. Study is the *work* which interrupts the *life*, introduces an embarrassing and inconsistent element into it. The faculty has no part in the *life*; it organizes the interruption, the interferences.[6]

On the other hand, as Kant well knew, the activities of pure reason cannot be fulfilled through their own exercise. The noumenal cannot be understood without an understanding of the phenomenal; the curriculum does not stand on its own shoulders but on the shoulders of life itself. The *trivium* and the *quadrivium* do not speak for the whole of life, nor even autonomously for themselves. They gain their meaning in part through their participation in life.

Pure reason or the curriculum fails to obtain its own objectives in isolation from the practical reason or student activities because, while the curriculum rigorously excludes extra-local considerations from its methodology at many points, it is basically — if subtly — dependent upon such factors. From this confusion in part is derived the well-known disdainful connotation of "academic." The curriculum which turns its back upon student life concentrates of necessity upon a more and more rarified conception of its nature and purpose. This process was seen clearly by Edward Caird, who said: "Just because reason cannot find its ideal realized in the world, it seeks to realize that ideal for itself."[7] An education so truncated cannot serve the whole student, for it is unable by its own method even to achieve its own objectives.

The failure of pure reason to understand reality is most apparent in the effort to perceive the nature of man. The social sciences and other disciplines which employ this method tend to consider the person as an object. This leads to the objectivization or depersonalization of man, a prominent characteristic of not a few so-called scientific procedures. Paul Tillich has commented upon the caricature of man which results:

Isolated subjectivity appears in idealistic epistemologies which reduce man to a cognitive subject (*ens cogitans*), who perceives, analyzes, and controls reality. The act of knowing is deprived of any participation of the total subject in the total object. There is no *eros* in the way in which the subject approaches the object and in which the object gives itself to the subject. On some levels abstraction is necessary; but if it determines the cognitive approach as a whole, it is a symptom of estrangement. And, since man is a part of his world, he himself becomes a mere object among objects. He becomes a part of the physically calculable whole, thus becoming a thoroughly calculable object himself.[8]

The reason which tends toward objectivization and abstraction ends up denying the fundamental nature of man and his individual and social behavior.

It is clear, moreover, that the curriculum and student activities cannot really be deposited in tight and exclusive compartments. One need only look through college catalogues to see that activities one university deems curricular are in others considered co-curricular, and vice versa. Historically, there has been a notable movement of activities in higher education between the curriculum and the co-curriculum. In other words, the contrast between the curriculum and the co-curriculum is formal at best.

Actually no ultimate line can be drawn between them, as F. C. S. Schiller points out in his discussion of F. H. Bradley's paper on "Truth and Practice":

It is not our intention to turn dualists, to prove that Theory and Practice are fundamentally different, and foreign to each other, and then to enslave Theory and Practice, Intellectual to Will. . . . We contend rather that there can be no independence of theory (except in popular language) and no opposition of practice, because theory is an outgrowth of practice and incapable of truly "independent" existence.[9]

So, intellection without action leads to an "unearthly ballet of bloodless categories." Or as Ralph Waldo Emerson put it in his essay on "The American Scholar": "The true scholar grudges every opportunity of action passed by, as a loss of power. Action is with the scholar subordinate, but it is essential. Without it, he is not yet man." Unfortunately, Emerson gave outright precedence to reflection. It may be that neither element in man's efforts to apprehend reality is superior. One cannot give the award for a prize-winning rose to a race horse.

It must likewise be made clear that student activities is not autonomous in the search for ever deepening expressions of reality. The belief that student activities is independent of the curriculum and the same general rules of operation as the curriculum is perhaps the most flagrant failure of most student activities programs. Too often the repeatedly quoted statement on student activities by John Henry Newman is used by devotees of student activities as a justification of their high calling. Said Newman:

I protest to you, Gentlemen, that if I had to choose between a so-called University, which dispensed with residence and tutorial super-intendence, and gave its degrees to any person who passed on examination in a wide range of subjects and a University which had no pro-fessors or examinations at all, but merely brought a number of young men together for three or four years and then sent them away as the University of Oxford is said to have done some sixty years since, if I were asked which of these two methods was the better discipline of the intellect. . . . if I must determine which of these two courses was the more successful in training, moulding, enlarging the mind, which sent out men the more fitted for their secular duties, which produced better public men, men of the men whose names would descend to posterity, I have no hesitation in giving the preference to the Univer-sity which did nothing, over that which exacted of its members an acquaintance with every science under the sun.[10]

Happily, however, this random quotation does not bear out Newman's complete thought on the matter, for is it not a relatively isolated "gem" within the general framework of his educational philosophy which in its totality denies the statement itself? Certainly Newman would be one of the last to deny the need for formal procedures and controls in education.

Efforts to erect a student activities province within higher education, primarily for the sake of keeping the students happy and of occupying the professional interest of those charged with responsibility for such programs, are a lamentable sign that some universities lack important unifying purposes, and that they are operating under educational phi-losophies which are as unsound as Don Quixote's Rosinante. Many uni-versities have allowed their student activities programs to become in-distinguishable from urban community centers.

The question may be asked of such student activity programs, as curriculum committees of faculties usually ask of suggested courses: "By what reasoning is it claimed that this activity contributes to the fulfillment of the basic task of the university?" The casual development of student activities on many campuses would seem to indicate that this question is seldom raised. Faculty members (and some administrators as well) often have little interest in and knowledge of activities programs; therefore they do not ask. In these circumstances, programs are commonly left to themselves to grow in haphazard ways. On some campuses the lack of faculty responsibility for activities is sadly defended as an expression of the "rights of students." The idea that the faculty should be as active in these programs as in fulfilling their curricular responsibilities is viewed with astonishment by many faculty members, administrators, professional personnel workers, and students. What university, for example, requires its faculty to spend at least half its time in student activities? [11]

The failure of this *laissez-faire* attitude toward activities is currently apparent in the unsatisfactory role which student political groups are playing on some university campuses. Part of the increased attention being given to political clubs is due to the tightening of national attitudes which is a direct effect of the present international unsettlement. But part is due also to the fact that the role of political organizations on the campus remains undefined. That is, what uniquely or commonly are the manner and the degree in which student political organizations contribute to the central task of the university? The answer is not always heartening or clear. But the question, having been asked, must be answered, and it opens a new era in university maturity. In the past decades the question was raised by university administrators, faculty and others, of athletics. Does the curriculum exist for the sake of athletics, or is the reverse true, and if it is true what does the answer concretely mean for the organization of athletics? That the reverse is true is almost universally accepted. Now this same question is being asked of student political organizations.

The primary educational dilemma of the university as it surveys its responsibility toward student political groups is found in the contrast between the sense of commitment and the demand for objectivity:

Some of the qualities required in the thinker are the opposite of those which the practical politician should possess. The latter must be a man of resolute will and even a certain one-sidedness, who having chosen one path, follows it without *arrière pensée*. The thinker must look at a question from all sides and must constantly return to his starting point to make sure that no error has crept into the argument though, in action, this would produce some indecisiveness. [12]

Politics requires a deep and abiding sense of commitment from the participant. He accepts a program which expresses the power interests of a special group or minority. He joins with others who have a sense of commitment toward their own interests in the effort to realize the group's objectives. This sense of commitment is a basic psychological factor in the activities of all student political groups. It is implied in student political study groups, and it becomes sometimes embarrassingly apparent in the specific behavior of student political action groups.

On the other hand, the task of the university requires objectivity. Partisan interests are transcended in the effort to grasp an advanced understanding of reality. The psychological demand, therefore, for the student as well as for the teacher is that they give up their preconceptions and special viewpoints in the search for reality. Teachers know full well the difficulty they encounter in asking students to overcome their special biases. So often students learn the "content" of courses but fail to achieve a corresponding change in their attitudes. They fail to grow as total persons because of their commitment to special values. They fail to be truly scholars. As Abraham Flexner said, the scholar has no practical responsibility for the trouble he makes; it is his business and duty to preserve his independence and irresponsibility. But he must go on thinking; in that realm his responsibility is of the gravest. And, perhaps, in the fullness of time, the very license of his thought may, without intention or forethought on his part, suggest inventions or profoundly influence solutions, as it has done hithertofore.[13]

Is this not what Hegel claimed when he said that "cool passion" is responsible for all the significant achievements of history?[14]

It is a dubious battle which is restricted to words alone. But words, after all, have meaning. Perhaps in the context of this discussion the term "liberal education" ought to be explored a bit. The older concept of liberal education defined it as that kind of education which freed the learner from his prejudices and partial interests. Liberal education is supposed to liberate. This meaning in the Christian-Hellenic view of the nature of the university has been ably delineated by Sir Walter Moberly:

First, it is "liberal" as opposed to "servile." That is, it aims at mental development for its own sake and not for any ulterior end. It seeks, not to make the student an effective tool to serve someone else's purpose or to give him power to make tools of others to serve his own purpose, but to train him to recognize, to respect and to delight in, what is intrinsically true, good and beautiful. It does so simply because this is a want of man's nature and in its satisfaction he fulfills himself.[15]

If these things are true, what effect should they have upon student political organizations? What changes in current student activities are implied? Although a final or universal answer is difficult to give, certain "signs" can be considered encouraging. For example, campus political activities require of the student the same high standards of critical thought which obtain in the classroom. This claim is equally valid for the whole range of student activities, but its relevancy needs particular enforcement in student political activities. This means that mere participation in political activity has no intrinsic merit. The claim that students need to participate in political action in order to learn how to live in the "world" is clearly invalid. Experience is a teacher of all things. Cannot a student learn to be the worst sort of backroom, wardheeling politician as well as a local "statesman" if he is permitted to enjoy politics devoid of educational standards? How can the university fail to apply educational standards, especially those deriving from its peculiar function in the community, to student political activity? If the student needs no guidance in his political expressions, why does he seemingly need it elsewhere, as in the classroom?

Of course there are dangers in these suggestions. It would be intolerable if the university acted to censor the content of political activity unless that activity was specifically restricted by law. But the dangers of not assuming an educational responsibility toward student political activities are also great. It is not easy to sit by idly, watching generation after generation of so-called intellectuals acting frankly and deliberately in the name of a "politics" which involves the degradation of simple but basic principles of objective reason and ethics. No wonder political science professors are constantly amazed that so little of their classroom teachings is discernible in the actions of former students who enter politics. Student activities is indeed a laboratory of the university, just as there are other laboratories in the physical and biological sciences or workshops and institutes in other areas of university life. But this laboratory also requires trained leadership. It, too, needs to be genuinely related to the chief purpose of the university.

The advantage of the interpenetration of the curriculum and the extra-curriculum in the political science sphere is ably illustrated historically in the lives of social and political leaders who achieved the proper synthesis between reflection and action.[16] William Ewart Gladstone provides a fair example. At Oxford, Gladstone was most active in the curriculum and the co-curriculum. In December, 1831, he crowned his curricular career by taking a double first-class. The range of theoretical interest which he displayed in his college life is still mentioned, especially by commencement speakers. But, more important, Gladstone allowed no separation to exist between the curriculum and student activities in his own life. The Whig Reform Bill of 1832, for example, caught his interest. He undertook extensive reading in order that he might talk intelligently about the subject. The Bill fructified his classroom learning. Nor did Gladstone forget his classroom training when he spoke vigorously against the bill. One of his biographers remarks upon the qualities of the classroom which the statesman carried over into his life of action:

Among the purely intellectual effects produced on Mr. Gladstone by the discipline of Oxford, it is obvious to reckon an almost excessive exactness in the statement of propositions, a habit of rigorous definition, a microscopic care in the choice of words, and a tendency to analyze every sentiment and every phrase, and to distinguish with intense precaution between statements almost exactly similar."[17]

No one is required to agree with Gladstone's political views. But can we not hope today that student political activities will take on in greater measure the more serious tone and temper of the curricula in our universities and colleges? How can this be achieved unless by our direct effort?

Certainly another possible consequence of rethinking the role of the political club on the campus is a recasting of the structure of student government. The older meaning of "student self-government" was self-contradictory, for the significant areas of the university's concern were never given over to the control of students no matter how the students were organized. To think of student self-government, moreover, as it has been considered in the past seems to suggest that there is in fact a deep division of interests and responsibilities within the university, and that the students have organized their own sphere, perhaps in a defensive fashion.

Again, in some instances, the fundamental reason for student government has been obscured by an overconcentration on "a vote for every student." The basic objective of student government is not that of providing a voting apparatus by which individual students can purge themselves of arduous responsibility or satisfy deep-seated needs for status, but to establish faculty-student formations which are related to the fulfillment of the fundamental aim of the university. Neither faculty inexperience nor alleged students' rights should blur the first principles.

The need for recasting the structure of student government has been realized in a number of colleges and universities. Antioch College has rethought the problem and reordered the structure of the entire college about it, as described by Algo D. Henderson:

What is needed is some mechanism to bring faculty and student together. This is important for several reasons: the typical campus problems are of common concern to faculty and students, and need the unified attention of a single group; the segregation of students into a student government is deficient as a method because ordinarily the students are permitted only nominal authority and responsibility; and in the light of the primary educational purpose involved, it is of the essence that the faculty be in some relationships to student problems through which they can stimulate, counsel, and instruct. Student government as it is commonly practiced should therefore be eliminated; and a new form of social organization, including all members of the institution, should be created. This would be a community government. The Antioch College Community Government, for example, is modeled after the commissioner-manager form of municipal government. But it is not alone a "government" in the narrow sense; it is in reality an extension of the classroom, in part a redefinition of the classroom; it is at the same time part and parcel of the counseling program. It not only ties in these aspects of the college program with its own objectives, but also serves as a particular organization through which to search for the best means of harmonizing individual freedom with group endeavors.[18]

This conception of the university, incidentally, is close to the original use of "university." In recent years "university" has often been defined as a social institution devoted to universal knowledge, a meaning apparently not originally intended. In medieval times "university" meant merely a number, a plurality, an aggregate of persons. Later the idea of corporateness entered into the meaning of the term. The *universitas vestra* was a letter addressed to the collective scholarly community, to "the whole of you." Ideally, in all its activities, the university needs to assert and to maintain constantly that quality which Alfred North Whitehead ascribed to abstractive hierarchies, namely, "connexity."

Throughout the foregoing discussion student political activity has served to illustrate the application of the fundamental principle of viewing the university in terms of its basic unity of purposes, that of apprehending reality in all its forms. Certainly political activity in which seemingly legitimate partisanship is most evident is a difficult example to use as an illustration of the general principle; yet it is well to face the obstacles rather than the points on which there might be ready agreement. Further analysis will be required in order to show that all student activities demand at their best the same standards of intellectual integrity which characterize the classroom at its best. The requirement of objectivity and impartiality is as pressing a claim in student activities within the university as it is in the classroom. Special interests and prejudices within individuals and groups need examination and rectification. A university which fails to perceive its role as a rectifier in all university-connected spheres of life is not living up to its essential function in society. It cannot rightfully permit one area within its concern to operate under standards lower than those it requires in other areas.

The apprehension of reality, it has been claimed, requires both contemplative and practical activities.[19] The role of student activities in part is to supply the practical opportunities whereby students are able under all the requirements of intellectual endeavor to apprehend a phase of reality. The role of student activities, then, is to supplement the classroom by providing extended and different means of fulfilling the requirements of education. There is no antithesis between the classroom and student activities. At many points they are one in methodology; in purpose they are indistinguishable — they are alternating and interpenetrating means of enabling the university to be itself. Student activities, moreover, cannot be viewed as a service to students in the sense that this meaning is implicit in some philosophies of student personnel services. Student activities has a legitimate claim upon the university for a basic role in the total education of the student. It should no more be conceived as a service than mathematics, sociology, or physics.[20] All are needed activities within the university. Together they assist students toward attaining a full understanding of reality.

⤙ 12

Faculty-Student Cooperation

THE authentic basis of faculty-student cooperation is the nature of the university as a social institution committed to a broad range of purposes. These may be summarized in briefest form as the apprehension of reality in all its facets. The apprehension of reality, however, requires two alternating efforts: contemplation and action. The curriculum represents the contemplative aspect of the university, the co-curriculum, including student activities, the active aspect.[1] Actually, the primacy of the goal of the university and the very nature of human experience indicate that contemplation and action are interchangeable methodologies within the several sections of the life of the university.

There are aspects of the curriculum which rightly give expression to the activist efforts of faculty and students in their apprehension of reality. Similarly, student activities requires intellectual integrity, objectivity, and the overcoming of simple partisanship. On the basis of this outlook, moreover, it may be claimed that the faculty and the students are the most fundamental personnel in the university. All others are, in a degree, auxiliary. All others exist to enhance the relationships between the faculty and the students. Constant and constructive cooperation between students and faculty is therefore one of the most important values in university education.

NOTE: This chapter is based in part on my article, "Values and *Disvalues* of Faculty-Student Committees," *Personnel and Guidance Journal*, 35 (1957), 289–292, reproduced here in modified form with the permission of the publisher.

151

To conceive of the university as a social institution also helps clarify the basic teaching relationship which exists between the faculty and the students. Unlike other social institutions, the university exists unequivocally for the purpose of having one generation share its findings and insights regarding reality with a younger generation. In part, the family as a social institution possesses the same aim: instruction of the younger by the older. The university, however, presumably is free of the private values of particular families; it stands for the truth, for reality at large. The family may teach its members to discriminate against minorities, no matter what the general views may be in society. The university, contrariwise, does not follow anyone's personal preferences or biases as a basis for its teaching. It is committed to discover the objective truth regarding the subject. Whether an individual is willing to abide by the knowledge available is largely the responsibility of the person, not the institution. So far as teaching is concerned, however, the family and the university have overlapping functions. Not always does the family simply teach its prejudices; not always does the university maintain an openness to reality.

Other social institutions are conducted in relation to committed values. The churches differ from other organizations in the community in that they are devoted to those truths which form the basis for men's ultimate commitments, namely, God. The religionist is not neutral in his allegiance, otherwise he would not be a member of a particular church. Only those persons who have faith in the ground of being as defined and described and worshiped in a special communion can be said to be members of the church. The church, then, differs from the university. The university can never become the church, nor should it seek to be, as sometimes happens. The university is itself.

So it is with the various social institutions in society. Each exists for particular and committed purposes. The university also exists for such purposes, except that its broad aim is to apprehend reality. It is committed to that primary purpose. Because the university is a distinctive social institution, it has a distinctive role in relation to the student. The teacher and the student are assembled within the university to engage in a joint enterprise: to apprehend reality. The student admittedly does not understand reality as fully as his teachers; this assumption runs through the nature of the relationships between students and faculty in the university. The teacher, however, is not one who has comprehended the full nature of reality. He, too, is a learner in many of his activities; he and the students are co-learners.

Yet it is fair to say that no teacher would be qualified as a teacher if he did not have a deeper and broader understanding of the nature of reality (or that part of it which has become his special subject matter) than does the student. The student and the teacher are not equals in many important respects: age, experience, learning, responsibility. Any doctrine of university organization which admits students and faculty as equals is, so far as the central task of the university is concerned, wild-eyed sentimentality.[2] It is false to the facts of the social requirements made of the university by the community. It is a distortion of the basic definition of the university as a social institution devoted to teaching and learning. Because the faculty has been organized for the direct purpose of teaching the students, they are by status, training, and desire the basic personnel category in the university along with the students.

The university as a social institution implies in other ways that the faculty and the students are the indispensable personnel. The organizational nature of the university calls for the guidance by the more experienced of the less. The fact that a function of the university is the transmission of knowledge constitutes another. The fact that the university legally (*in loco parentis*) has a major responsibility for the life of the student is another. In these and other ways, the university exists primarily because there are people who wish to learn, and because there are people who are qualified to teach them.

Acceptance of this view of the nature of the university places tremendous and basic responsibility for the activities of the university upon the faculty. The faculty performs the chief role in the university, even beyond that of the students. Administrators, student personnel workers, and others have an auxiliary (*untergeordnet*) or assisting relationship to the primary one between faculty and students. The administrator is in many regards a facilitator. He seeks through his own sphere of responsibility to enable the relationships between the faculty and the students to be most effective. So, too, for the student personnel worker. He does not operate an autonomous sphere of responsibility. He too is ancillary; he seeks at his best to facilitate the most effective relations between faculty and students.

Admittedly student personnel workers by reason of their specialized training are not always or even generally willing to act as the facilitator. Often they view their own relations with students to be at least as important as the faculty's and in a few instances to be more significant. Their status in some universities as an arm of the administration occasionally encourages unwarranted feelings of detachment and superiority. Certainly their philosophy of "the whole man" has abetted the sense of superiority. But in actuality they should find their most challenging and responsible role within the university in contributing to the enhancement of relations between faculty and students.

To say that the student personnel worker should hold a facilitating role does not mean that his function is exclusively auxiliary. As was argued in the last chapter, his function cannot be lightly dismissed as second-rate. It is part and parcel of the basic task of the university. Even so, it is not given to the student personnel worker to manage and control this function, for that responsibility belongs primarily to the faculty. Student personnel workers, therefore, find their meaning within the university in relation to the manner in which the faculty conceives and practices its responsibilities to the students.

Since the faculty and students hold the basic teaching and learning tie within the university it is well at this point to examine in detail what relationships exist between them in a concrete sphere of mutual concern. Many such areas might be considered for examination. The one chosen here is representative of the nature of the relations involved and the variable solutions which possibly should be sought: faculty-student committees.

The 1955 study by the United States National Student Association, *Student Government: Student Leaders and the American College*, reviewed among other topics the operation of faculty-student committees in American colleges.[3] The findings of this project supported by the Ford Foundation are enlightening despite the nonvaluative orientation of the total effort, and they will undoubtedly receive the attention of students, faculty, and administrators in many colleges. Especially of interest in the present consideration is the range of opinion reflected on the theme of faculty-student committees. This suggests that the time is ripe for a re-examination of the values and disvalues of these commonly accepted committees.[4] The extent to which criticisms of the faculty-student committee were expressed in the Association's research gives a fresh opportunity to consider certain of the pros and cons.

First among the several disvalues in permitting student participation on what otherwise would be faculty committees is discontinuity. The college's chief responsibility is to ensure that a complex organization of educational and other activities is maintained for the benefit of the students. These services require a high measure of "time-binding" in order to be effective. The generally recognized fact in educational administration is that the faculty and the administration possess a relatively high degree of stability and permanency while the student body is ever changing. Indeed, student representatives to faculty-student committees usually change every year; some even each term (taking graduation, leaves, elections, and similar factors into account). Faculty-student committees repeatedly find that they have discussed long and deeply certain problems within their provinces only to have a change in student membership raise the same problems, requiring repetitive discussion and decision.[5] This may be institutionally wasteful.

Second is incompetency. It is assumed that a committee, to be truly effective, holds some degree of competency for the responsibility given it. To place persons of low competency on a responsible committee is to nullify the committee's function. Students generally do not possess sufficient knowledge and understanding to be granted positions on committees for which the faculty (in terms of educational or even legal responsibility) should be held accountable. A committee evaluating research methods and programs should have no student members, not because students are not liked, but because they lack the proper qualifications for this service. May not the same claim be made, more or less, for problems related to admissions, honorary degrees, finances, legislations, and graduation requirements?

Third is immaturity. Committee work which regularly requires the participation of faculty members calls for the ability to arrive at mature decisions affecting the various groups within the college. The administrator who spends the greater part of his time working with the complexities of institutional organization, with the problems related to associations of colleges and professional groups, and with the community, often feels that considerable experience as well as intellectual prowess and good will are required for successful management. Often the administrator senses that not even the faculty fully appreciate the complexities of certain academic situations. How then is it possible that students — young, immature, lacking in responsible experience —

should be able to share in the making of mature decisions affecting the totality of the institution or some significant part of it? Are not students lacking in the very quality for which they are being educated and for which the college at its best stands — mature responsibility?

Fourth is the limited time of students. The Association's study interestingly relates that one administrator suggested that students not serve on institutional committees because "it is the duty of the administration to do as much as it can for the student so that he is not overburdened by extra-curricular chores."[6] The assumption, of course, is that classroom responsibilities are not only of primary importance in securing a college education, but call for the curtailment of serious demands upon the student's time in "extra-curricular chores."

Fifth is lack of authority. In most colleges responsibility for the operation and development of the institution is imposed by law upon a board of trustees, an administration, and a faculty. The degree of responsibility granted to each varies from college to college and there is an observable difference between theory and practice. Yet in the main, student bodies are not given technical responsibility for administration. The presence of students on institutional committees in which students finally have no legal duty may compromise the task and function of those who hold responsibility. It may give students a false conception of the administrative distinctions common to colleges as well as all organizations of any size in the community. If, as the Association's report states, student governments are interested in the "improvement and expansion," with no clear conception of institutional limitations upon function, then it may be that to encourage faculty-student committees, especially in areas where students hold no legal duty or professional responsibility, is to encourage a sort of collegiate demagoguery.[7]

Sixth is power-mindedness. In some instances students have tenaciously held to an exact and mathematical conception of democracy and have wished to be equally represented on faculty-student committees. In a few colleges students do possess equal representation on some committees. Whether or not such equal relations with the faculty exist, there can be detected in the attitudes and actions of students (either individually, in groups, or through student governments) a concern for their own legally undefined or denied status. They speak in moments of emotion as if they were employees of the college with the contractual privileges of workers in the industrial world, or as if their situation were roughly comparable to that of the citizen in the general political community. Both concepts are sadly inadequate and fallacious. Not even the faculty may be considered purely as employees of a college (witness the ambiguities that so-called academic freedom and the tenure laws raise on this point). Certainly the college or university is everywhere recognized legally to be *in loco parentis* so far as students are concerned, rather than as an employer. As for the "political student," the Association's report admirably perceives:

in the political community, anyone who is twenty-one has the right to participate in determining the way the community is run, but the college is a bureaucratic organization, an institution rather than a political community, and in the college the student is not only in the sociological position of a client, but as well is in the legal position of a child.[8]

The values of student participation in institutional committees have been elaborated on many occasions, especially in recent years. By and large these values may all be subsumed under the general heading of "educational," although a more discriminating analysis may prove to be fruitful.

First, educational values (taken narrowly) in student participation on college committees include personal and citizenship factors or goals. The personal aspect of the general educational goal has been variously formulated. Briefly, it signifies the growth and enhancement of individual personality. The student who participates in as wide a range of educational experiences as possible may be said to be growing personally, to be enhancing his personality. His membership on institutional committees, therefore, is educational because it contributes to his personal development.

As to citizenship, participation on institutional committees aims at developing the social leadership potential of the student. It is assumed that college leadership is positively related to later leadership in the community. Community leadership may be expressed not only professionally in terms of acknowledged professional competence in law, medicine, religion, teaching, or other fields; it also connotes the leadership of the citizen as citizen in the manifold affairs of the community. So far as student membership on college committees is concerned, it is hoped that the student will learn how to be a leader not only by participating in student activities groups, but also by sharing responsibility with intelligent and concerned adults. It is believed that the student is called upon for the full exercise of his knowledge and skill in faculty relations and in attacking serious problems. For the young to be in association with adults on committees is similar to the situation of the child who learns how to be adult through association and sharing with his parents.

In addition to the educational values achievable through membership on committees, it is thought by many that the sharing of responsibility with students in certain areas is indispensable to the successful operation of the college. The leading example here, fundamentally a direct concern of the students themselves, is student activities. On this point the claim is made that no one knows better than the students what they wish to do and how they wish to achieve their own purposes. One can't legislate a pleasurable (and successful) party, it is said. Obviously on this score much can be said for active student participation and even student control of certain areas in their own activities. In such matters the faculty appear to be "elder statesmen" or friendly advisers rather than persons who hold legal responsibility for a particular enterprise. On those committees which regulate these activities it may be desirable not only for the students to have equal representation but even a predominance of the membership. Here the argument of technical incompetence does not hold, since the students quite often are more skilled than the faculty.

The third value is institutional morale. Having students serve on committees may help to develop an awareness among students of the "realities" and perplexities of the total life of the institution. When impatient with certain aspects of the curriculum or the administration, students may then discover through their representatives, who have a chance to work closely with faculty members on these problems, that at least "there is more than one point of view." Under certain controls, it may be wise to permit student newspapers to "sit in" on some faculty and faculty-student committees in order that the genuine concern for the betterment of the college may filter through the newspaper to the students at large. It is obvious (and the Association's study supports this view) that on many campuses antagonistic feelings create a real chasm between the students on the one hand and the faculty and administration on the other. This chasm probably broadens and deepens unless there are unrelenting efforts to build bridges of understanding if not of agreement between the young and their elders. Student membership on college committees provides one bridge of understanding. Despite serious limitations, then, the participation of students on faculty-student committees in specific areas and under carefully defined limitations seems to be not only permissible and advisable but even necessary and desirable.

The examination of the relations between faculty and students on committees has been undertaken merely as an illustration of the manner in which the interests of the faculty and the students converge and diverge within the college or university community. As in every human situation, a variety of values and disvalues is involved in relations between faculty and students. Oversimplified, monolithic, sloganic "answers" to the complex problems of faculty-student relations are to be shunned. Ideas of extreme egalitarianism by which everyone connected with the university is thought to have "one vote" in the determination of the university's policies constitute a distortion of democracy and of the institutional character of the university.

As is evident from the foregoing discussion of faculty-student cooperation on committees, the student personnel worker is not directly or necessarily involved in all faculty-student relationships. Occasionally he may have a role in counseling both faculty members and students on certain problems. He may contribute from the storehouse of his experience to the more effective functioning of both faculty and students. He may be helpful in others ways. In most situations, however, he is not the basic agent of carrying out the purposes of the university. Here students have their obligations, too, but the faculty is charged with the primary responsibility.

⤙ 13

Professionalism

ONLY a very small fraction of student personnel workers actively considered the field as their chosen career from the time of high school. The present corps has been organized mainly out of personnel who originally planned to enter other fields. Although no conclusive study has yet appeared to show the multiplicity and variety of backgrounds of current workers, it can be supposed that among them are elementary, secondary, and college teachers; social scientists; ministerial students; persons who considered different areas of social work; psychologists of one sort or another; student leaders who gave up previously considered vocational goals; miscellaneous persons who could not succeed in other fields; women wanting merely an interim job until married; and so forth.

Apparently many student personnel workers have fallen into the field without ever clearly making a profound vocational choice, much in the manner of William Beesley in Kingsley Amis' novel. Beesley, an instructor in medieval history and culture, when asked how he chose his field of specialization, replies:

The reason why I'm a medievalist, as you call it, is that the medieval papers were a soft option in the Leicester course, so I specialized in

NOTE: This chapter is based in part on my article, "Professionalism and the Christian Faith," *Lutheran Quarterly*, 8 (1956), 33–42, and on materials originally published in the "Letters to the Editor" section, *Journal of Counseling Psychology*, 4 (1957), 248–250, reproduced here in modified form with the permission of the publishers.

them. Then when I applied for the job here, I naturally made a big point of that, because it looked better to be interested in something specific. It's why I got the job instead of that clever boy from Oxford who mucked himself up in the interview by chewing the fat about modern theories of interpretation. But I never guessed I'd be landed with all the medieval stuff, and nothing but medieval stuff.[1]

In more recent years a larger number of persons have become aware of student personnel work as a career, and have trained specifically for the work.

It is difficult, despite the growing literature on occupations, to understand fully why persons become interested in particular careers.[2] It seems appropriate to think that vocational choices are made in the light of the total configuration of the personality needs of the individual, yet even this comprehensive explanation requires critical analysis for there seem to be individuals who fail to fit the pattern precisely. If the self has the ability to transcend itself, it is possible to understand that some people do not act in simple ways to fulfill their chartable needs. To assert that persons always act in conformance with their personalities would deny to men the important fact of their finite freedom. It is the freedom of man which determines behavior within the limits of personal destiny. To ascribe needs as the controlling factor in human behavior is to establish in its extreme form the kind of mechanistic, deterministic psychology of the person which the nature of man essentially denies. Yet the needs of men are one of the significant determining elements in behavior, along with other situational, historical, and cultural factors.

A widely held supposition states that men make personal choices in the light of what will benefit them most materially. Although Marxism is undoubtedly the most strenuous and systematic statement of this outlook, Marx himself did not fully subscribe to it. He pointed out the necessity for the presence of a noneconomic idealism in the establishment of trade unions:

If the first aim of the general resistance was merely the maintenance of wages, combinations [of workers] at first isolated, constitute themselves into groups as the capitalists in their turn unite in the idea of repression, and in the face of always united capital, the maintenance of the association [union] becomes more necessary to them than that of wages. This is so true that the English economists are amazed to see the workers sacrifice a good part of their wages in favor of associations.

which in the eyes of the economists, are established solely in favor of wages.[3]

Wages, an economic gain, are placed second to the desire to achieve association, in the view of Marx. The so-called materialist transcends his doctrine.

Contrariwise, Adam Smith believed that men do act consistently in relation to economic values — an idea seemingly inconsistent with Smith's broader views of human nature. As a professor of moral theology in a Scottish university, Smith's main purpose in pursuing economic theory was to extend his theological system's implications clearly into the work world. Theologically he believed that man is a spiritual creature who acts in a spiritual world. Yet, he was able to say in speaking of the professions: "We trust our health to the physician, our fortune and sometimes our wealth and reputations to the lawyer and attorney. Such confidence could not be safely reposed in people of a very mean or low condition. Their reward must be such as may give them that rank in society which so important a trust requires."[4]

Smith relied for leadership in society not upon spiritual conditions or motivations, but upon "rank" and "reward." These symbols in his estimation prevent disastrous social anarchy and through complex specialization enable men to attain collectively the good life.

The historic and cultural evidence in American society points to the fact that men have sought to increase their status upon the basis of work, thereby to rise above the social position held by their forefathers. Higher status most often depends upon specialization, which requires long and technical training. The person who seeks to increase his status in the community will consider those vocations which possess the elements of exclusiveness and specialized training. The modern trend toward the "social division of labor" has encouraged this development in part, and has also paralleled it. As a result of this striving for status and the accompanying specialization, the role of higher education in society has greatly expanded in volume and significance. Higher education today is almost a necessity for the person who wishes, within the bounds of average chances, to achieve a higher status than that of his family's in the community.[5]

In the light of these changes in society, along with contributing psychological and economic forces, the number of specializations in the economy has rapidly increased, together with the number of work functions which seek the appellation of profession. "Profession" still connotes a high degree of specialization and a concomitant high status in society. At the present time there is little agreement on what constitutes a profession in the technical sense. The term is largely employed by people traditionally identified with the professions, as a legitimate expression of their status: physicians, lawyers, clergymen, and the like. But it is also used by workers who wish to attain the community acceptance commonly granted members of the legitimate professions. The use of "profession" sometimes merely asserts the individual's desire to be respected by those who do not have his specific training. It may be used as a bargaining instrument for higher wages. It may be adopted as a personally consoling measure by people who lack the ability or the preference to succeed in one of the traditional professions. The term may be used, moreover, to describe the status of those who work in positions ancillary to the traditional professions. A look into the historical growth of professionalism may throw light upon the present situation of the student personnel worker and his often repeated claim to professional status.

Professionalism, in quick summary, began under the sponsorship of the church in the medieval period. Later, it broke away from spiritual premises and controls as relations between church and society changed in the Renaissance. Then it developed into the patchwork fragmentation of more recent times, on a so-called secular basis.

In the medieval period all work related to the fundamental theme of Christianity. The physician, priest, lawyer, and others believed that their work was related to God and His will for them and for society. The intensity of such belief varied, of course, but its pervasive significance can scarcely be doubted. The professional was not aware of a divorce between his service to God and his service to man. The development of a keener religious sensitivity was considered a legitimate effort on the part of the professional. Increased knowledge and skill derived not only from human strivings; it came chiefly through religious devotion and consecration. Those who sought entrance into the professions were carefully screened at times by the religious authorities so that the recruit's spiritual life as well as his professional promise came under scrutiny. The ethical problems which nowadays have become the province of committees of professional associations found their expression and solution in the universalizing ethics of the Church.

The Christian worldview gave the motivational support and the philosophy to early professionalism. A large number of the professionals of that period were actually priests who believed that their vocational calling included the services which now the secular professions perform.

Under the impact of the forces which were made alive by the Renaissance and the Reformation, the older notion of the professions was seriously modified. The sacerdotal conception of the Christian ministry gave way to the pastoral: the ministry as the all-embracing vocation of the educated man, and the sense that all work finds its meaning in relation to God, broke down. The clergy, facing an ever more complex society, assumed a professional function, the pastoral, as its own. It thus cut itself off from the openminded attitude it possessed in earlier days toward all professional functions; in a sense it gave these over to a growing body of persons who stood only partially under the influence of the churches. In other words, the ministry became a profession side by side with other professions. Each had its clear claim on an area of knowledge. Each tended to seek its own technical and ethical solutions.[6] Each tended to band together, not in the church, but in a common association of fellow workers. The professional person, similarly, no longer sought his fulfillment simply in service to God and man. He was able to recognize his own selfhood as a relatively independent and autonomous rationale for activity. Self-advancement became a worthy reason for professional activity. The professional person laid more stress upon his own satisfactions in work than on his obligations under God to the service of God and man. He himself became a key element in the life of professionalism. It is not true that the professional person in this era thought of himself as opposed to Christian teachings or the church. He simply had less use for them. He was able to find a basis for his professionalism in personal and social values.[7]

As time proceeded, the influence of the church further eroded. Professional bands no longer looked to the church as the inspiration of their special social function. Many came even to deny a relationship to the church. It became apparent that professional persons no longer depended upon Christianity as a supporting philosophy for professionalism. They saw at least as much value in secular explanations. Philosophy to a degree took the place of theology; later, philosophy was supplanted by the sciences and other disciplines. Both in organizational attachment and in philosophical underpinning the rising professions became independent of Christianity.

The professions flourished and multiplied. Since they gained their social sanction from within themselves rather than from the church or some other social body, they were in perfect freedom to establish themselves. As a result of their proliferation not only into areas of specialization but also into schools of thought within these areas, the need for professional education soon became pressing. Professional education, of course, had been associated with university training prior to this period (note Salerno, Bologna, Basle, and Leyden, for example, for medicine), but in the secular era the increase in the number and variety of training programs closely paralleled the rise of the professions. As the professions found a profitable following outside the churches they required an increased membership. Membership was controlled through educational requirements.

The curricula of the modern universities are a far cry from the *trivium* and the *quadrivium* of their medieval counterparts. Under the need for specialists the modern universities have reflected rather than controlled the divisiveness, lack of coherent philosophy, and the rapid changeability of the fragmented professions. The resulting array of schools, colleges, universities, divisions, departments, and courses reflects the intrusive demands of secular professionalism. Everybody had to have his special status; the universities were agents for the training of such persons; the universities, therefore, had to be fragmented in their offerings. In more recent years, however, a tendency to counter overspecialization with "general education" has emerged. Usually this general education is less general than it may seem to the unsuspecting observer. In the main, general education has come to mean preliminary collegiate education — education prior to specialization. It has not solved the fundamental problem of the fragmentation of knowledge, nor has it offered any vital principle of coherence for the student's mind. Thus a key to the understanding of the current plight of higher education may be found in the unchecked growth of professionalism.

The professions, during the period of their development, not only increased in numbers and in the sense of fierce specialization; they also entertained a biting competitiveness and differentiation within their ranks. What originated as a relatively coherent profession with common ethical standards and methods became a profession with antithetical first principles of practice, clear differences as to what constituted good practice, and the resulting educational institutions which both expressed and enforced this divisiveness.

Social work may be taken purely as an example of this tendency. Social work secured professional possibilities, according to some observers, with the rise of the New York School of Social Work in the late 1890s. Prior to this time, social work still represented the efforts of the religiously inspired person, often within the bounds of his religious community, to provide aid to the less fortunate. The founding of specialized schools of social work marks the time at which social work changed from a relatively dependent vocation, if such it may be called, to a relatively independent profession. Social work claimed at this turning point that the field comprised an independent body of knowledge and skill, that it was teachable. Persons who wished to become social workers — to join the ranks of those who managed the training and the practice — had of necessity to attend a school of social work. In this way the rise of yet another division of training within the university was related directly to the coming of age of another profession. Social work, in the words of a former dean of the New York School of Social Work, had changed from a "cause" to a "function."[8] By this he meant that social work no longer was a loosely organized movement which called upon an individual's humanitarian motives for activity. It was an ordered function, carried on by professional workers, in the community.

In its earlier professional period social work was not a self-contained, harmonious "function." As soon as the word profession was breathed for social work a series of further divisions occurred within the field. Instead of there being just one kind of professional person — the social worker — there were many: the family caseworker, the child guidance worker, the medical social worker, the group worker, the community welfare organizer, the psychiatric social worker, the social work researcher, the social administrator, the worker in children's institutions, and so forth. The growth of divisions for a period of decades was one of the most significant features of social work professionalism.

Divisiveness in social work also occurred on the basis of schools of thought. Originally the social environmentalist views of Mary Richmond seemed to predominate.[9] Then with the rise of psychoanalytic influence, social work became deeply affected by Freud's teachings.[10] The period of the economic depression strengthened the environmentalist tradition. The psychology of Otto Rank, moreover, came to have a widespread influence upon social workers.[11] This resulted in a number of agencies becoming devoted to the application of his principles in opposition to those agencies which recognized the primacy of psychoanalytic insights. In addition other schools of thought, including the Thomist, came into being.[12] The disorganization of thought and the increase in professionalization have gone hand in hand within social work.[13]

More recently, however, notable efforts from almost every quarter within social work have sought to stem the tide of divisionism. There have been attempts to establish "generic principles" by which all specializations within the field might be tied together. Graduate schools have abolished the reflection of overspecialization in the field from their curricula. The national associations which formerly had organizationally defined extreme specialization have given way to a single association. In these and other ways social work is seeking to face the problem of professional divisiveness.

Social work in this context has been used as an illustration of a principle of historical development within the professions. Its pattern very well fits that of a number of other professions; the parallels with student personnel work are hopefully apparent. Student personnel work has entered its phase of professionalism within the last seventy-five to one hundred years. It has been slower in its development, although the general pattern seems to have run true to form. Like social work it is characterized by dependence on philosophies of practice borrowed largely from other disciplines and professions. It also has been characterized by rapid overspecialization to the point where no one function seems to form the basis for the total operation. Even counseling psychology, suggested by some as the ideal basis of training for all student personnel workers, falls seriously short of providing the student activities worker with the background he deems necessary.[14]

Yet, the very fact that some form of training is being suggested as the primary basis is hopeful. It may mean that the divisiveness within student personnel work has run its course, and that now efforts at reconstruction can fruitfully begin. Organizationally, however, the field is still rampant with a large number of overlapping associations which purport to claim the ultimate allegiance of their members. Student personnel work, by almost any available criteria, has surely not come of age. It, too, must be understood in the light of the historical development of the professions, and as a late feature of the general disorganization of knowledge and the self-assertiveness of special bands of would-be experts.

The foregoing analysis of professionalism indicates, among other things, that the professions themselves under their own autonomy have been unable to solve the problems both of general knowledge and of their own internal coherence. The educators who have considered the same problems have also failed, unable to impose any system on the training of professionals. Not only have they failed to integrate specialized education into general education, they have remained far from agreement as to what content and methods produce the most desirable form of professional education. In the face of these failures, and for positive reasons also, communities have felt a need to protect themselves against educators and professionals alike. The common means for securing this protection is through government. Licensing of professionals has proven to be the most suitable method employed by government for insuring at least a minimum of sound education and practice. The licensing may take the form simply of requiring a candidate to pass an examination. It also may be more elaborate, and involve prescriptions of prior education, character, and so forth. Even though the requirements of the community may not be in harmony with those of the professional associations nor with the thought of the educators, they nonetheless serve a function in establishing a floor under the professions so far as practice is concerned.

Licensing, however, has not played a fully meritorious role in the rise of professionalism. Although it has protected the community and tended to unify the requirements, educational and professional, of the various professions, it also has led to a situation in which the universities have virtually ceased to maintain the final control over what within the range of university experience should be the ingredients of professional training. The universities have been content to educate students to meet the requirements of community acceptance. Such acceptance may fall far short of what is ideal, in the opinion of intelligent men, or even of what is reasonably desired and attainable. They have been too content merely to accept the task of training students in techniques, without insisting upon knowledge which professionals may mistakenly consider to be frilly or impractical.[15]

If licensing were taken as a common requirement of the professions, student personnel work, at least in higher education, could not be considered a profession, since licensing of such workers does not exist. On this point alone, the claim that student personnel work is an autonomous profession would collapse. It is true that there have regularly been attempts to secure some sort of professional organization by which ultimately the professional claims of student personnel work might be impressed upon the community sufficiently to lead to licensing. At the present time such a future seems far distant, if ever attainable. Perhaps it is not even desirable. Of course licensing of guidance personnel in the "lower" schools is widely developed.

On this score it is valuable to note that the criteria of a profession have been established with some care.[16] John G. Darley, who follows the older version of the criteria, lists the following standards: existence of a social need; existence of specialized knowledge and skill; the power of imposing the standards of recruitment and training; development of a system of ethical codes; and legal recognition. In relating these criteria to student personnel work, Darley says:

By these criteria, which I think are sociologically sound, only parts of the total student personnel program have any claim to being professional or should seek professional status. But personnel workers all tend to act as if they were well along the social trail that leads to full professionalization . . . I suggest that one of the problems of higher education is that it is hag-ridden enough by compartmentalization and that we cannot bear very many more separate professions in the entire enterprise. If we act like a profession in our various specialities, if we as personnel workers make certain claims to glory based on the criteria of a profession, but if we are not perceived as having earned this status, we may draw down upon our heads in our local institutions the ridicule, the exasperation, or the rejection of those upon whom we depend and those whom we, as members of the personnel group, serve in higher education.[17]

In recent years many student personnel workers have sought to meet the requirements of other professions — usually in some aspect of applied psychology — as a means of securing professional status within the university.[18] While commendable in themselves, such efforts do not constitute professional attainment in student personnel work, nor do they directly and sufficiently relate to the requirements of the field as a human relations activity within higher education. They are all too likely to impose upon the student activities worker a dual loyalty which at best may be stimulating, at worst frustratingly schizophrenic.

In part, the denial of recognition to student personnel work as a profession is owing to the fact that it has had to establish itself as a latecomer within a more settled and traditionally organized intellectual community, in which its assertions to competence are frequently and properly met with attitudes of skepticism. Nor do constant assertions of their professionalism by the workers create the reality; unfortunately, the opposite result may occur. Their assertions reflect the institutional power predicament of the workers. Social institutions constitute systems of social power.[19] This power is organized both internally and in relation to the community. In keeping with the general trend in society toward increased status through professionalization, the workers desire to be recognized as professionals. Such recognition is frequently expressed in the signing of letters, where the Ph.D. may be attached to the name as a means of reminding the uninitiated that they are not partners in the mysteries of the would-be profession.

But the more pressing and threatening attitudes are brought against student personnel workers from within the university. Internally the power system of the university can be most limiting and degrading. Its effects are feared by student personnel workers, since they appear to be the target of much of the attack of the older and more settled professions. David Riesman has written of the "obscurantism, old and new" which exists within the university.[20] It is his claim that the older disciplines are inclined to be obscurantist in relation to the new. History, for example, looks down its nose at anthropology and is critical of the methods, the terminology, and chiefly of the success of the newer discipline. So it is with student personnel work. The older disciplines tend to feel threatened by the newer developments within higher education. They are inclined to love the good old days — days, it generally turns out, that never were.

The newer disciplines are placed in a somewhat defensive position within the university. They sometimes find strength in banding together, both for their own comfort and for actual tests of political strength in the councils of the university. In this power struggle student personnel work may find itself most sympathetic with the disciplines of psychology, education, home economics, sociology, anthropology.

The student personnel workers' need for status and acceptance within the university is indicated by their constant use of the term "professional." Sometimes appearing to be fixated on this notion, they wish everyone to know that what they do is professional before anything else. They are overly inclined to represent their field as monolithic in its findings and attitudes. At most they find it difficult to explain to laymen what it is that they do that makes their activities not only professional but needed in the university. At least they like to induce the required attitude of respect on the part of others before they proceed to explain their activities. They have become members of another "veto group" which feels the responsibility to judge all others in terms of presumed vested interests.[21]

Isolation is another response which has characterized the role of student personnel workers in the power struggle within the university. The workers have retired within the citadel of what they consider their private province of responsibility. Some exclusiveness is required by all social functions as a means of asserting the specialized character of the activity. Yet it also has its baneful aspects. Within the university it has meant that the workers have often been cut off from the rest of the university personnel. As Darley puts it: "Professionalization leads to a certain amount of separatism — a separation of us as personnel workers from others in the academic enterprise."[22] This isolation is a means of meeting the power struggle by withdrawing from it, of staking one's claims to a restricted area of activity, and of erecting bulwarks against outsiders.[23] As a consequence the workers in many universities are simply not well known in and about the institution by the faculty and others. They may not take part in scholarly discussions with the faculty to the same degree as do members of the so-called academic departments; they may not act as often as faculty advisers to student groups outside their sphere of interest; they may not be socially proficient in "selling" their specialty in the faculty marketplace. They may be content with waging merely a defensive operation against possible encroachments on their duties.

The workers also tend to become separated among themselves. Increasingly a spirit of subspecialization has developed within the field. Counselors pride themselves upon their differences of training and aspiration. Dormitory personnel may feel that they have little in common with counselors. Those who work with groups may feel that the nature of their activity is greatly removed from those who work with individuals. And so it goes. The fact is that increasingly members of the subspecialties are inclined to think that they are not competent to speak about the problems and goals of those in other subspecialties. This development is a form of isolationism which promises to increase even further, since there does not seem to be available the philosophic underpinning required to overcome divisive specialization and pseudo-professionalization.

Again, a method of meeting the irritations and frustrations of the university power situation is to take refuge in *mystique*. This reaction is in a sense a variation of withdrawal since it depends upon the conception of the worker as the keeper of the sacred values. Similar to a priest, the worker supposes that he understands the nature of the mystery of mysteries. It is his function to mediate the mystery to the unwashed of the university community. The definition of the mystery which is protected varies. One example places it in the skill of the worker, the claim that there is an efficacy to his activities which is not available to the uninitiated. This view makes skill a mysterious factor in human experience, attainable only by a select few. The layman should not seek it; he should not be offered assistance in securing it by the professional; he should only know enough to avoid claiming that he has any ability in the performance of duties requiring the skill. This attitude sometimes takes the extreme form of wild consternation on the part of the student personnel worker who hears of a faculty member who has attempted to counsel a student.

Another example of the mystical defensiveness of the student personnel worker is his attitude toward the confidentiality of student information and records. Confidentiality is a perfectly legitimate concept within the university, as it is within other social institutions. Yet the student personnel worker has employed it at times in a distorted manner which reveals his peculiar position in relation to the academic community. Confidentiality is thus defined by some workers almost solely as whatever the practitioner keeps from others. It is assumed that when nothing is ever revealed about a student to anyone, the principle of confidentiality is being observed to the letter. Actually, one hundred per cent, absolute confidentiality exists almost never.

Confidentiality does imply that proper restrictions govern the use of information obtained from persons in a close personal relationship. It signifies also the conditions under which information is to be used as well as restricted. It probably would be entirely beneficial if the word confidentiality were banned from the language of the student personnel worker, and if the realities sometimes subsumed under this term with dogmatic emotion were discussed one by one as circumstances developed. A ritualistic imperviousness to institutional requirements is surely not the measure of the problem.

The student personnel worker all too often adheres to a doctrine of confidentiality which creates problems for himself in his relations with others, and which may not fulfill his intentions however sincere his practice. The worker tends to assume that the faculty member should tell him everything he knows about a student, but that he himself should reveal nothing or next to nothing under the guise that he, of necessity, must practice the principle of confidentiality. There is little wonder that the student personnel worker is put on the defensive by adopting this attitude in dealing with the faculty.

The worker may properly resist the inquiries of an administrative officer of the university who is contemplating a disciplinary action.[24] Such reluctance on the part of the worker may satisfy his image of himself as the keeper of the mysteries, but it will hardly mollify the feelings of the faculty and the administration. In fact, it constitutes an unnecessary and illogical application of an alleged professional spirit. In order to enjoy such complete autonomy the worker should be self-employed. As such he would have the right, under the code of suitable professional practice, to determine his own policy so far as confidentiality is concerned. He could in fact maintain the one hundred per cent type of confidentiality, although there are indications that this is practically impossible.

The worker within the university does not determine his own policy, although he may share in its determination.[25] But he should expect no more than to obey the final determination of the institution's policy in regard to confidentiality. Ultimately, matters of policy for the institution as a whole are the responsibility of the policy-determining committees, administrators, and the legally constituted and controlling board of trustees. Of course he may seek to use his persuasive influence to modify the university's policy, but whatever it may be at a given time it is his policy so far as his activities are concerned.[26] For the student personnel worker to assume that only he fully appreciates the concept of confidentiality, or that only his view of its meaning should

dominate the university, is but another example of his defensive position in relation to others.

One more illustration of the manner in which the student personnel
worker seeks to enforce his status within the university is his use of
special terms. Many persons within the field and without have commented upon the jargon of the worker. Perhaps the most striking and
unexamined of the battery of such terms is "the whole man." Comment
has been made previously on this point. Other terms which contain
ambiguities are personality, adjustment, self-realization, guidance,
counseling, advising, personnel, services, manipulation, confidentiality,
permissiveness, psychotherapy, group counseling, group work, professional, vocational. The number is large and seems to be ever increasing.
Probably the specialized terms of psychology are the most prevalent,
although sociology and other disciplines are heavy contributors.

Special terminology, of course, has a legitimate role to play within
any field of inquiry or activity. A discipline has a right to define common or uncommon terms in ways which are helpful for the discipline's
purpose. Yet esoteric terms are not always necessary to increase meaning. Regularly the most connotative terms are those which have borne
long and common usage in the speech of large numbers of people.
Despite the need for special terms, a discipline at its best stands ready
at any time to translate its jargon into the language of members of
other disciplines or of the newspaper reader.

It is not clear to what extent the eagerness of student personnel
workers to use special language is based upon their need to become a
profession and thus acquire status, upon the legitimate requirements of
clarity and preciseness, or upon the defensive reactions apparent in
their relations with the more established academic professions. It is
probably a reflection of all three. At any rate the problem of the worker
in the power conflicts of the university is not readily met by recourse
to artificial stratagems of verbal warfare.

No one is wise enough either to understand fully the present professional problems of the student personnel worker or to suggest final
solutions. The present situation of the worker seems to consist largely
of the following disadvantages: student personnel work does not exist
as a profession; the worker's claims that he is a professional usually
meet with suspicion; he often has to band together with colleagues
in related disciplines to gather strength in meeting university power

conflicts; he also tends to withdraw from facing the full implications of his status and his activities. While some highly knowledgeable persons of long experience in the field believe that student personnel work is developing in as sound and constructive a manner as is possible, there is some reason for doubt. From an institutional viewpoint any effort toward separation of knowledge and practice is questionable.

It well may be that the whole field of student personnel work needs to acquire a new philosophy and a resulting rationale of its place within the university.[27] There are some evidences that a new philosophy is being formed. In part it is the amplification of attitudes and standpoints which have been apparent from the beginning of the work. In other respects it is resulting from fresh examinations of the interrelatedness of the several fields of knowledge and practice, and the realization of the compelling claims of the total university. Edward J. Shoben, Jr., has suggestively summarized this development:

Student personnel workers will most probably make their finest contributions by articulating themselves more explicitly with the rest of the educational enterprise, by finding greater commonalities with instructors and investigators, and by broadening both their professional horizons and their basic knowledge. The personnel movement is no longer a protest against the neglect of learning opportunities in student life outside the classroom. It is an organized effort, currently undergoing a significant degree of professionalization, to capitalize on such opportunities in distinctive ways but in the service of the same goals that justify and animate the educational process generally.[28]

Formulating a genuine philosophy will be difficult. The path to the attainment of this reorientation of student personnel work is strewn with the debris of past mistakes, shallow or even nonexistent philosophies, petulant arrogance regarding mission and status, superficial research, and other resistances to genuine advancement. Nonetheless, there have been authentic gains: the existence of graduate training programs, increased recognition of the significance of the field, a clearer administrative place for the field within the university, the strengthening of groups and associations of workers, new knowledge and skill, and in places, adequate leadership. The task of reorientation will be arduous; more errors will be made; yet the challenge is appealing and worthwhile.

NOTES AND INDEX

Notes

Chapter 1. Perspective

[1] *The New York Times*, March 26, 1958, p. 11. Later, however, "a man who can remember" reported that the Secretary took the side of those who were outraged by Voltaire's slur on Joan of Arc against the faction that agreed with the French man of letters. See *The New York Times*, March 31, 1958, p. 17.

[2] *Newsday*, November 29, 1956, p. 43.

[3] *The New York Times*, December 4, 1956, p. 30.

[4] *The New York Times*, October 3, 1956, p. 17.

[5] *Ibid.*

[6] *The New York Times*, December 15, 1956, p. 18.

[7] *The New York Times*, March 4, 1957, p. 48.

[8] *The New York Times*, June 8, 1958, p. 69.

[9] Philip E. Jacob, *Changing Values in College* (New York: Harper, 1957).

[10] *The New York Times*, March 3, 1957, p. 9. The plight of students under Soviet domination, however, is quite different. See Maria Yen's *The Umbrella Garden: A Picture of Student Life in Red China* (New York: Macmillan, 1954).

[11] *The New York Times* editorialized in favor of the Latin American students. See June 17, 1956, p. 22.

[12] Student life in the medieval period has been described by U. T. Holmes, *Daily Living in the Twelfth Century: Based on the Observations of Alexander Neckham in London and Paris* (Madison: University of Wisconsin Press, 1952); R. S. Rait, *Life in the Medieval University* (Cambridge [England]: The University Press, 1912); and C. H. Haskins, *The Rise of the Universities* (Ithaca, N.Y.: Cornell University Press, 1957).

[13] Hastings Rashdall, *The Universities of Europe in the Middle Ages* (Oxford: The Clarendon Press, 1936), vol. 1, pp. 334–335. This is clearly the best source on medieval university life.

[14] Crane Brinton, *The Anatomy of Revolution* (New York: Vintage Books, 1957).

[15] The meaning of professionalism will be discussed in Chapter 13.

[16] Despite some demurrers, the old term which partly expressed in negative fashion the idea of voluntarism, "extracurricular," is now *passé*. "Extra" gives a connotation of not necessary, something that can be done without. Currently the

term "student personnel services" has wide currency, although "co-curricular" is employed to show the relationship between the compulsory curricular and the voluntary noncurricular aspects of the university. Another term to describe student personnel service in secondary schools appears in the title of a book: see Louis R. Kilzer, Harold H. Stephenson, and Orville Nordberg, *Allied Activities in the Secondary School* (New York: Harper, 1956).

[17] In 1955 Yale University took certain steps "to place classroom studies ahead of athletics, week-end parties or extra-curricular campus activities." This decision, a result of an eighteen-month study by a committee of fourteen faculty members, definitely limited various kinds of noncurricular activites. See *The New York Times*, May 11, 1955, p. 33.

[18] Alfred North Whitehead put the matter thus: "We must take it as an unavoidable fact that God has so made the world that there are more topics for knowledge than any one person can possibly acquire. It is hopeless to approach the problem by way of the enumeration of subjects which every one ought to have mastered. There are too many of them, all with excellent title-deeds . . . what I am anxious to impress upon you is that though knowledge is one chief aim of intellectual education, there is another ingredient, vaguer but greater, and more dominating in its importance. The ancients called it 'wisdom.' You cannot be wise without some basis in knowledge; but you may easily acquire knowledge and remain bare of wisdom . . . wisdom is the way knowledge is held." See *The Aims of Education* (New York: Mentor Books, 1949), pp. 40–41.

[19] There is no intention in what has been said to suggest that knowledge and skill are unrelated. It is clear that Karl Mannheim is correct in his assertion that the present-day culture crisis rests to a significant degree upon the divorce of "functional" from "substantive knowledge." Student activities, however, is liable to the charge that it places more stress upon techniques and methods than it does upon the causes and consequences of human behavior. See *Man and Society in an Age of Transformation* (New York: Harcourt, Brace, 1940).

[20] Small groups have lent themselves to some effective research. For example, Eric F. Gardner and George G. Thompson have introduced a new approach for the measurement of social relationships and group structures in small groups, using nine of the fraternities of a large university. See *Social Relations and Morale in Small Groups* (New York: Appleton-Century-Crofts, 1956).

[21] There is an affinity between student activities as education and what is sometimes called "functional education." Functional education is said to consist of various out-of-the-classroom activities which are directed by the university for the fuller education of the students. Within this definition fall collegiate programs which strongly stress work-study requirements, community experience programs whereby prospective teachers, social workers, and others are placed under supervision as volunteers in social and health agencies in the community, the field experience programs of graduate and specialized (vocational) institutions, certain kinds of "laboratory" activities in the sciences, and so forth. Functional education, like student activities, is a relatively unorganized and unsystematized educational sphere.

[22] There is growth under such circumstances in what Harold D. Lasswell has termed "the self-system of the person." For a description of this process, see his "Democratic Character," in *The Political Writings of Harold D. Lasswell* (Glencoe, Ill.: The Free Press, 1951).

Chapter 2. Background

[1] Even the word "university" connotes student organization. "Historically, the word university has no connection with the universe or the universality of learn-

ing; it denotes only the totality of a group, whether of barbers, carpenters, or students did not matter. The students of Bologna organized such a university first as a means of protection against the townspeople . . . Victorious over the townsmen, the students turned on 'their other enemies, the professors.'" C. H. Haskins, *The Rise of the Universities* (Ithaca, N.Y.: Cornell University Press, 1957), p. 9.

[2] Originally "college" meant something quite different from its current connotation. In the medieval period it was merely an endowed hospice or a hall of residence. As Hastings Rashdall points out: "The object of the earliest college-founders was simply to secure board and lodging for poor scholars who could not pay for it themselves." In time, however, the colleges became centers of both living and organized teaching. See Hastings Rashdall, *The Universities of Europe in the Middle Ages* (Oxford: The Clarendon Press, 1936), vol. 1, p. 500.

[3] Some student personnel workers erroneously think that their specialization developed relatively late in the history of American higher education: "Formal college personnel work really began with the work of the early deans of women and probably dates back to the first coeducational institutions." This view ties student personnel work to the introduction of such specific personnel as deans of women and men. See Ruth Barry and Beverly Wolf, *Modern Issues in Guidance-Personnel Work* (New York: Teachers College, 1957), pp. 19–20. An accurate account is given, however, by Eugenie A. Leonard, *Origins of Personnel Services in American Higher Education* (Minneapolis: University of Minnesota Press, 1956).

[4] *Ibid.*, p. 3. The historical comments which follow this quotation depend at a number of points upon Professor Leonard's pioneering book.

[5] *Ibid.*, p. 114.

[6] A brief history, yet with more detail than is offered here, is presented by Ruth Barry and Beverly Wolf, *op. cit.*, pp. 19–26.

[7] There is a systematic account of some of these changes, although in a different format, in *The Year Book of Education: 1955* (Yonkers, N.Y.: World Book Company, 1955).

[8] Ernest W. Burgess, and Harvey J. Locke, *The Family: From Institution to Companionship* (New York: American Book Company, 1945), especially pp. 21–22.

[9] See "Family Life Education," *Social Work Year Book: 1957* (New York: National Association of Social Workers), pp. 239–244.

[10] See Émile Durkheim, *De la division du travail social* (Paris: Librairie Felix Alcan, 1938), now available in translation by George Simpson, as *Émile Durkheim on the Division of Labor in Society* (Glencoe, Ill.: The Free Press, 1947).

[11] Peter M. Blau, *Bureaucracy in Modern Society* (New York: Random House, 1956), p. 17.

[12] Those who regret this development well may give attention to Nathan M. Pusey's comment: "The character of our education has changed with our society. Wasting time in lamenting the passing of an earlier, more restricted, more 'classical' period is of little profit. It is not likely again to be possible, nor in my judgment would it be wise, to try to cut back or restrict the numbers of those who are permitted to make what they can of the advantages of formal education, beyond high school." Quoted from "The Exploding World of Education," *Fortune*, September 1955, p. 198.

[13] Walter Moberly, *The Crisis in the University* (London: SCM Press, 1949), pp. 57–58.

[14] William H. Whyte, Jr., *The Organization Man* (New York: Simon and Schuster, 1956).

[15] The original formulator of the "Protestant ethic" is probably Max Weber, *The Protestant Ethic and the Spirit of Capitalism* (New York: Scribner, 1930).

[16] Barbara Ward, *Faith and Freedom* (New York: Norton, 1954). It is interesting to note that another leading Roman Catholic thinker, the French philosopher and

theologian Jacques Maritain, says that talk of American materialism is "no more than a curtain of silly gossip and slander." See *Reflections on America* (New York: Scribner, 1958).

[17] It is not claimed here, contrary to certain aspects of the philosophy of John Dewey, for example, that change, uncertainty, and conflict are ultimate traits of social experience. See *Reconstruction in Philosophy* (New York: Holt, 1920), pp. 96, 183. It is clear that some values persist and even grow stronger as the years advance. Frederick Jackson Turner shows how such frontier attitudes as assertiveness, restlessness, shrewdness, optimism, tough-mindedness, adventurousness, self-respect, ingenuity, developed in generations of American pioneers and spread to the more settled and conservative urban centers of the country. See *The Frontier in American History* (New York: Holt, 1921).

[18] Lewis Mumford puts it this way: "The period through which we are living presents itself as one of unmitigated confusion and disintegration: a period of paralyzing economic depressions, of unrestrained butcheries and enslavements, and one of world-ravaging wars . . . a loss of communion between classes and people, a breakdown in stable behavior, a loss of form and purpose in many of the arts . . ." See *The Condition of Man* (New York: Harcourt, Brace, 1944), p. 14.

[19] A constant temptation for student personnel workers as well as others is to seek a return to the "idyllic" conditions of an imagined past. In the light of the changes which have been described for society as a whole it is interesting to note the preachments of Rexford Guy Tugwell in his *A Chronicle of Jeopardy: 1945– 1955* (Chicago: University of Chicago Press, 1956). Prominent as a "brain truster" of the 1930s, he finds little courage to face the future except in terms of certain "evils" and "solutions" of the past. He speaks scathingly of the "economic royalists," the "malefactors of great wealth," the "interests of scarcity" — the whole company of New Deal scapegoats. His solution to the present national and international dilemma lies in dragging ourselves back to the golden days of the 1930s. The parallel to this kind of analysis occasionally occurs in student personnel work circles in several forms, including that of longing for the highly simplified and personalized situation which characterized the university in former times. For a description of the problem in educational theory, see also "The Wastelands Revisited," by William Lee Miller, *The Key Reporter*, January 1956, pp. 2, 5–6.

Chapter 3. Shortcomings and Problems

[1] Originally formulated by William F. Ogburn, the concept of "cultural lag" is described in *Social Change* (New York: Huebsch, 1923).

[2] Two educational philosophies with different views on this subject are "progressivism" and "reconstructionism." They are described in detail in Theodore Brameld's *Philosophies of Education in Cultural Perspective* (New York: Dryden, 1955). Also, Brameld's *Toward a Reconstructed Philosophy of Education* (New York: Dryden, 1956), which especially discusses "reconstructionism."

[3] John Dewey, *Reconstruction in Philosophy* (New York: Holt, 1920), p. 177.

[4] A good source of questioning on this score is Howard E. Wilson's *American College Life as Education in World Outlook* (Washington, D.C.: American Council on Education, 1956). He asks, for example: "Can the ideal of a collegiate way of life which gives learning higher priority than it gives football, which makes the student center as much a house of thought and esthetics as a house of play, be realized under modern conditions?" Wilson makes a strong case for the need of a better bond between the curriculum and the extra-curriculum in the student's intellectual life.

[5] Carl L. Becker, *Freedom and Responsibility in the American Way of Life* (New York: Vintage Books, 1955), p. 64.

⁶ Alfred North Whitehead, *The Aims of Education and Other Essays* (New York: Macmillan, 1929), pp. 41–42.

⁷ The faculty report on "the new program" at Amherst effectively makes this point. See Gail Kennedy, ed., *Education at Amherst: The New Program* (New York: Harper, 1955), pp. 120–121.

⁸ Charles A. Siepmann, *Radio, Television, and Society* (New York: Oxford University Press, 1951), pp. 175–176.

⁹ A somewhat different but nevertheless instructive view of this development is presented in Esther Lloyd-Jones and Margaret Ruth Smith, eds., *Student Personnel Work as Deeper Teaching* (New York: Harper, 1954), especially in the first chapter.

¹⁰ The relations between science and goals have been described as follows: "Science does not give us goals, but men use their knowledge to broaden and refine and increasingly achieve their human aims. And they use their growing knowledge of themselves to work out what their aims are and to distinguish increasingly the spurious from the genuine. A full scientific understanding thus molds their way of looking at the world. They see themselves at every point as active creators out of the past and into the future." See Abraham Edel, *Ethical Judgment: The Use of Science in Ethics* (Glencoe, Ill.: The Free Press, 1955), p. 339.

¹¹ Harvard University, *General Education in a Free Society*, Report of the Harvard Committee (Cambridge, Mass.: Harvard University Press, 1945).

¹² Huston Smith, *The Purposes of Higher Education* (New York: Harper, 1955).

¹³ Mary McCarthy, *The Groves of Academe* (New York: Harcourt, Brace, 1952), p. 62.

¹⁴ Walter Lippmann, *The Public Philosophy* (Boston: Little, Brown, 1955).

¹⁵ Ruth Barry and Beverly Wolf say: "The greatest needs today in the area of guidance-personnel procedures and practices are to examine the present methods; to question the assumptions on which present practices are based; to look at current needs and to consider whether present procedures are adequate to meet these needs; and to dare to experiment outside the framework of what is." See *Modern Issues in Guidance-Personnel Work* (New York: Teachers College, 1957), p. 149.

Chapter 4. Education as a Social Institution

¹ Edward J. Shoben, Jr., claims, in the psychological tradition, that student personnel work exists mainly as "a socialization agent," and as an expression of the need for the workers to devote "a proper portion of their time to contributing to the totality and contours of available knowledge through research and scholarly activity." There is a question as to whether some universities consider such workers to have functions other than that of providing a "service station" for ailing students. It may be doubted too whether many of such workers consider themselves responsible for "research and scholarly activity." Professor Shoben laments the paucity of research contributions elsewhere. See "Annual Business Meeting," *Counseling News and Views*, 9 (1956), 4. See also "A Rationale for Modern Student Personnel Work," *Personnel-O-Gram*, 12 (1958), 9–11. Shoben's "socialization" idea seems to fit "the adjustment view" of the aims of student personnel services as analyzed by Ruth Barry and Beverly Wolf in *Modern Issues in Guidance-Personnel Work* (New York: Teachers College, 1957), pp. 45–46.

² See Bronislaw Malinowski, "The Group and the Individual in Functional Analysis," *American Journal of Sociology*, 44 (1939), 938–964; and "Culture," *Encyclopedia of the Social Sciences*, 4, 621–645. Ruth Barry and Beverly Wolf (*op. cit.*) discuss eight "approaches" which dominate the student personnel field, historically and currently. One, "the integrated view," comes closest to meeting the conditions of an adequate conception of student personnel work as contained in

this book. They say: "This approach to guidance-personnel work is mainly in the theoretical stage. New procedures and organizational arrangements that might implement it have not been developed. The integrated view represents in theory, however, the most radically different approach to guidance-personnel work" (p. 52).

[3] Gerard De Gre, *Science as a Social Institution* (New York: Random House, 1955); Helen Witmer, *Social Work: An Analysis of a Social Institution* (New York: Farrar and Rinehart, 1942).

[4] James K. Feibleman, *The Institutions of Society* (New York: Macmillan, 1957).

[5] It is well to note, with James Bryant Conant, that the greatest variety exists in higher education in the United States, both qualitatively and in specific types of institutions. He claims that it is time more frankness entered into discussions of American higher education so that the "enormous differences" existing between institutions called universities be recognized. See *The Citadel of Learning* (New Haven: Yale University Press, 1956). Norman Cousins has also noted that it is incorrect to identify higher education with the colleges of the country: "the average college graduate of 1955 may be no better equipped than the average high-school or even elementary-school graduate at the turn of the century." See "Beyond the Classroom," *The Saturday Review,* September 10, 1955, p. 24.

[6] Of course education in certain formulations has many purposes rather than one. See Fred M. Hechinger, *An Adventure in Education: Connecticut Points the Way,* with a commentary by Norman Cousins (New York: Macmillan, 1956). Moreover, it is obvious that the goals are not entirely static. Alfred Whitney Griswold has analyzed the crucial tasks facing the university today in the light of the new age of specialization and science. He asks what is worth preserving of the older university tradition. See *In the University Tradition* (New Haven: Yale University Press, 1957).

[7] W. H. Auden, "Under Which Lyre: A Reactionary Tract for the Times," Phi Beta Kappa Poem, Harvard, 1946, *Nones* (New York: Random House, 1950), pp. 69–70.

[8] See Ruth Barry and Beverly Wolf, *op. cit.,* pp. 175–176, 178.

[9] Report of the Harvard Committee, *General Education in a Free Society* (Cambridge, Mass.: Harvard University Press, 1945).

[10] In "Reappraisal of the University," Kenneth Lindsay as an educator examines the varying aims of education in the free societies of the West, and concludes that a unified approach is needed. See *The New York Times Magazine,* June 5, 1955, pp. 10ff.

[11] Harry D. Gideonse, *Biennial Report of the President of Brooklyn College for the Academic Years 1955–1957* (Brooklyn, N.Y.: Brooklyn College, 1957), p. D-4 (1).

[12] See Roy R. Senour, Jr., "Students as Advisors to Student Organizations," *Personnel and Guidance Journal,* 35 (1956), 112–114.

[13] Frances E. Falvey, *Student Participation in College Administration* (New York: Teachers College, 1952).

[14] By "charter" is meant the collection of public and private, formal and informal rules and regulations which gives an institution its original basis for existence and for its continued existence in time.

[15] One of the best discussions of the nature of the charter is provided by Max Weber, although his attention is directed to the nature of bureaucracies. See *From Max Weber* (New York: Oxford University Press, 1946), pp. 196–244; also *The Theory of Social and Economic Organization* (New York: Oxford University Press, 1947).

[16] Although in a critical and hectoring spirit, Thorstein Veblen has written a

chapter on the subject. See *The Higher Learning in America* (New York: Sagamore Press, 1957), Chapter 3, pp. 98–107.

[17] An example of oversimplification is the following definition of education as "the process whereby persons intentionally guide the development of persons" — overly simple because it magnifies the personal relations apparent in education to the sidetracking of the multiplicity of factors indicated in the definition of education in institutional terms. See Philip H. Phenix, *Philosophy of Education* (New York: Holt, 1958), p. 13. In fiction, the institutional complications of higher education are made clear and certainly important by Carlos Baker in his *A Friend in Power* (New York: Scribner, 1958). In non-fiction the same point is made for large-scale organizations by C. Northcote Parkinson in his *Parkinson's Law* (Boston: Houghton, 1957). So far as personnel is concerned, Professor Parkinson argues that the staff of any administrative department increases annually five to six per cent "irrespective of any variation in the amount of work (if any) to be done." This "law" he illustrates in detail with several cases, including that of the British Admiralty between 1914 and 1928.

[18] A striking study has been made of the hospital in somewhat similar terms. Hopefully a student activities worker could create a parallel study of the university. See William Caudill, *The Psychiatric Hospital as a Small Society* (Cambridge, Mass.: Harvard University Press, 1958).

[19] Philip H. Phenix, *Philosophy of Education* (New York: Holt, 1958), p. 60.

Chapter 5. The Nature of Man

[1] Ruth Barry and Beverly Wolf, *Modern Issues in Guidance-Personnel Work* (New York: Teachers College, 1957), p. 53.

[2] Hans Sedlmayr suggests that art also has been progressively losing its integrity, a tendency which began prior to the French Revolution. The resultant situation is one in which chaos in art is made into an artistic virtue. See *Art in Crisis: The Lost Center* (Chicago: Regnery, 1958).

[3] Ernst Cassirer, *An Essay on Man* (New York: Doubleday, 1956). This is the title of Cassirer's first chapter.

[4] *Ibid.*, p. 39.

[5] *Ibid.*, pp. 39–40.

[6] Nathan A. Scott, Jr., *Modern Literature and the Religious Frontier* (New York: Harper, 1958), p. 74.

[7] Stephen Spender, the British poet and essayist, thinks that the "angry men" who are writing today's novels will mature literarily as they grow older, and that later and wiser they well may lead "useful" lives. See "When the Angry Men Grow Older," *The New York Times Book Review*, July 20, 1958," pp. 1, 12.

[8] Charles I. Glicksberg, "The Literature of Absurdity," *The Western Humanities Review*, 12 (1958), 29.

[9] This is the description of Malone given by Samuel Beckett. Malone, the chief protagonist of Beckett's play, asks only that he be "neither hot nor cold anymore, I shall be tepid, I shall die tepid." In his tepid way he describes to his hearers the agonies of nihilism. See *Malone Dies* (New York: Grove Press, 1956). Nihilism is the open theme of many lesser works also. John Barth, the hero in *The End of the Road* (New York: Doubleday, 1958), is a gruesomely spirited professor of history who believes in a "cheerful nihilism." Even the romantically inclined, "cherry-blossom" culture of Japan apparently knows of nihilistic tendencies, evidenced by Osamu Dazai's *No Longer Human* (New York: New Directions, 1958).

[10] So are other people, for that matter. Lewis Mumford, who in recent years has turned to sermons on moral conditions, says that mankind has passed through four great transformations which have produced biological man, archaic man,

civilized man, and axial man. There is present in his thought clear reminiscences of the stage theory of human progress unscientifically developed by Herbert Spencer and others. See *The Transformation of Man* (New York: Harper, 1956).

[11] Reinhold Niebuhr speaks about the "unresolved conflict between the Olympian and the Dionysian, the rational and the vitalistic, principles in Greek thought." *The Nature and Destiny of Man* (New York: Scribner, 1945), vol. 1, p. 8. But, I prefer to permit Olympus to be the "arbiter" between the two principles or "the ground of existence." A review of the Apollo myths will affirm, I believe, the justification for my choice.

[12] Novels about university life quite often stress the seamy side of life. Aside from novels mentioned elsewhere in this volume, Nathaniel Burt in *Make My Bed* (Boston: Little, Brown, 1957), tells the story of a sordid triangle; Charles Thompson's *Halfway Down the Stairs* (New York: Harper, 1957), is centered upon a Cornell coed with an insatiable thirst for men; Eileen Bassing's *Home before Dark* (New York: Random House, 1957), depicts the cheapness of spirit which sometimes pervades academic halls; Robertson Davies' *Leaven of Malice* (New York: Scribner, 1955) involves poison-pen sketches and "organized whee"; Howard Nemerov's *The Homecoming Game* (New York: Simon and Schuster, 1957) shows how chicanery enters into collegiate athletics; Richard Frede's *Entry E* (New York: Random House, 1958) revolves about a drinking and sex orgy in a student's room.

[13] Nietzsche in *The Birth of Tragedy* probably overemphasizes his indebtedness to the Dionysian principle in Greek thought.

[14] See particularly the chapter by Reinhold Niebuhr in *The Christian Idea of Education* (New Haven: Yale University Press, 1957) for a balanced view of this dilemma.

[15] With reference to voluntarism this point is clearly evident in the following: "There is also a confusion about authority in a democracy. One faculty member said seriously, in speaking of a student, 'I didn't know whether to tell him he had to, or to be democratic and let him do as he pleased.' Democracy does not mean the absence of authority. The difference between democracy and totalitarianism is not in the degree of authority, but in its source and use." Esther Lloyd-Jones and Margaret Ruth Smith, eds., *Student Personnel Work as Deeper Teaching* (New York: Harper, 1954), p. 132.

[16] Alfred North Whitehead says that "the seventeenth- and eighteenth-century philosophers practically made a discovery which, although it lies on the surface of their writings, they only half-realized. The discovery is that there are two kinds of fluency. One kind is the concrescence which in Locke's language, is 'the real internal constitution of a particular existent.' The other kind is the *transition* from particular existent to particular existent." *Kairos* is the first, not the second meaning. *Process and Reality: An Essay in Cosmology* (New York: Macmillan, 1930), pp. 319–320.

[17] An instructive discussion of *kairos* may be found in Paul Tillich's *The Protestant Era* (Chicago: University of Chicago Press, 1948), pp. 32–51.

[18] Edmund Fuller, *Man in Modern Fiction* (New York: Random House, 1958). See also Amos N. Wilder, *Modern Poetry and the Christian Tradition* (New York: Scribner, 1952).

[19] Randall Stewart, *American Literature and Christian Doctrine* (Baton Rouge: Louisiana State University Press, 1958).

[20] Rebecca West asserts that Shakespeare's *Hamlet* has been seriously misunderstood because its readers and hearers have been psychologically unwilling to face the fact that Hamlet is tainted with "original sin," like themselves. She contrasts Shakespeare's Christian view of man with Henry Fielding's Pelagian view (from the fourth-century monk, Britain's most famous heretic, who taught that men facing

good and evil will choose good and therefore in time become perfect). Here also are the two traditions in longer perspective than that supplied by Spender. See *The Court and the Castle* (New Haven: Yale University Press, 1957).

[21] Stephen Spender, *The Creative Element: A Study of the Vision, Despair and Orthodoxy among Some Modern Writers* (New York: British Book Center, 1954).

[22] *The New York Times*, June 10, 1957, p. 19. Nathan A. Scott, Jr., has written a persuasive little book which invites serious consideration. See *Modern Literature and the Religious Frontier* (New York: Harper, 1958).

[23] Albert Camus, Nobel Prize winning novelist, finds man's plight to rest not upon the Oedipus complex, alcoholism, Marxism, etc., but upon the sense of estrangement. In *The Fall* (New York: Knopf, 1956), the hero, Jean Baptiste, is under Adam's curse, original sin. In *The Myth of Sisyphus* (New York: Knopf, 1955), a man in despair can believe in damnation but not in salvation. In *The Stranger* (New York: Knopf, 1946), a sad hero discovers in the final analysis that he does not know himself; he is a stranger to himself. For a more comprehensive view of Camus' thought, see Philip Thody's *Albert Camus: A Study of His Work* (New York: Macmillan, 1958); and Thomas Hanna's *The Thought and Art of Albert Camus* (Chicago: Regnery, 1958).

[24] A more popular but also more superficial example is Colin Wilson's *The Outsider* (Boston: Houghton, 1956).

[25] There is considerable evidence to show that the efforts of the Soviet Union have not met with success. The role of religious organizations today in Russia points to this fact. Also, the youth of the country, according to official complaints, often fail to understand and appreciate the advantages of the collectivist society. See *The New York Times*, July 13, 1958, p. 11.

[26] Martin Heidegger, for example, says that the self lives in the knowledge and dread of its own extinction, challenged to affirm its humanity by fulfilling its own potentiality in defiance of its creaturely finiteness. To do this the self must examine its conscience. There it finds its guilt. But Heidegger's guilt is not that of the Judeo-Christian tradition. Rather it is indebtedness (*Schuld*). Recognizing its indebtedness, the self secures an authentic existence. This existence is unique in the realm of reality and must be constantly affirmed against the pressing temptation to sink into anonymity and factitiousness. See *Heidegger* by Marjorie Grene (New York: Hillary House, 1958) for a fuller explanation.

[27] A good starting point would be Erich Kahler's *The Tower and the Abyss: An Inquiry into the Transformation of the Individual* (New York: Braziller, 1957). Professor Kahler believes that society is moving toward the abyss of self-negation. He is especially perceptive in his comments on French existentialism, in this connection. But he also tries to formulate ways by which the values of individualism and community may be enhanced (the tower).

[28] Gerald Sykes has pointed out that the times require the rethinking of fundamental positions. In his novel *The Children of Light* (New York: Farrar, Straus, 1954), the hero says: "We are a boy king in a murderous palace, a boy king whose father died unexpectedly. Either we are going to learn how to rule — and learn very soon — or we are going to lose almost as quickly as we got it the power we did not seek, did not want, and must keep if we are to keep life itself . . . We are *rethinking everything*. We have to — or perish. Every tradition we have is inadequate, including the revolutionary."

Chapter 6. Theoretical Constructs

[1] Alfred North Whitehead, *Science and the Modern World* (New York: Mentor Books, 1948), p. 36.

[2] A comprehensive account of a student personnel theory is found in Paul J.

Brouwer, "An Outline of a Personnel Philosophy of Education," *Student Personnel Services in General Education* (Washington, D.C.: American Council on Education, 1949), pp. 310–317.

³ See especially Chapter 2 in *Constraint and Variety in American Education* (Lincoln: University of Nebraska Press, 1956).

⁴ Charles Wesley Cannom, "Philosophical Principles," *Student Personnel Services in General Education*, ed. Paul J. Brouwer (Washington, D.C.: American Council on Education, 1949), p. 274.

⁵ *The Student Personnel Point of View* (Washington, D.C.: American Council on Education, 1949), reprinted in January, 1955.

⁶ Robert M. Hutchins, *Education for Freedom* (Baton Rouge: Louisiana State University Press, 1947), p. 37.

⁷ Theodore M. Greene, "The Surface and the Substance of Education," *Scripps College Bulletin*, 30 (1955), 22.

⁸ The contributions of "logical positivism" in this connection are outlined cogently in Richard von Mises, *Positivism: A Study in Human Understanding* (Cambridge, Mass.: Harvard University Press, 1951).

⁹ It must be realized, however, that present research methods are so severely limited both in effectiveness and scope that the basis for belief and action must in many cases (regularly the more important) rest finally on other bases than scientific verification. In fact, as Pitirim Sorokin has suggested, it well may be that in the realm of human nature and interpersonal relations the physiocratic categories and methods of social science stand in need of fundamental revision. Pitirim A. Sorokin, *Sociocultural Causality, Time and Space* (Durham, N.C.: Duke University Press, 1943).

¹⁰ Paul Tillich, *The Interpretation of History* (New York: Scribner, 1936), p. 72.

¹¹ Another interpretative effort has been provided by Harold Taylor with the categories of rationalist, neo-humanist, and instrumentalist. See "The Philosophical Foundations of General Education," *General Education* (Chicago: University of Chicago Press, 1952), Part I.

¹² Says Lancelot Hogben: "We can now envisage the possibility that the methods of physical science will one day claim the field of what can properly be called knowledge." Quoted in Richard Hertz, *Chance and Symbol: A Study in Aesthetic and Ethical Consistency* (Chicago: University of Chicago Press, 1948), p. 96.

¹³ Louis Arnaud Reid, "General Problems of Guidance in Moral Choice," *Year Book of Education* (Yonkers, N.Y.: World Book Company, 1955), pp. 60–63.

¹⁴ J. J. Bachofen, in commenting upon the influence of Virgil's *Aeneid*, says: "We children of the nineteenth century, who are commonly satisfied when we know what we shall eat and drink, how we shall dress, and on what pleasures we can count, are hardly capable of appreciating the pressure which lofty designs exercise over a whole people, even less of realizing the importance that great popular traditions like the saga of Aeneas have for the formation of the tribe." See *Der Mythus*, ed. A. Baeumler (Munich, 1926), p. 566.

¹⁵ Mary Parker Follett, *The New State: Group Organization, the Solution of Popular Government* (New York: Longmans, Green, 1918), p. 54.

Chapter 7. Values

¹ Charles Eugene Morris, "Evaluation of the Student Personnel Program," in *Student Personnel Work as Deeper Teaching*, Esther Lloyd-Jones and Margaret Ruth Smith, eds. (New York: Harper, 1954), p. 325.

² Leonard Bacon, "Sophia Trenton," *Ph.D.s* (New York: Harper, 1925), p. 19.

³ Edward B. Titchener, *Systematic Psychology: Prolegomena* (New York: Mac-

millan, 1929), pp. 69–70. Also, see William James, *Principles of Psychology* (New York: Holt, 1890), vol. 2, p. 640.

⁴ Ruth Nanda Anshen, *The Family: Its Function and Destiny* (New York: Harper, 1949), p. 5.

⁵ Ernest Mach, *Contributions to the Analysis of Sensations* (Chicago: University of Chicago Press, 1897). There are many parallel relations between modern positivism and Greek skepticism. See, in this connection, M. M. Patrick, *The Greek Skeptics* (New York: Columbia University Press, 1929).

⁶ Rudolf Carnap, *Introduction to Semantics* (Cambridge, Mass.: Harvard University Press, 1942). See also the writings of other "logical empiricists," such as Otto Neurath and Philipp Frank.

⁷ Richard von Mises, *Positivism: A Study in Human Understanding* (Cambridge, Mass.: Harvard University Press, 1951), p. 80.

⁸ Morris R. Cohen, *Reason and Nature* (New York: Harcourt, Brace, 1931), p. xii.

⁹ von Mises, *op. cit.*, p. 21.

¹⁰ Edward L. Thorndike's realistic theory of education falls into this trap, for example. The S-R bond psychology which is very influential in teacher education programs is a variant. He claims for quantitative reality rightly, of course, that "whatever exists, exists in some amount." Quoted from Harold Rugg, *Foundations for American Education* (Cleveland: World Book Company, 1947), p. 125. But Thorndike is asserting more. Quantitative reality is the whole of reality to him. Thus, he misses the whole point of value discussion. See also his *Selected Writings from a Connectionalist's Psychology* (New York: Appleton-Century-Crofts, 1949).

¹¹ Alfred North Whitehead also recognizes the complementariness of theory and research: "Science is a river with two sources, the practical source and the theoretical source. The practical source is the desire to direct our actions to achieve predetermined ends . . . The theoretical source is the desire to understand . . . Success in practice depends on theorists who . . . have been there before, and by some good chance have hit upon relevant ideas." See *The Aims of Education* (New York: Mentor Books, 1949), p. 107.

¹² George Herbert Mead thought otherwise. He says that ends must be re-examined as means come into conflict with each other. Unfortunately he did not suggest a dependable method for the re-examination of ends. See "Scientific Method and the Moral Sciences," *International Journal of Ethics*, 33 (1923), 229–247.

¹³ The following works of Weber are some that are available in English: *The Protestant Ethic and the Spirit of Capitalism*, tr. by Talcott Parsons (London: Allen and Unwin, 1930); *The Theory of Social and Economic Organization*, tr. by A. M. Henderson and Talcott Parsons (New York: Oxford University Press, 1947); *From Max Weber: Essays in Sociology*, ed. and tr. by H. H. Gerth and C. Wright Mills (New York: Oxford University Press, 1946).

¹⁴ Robert Ulich, *Fundamentals of Democratic Education* (New York: American Book Co., 1945); *Conditions of Civilized Living* (New York: Dutton, 1946); *Crisis and Hope in American Education* (Boston: Beacon, 1951); *The Human Career: A Philosophy of Self-Transcendence* (New York: Harper, 1955).

¹⁵ J. Donald Butler, *Four Philosophies and Their Practice in Education and Religion* (New York: Harper, 1951), p. 502.

¹⁶ See, for example, Paul Tillich, *Systematic Theology* (Chicago: University of Chicago Press; vol. 1, 1951, vol. 2, 1957, vol. 3, 1963). Professor Tillich's method of "correlation" appears to be most promising even for student activities theory. His language, moreover, most often is well adapted to so-called secular understanding.

¹⁷ I am not advocating a uniform agreement on fundamental values. Such would be stifling of individual and social growth, unrealistic in a democracy and episte-

mologically doubtful of success. David Riesman, in speaking of the assumption that "agreement on fundamental values is essential for democratic functioning," says: "The attempt to enforce such agreement seems to me to be a good way to bring on civil war . . ." *Individualism Reconsidered* (Glencoe, Ill.: The Free Press, 1954), p. 17.

[18] Tillich, *op. cit.*, vol. 2, p. 28.

[19] Robert S. Hartman, "Role of the Value Consultant," Part I, *The Tech*, February 17, 1956, p. 2.

[20] *Ibid.*, Part II, *The Tech*, February 24, 1956, p. 2.

[21] *Ibid.*, p. 2.

[22] *Ibid.*, Part III, *The Tech*, February 28, 1956, p. 2. The series consists of five parts.

Chapter 8. Intentions

[1] Of course, there are those like Thorstein Veblen who claim that the university does not aid in the adjustment of the student to such segments of the community as business activity. He felt that the training of the university and the aims of business are diametrically opposed to each other. See *The Higher Learning in America* (New York: Sagamore Press, 1957), p. 56.

[2] By "intentions of student activities programs" I mean to suggest the sum of attributes contained in the general concepts of aims and other teleological references.

[3] Wilfrid Sheed has pointed out that in the United States student songs stress sports and the hallowed tradition of the university, while in Europe the songs are heavy with nostalgia. None finds anything to sing about in studying. See "No Paeans to Pedagogues," *The New York Times Magazine*, November 26, 1956, pp. 70–71.

[4] Ernest Earnest in his *Academic Procession: An Informal History of the American College: 1636–1953* (Indianapolis: Bobbs-Merrill, 1953), pp. 186, 187, notes that universities "put a brand on students . . . witness a Princeton or Virginia Ph.D. who has done his undergraduate work at the same place." He also tells the following story: "A Wellesley girl returning by train to Virginia for the Christmas holidays happened to look at her watch. 'It's silent time at Wellesley now,' she said. Instantly a hush fell over the Wellesley girls traveling with her."

[5] Charlotte Devree writes on the "progressive education type" of college girl who, if she is a Bennington student, is apt to develop into a stylized product, characterized by a maximum of artistic self-expression coupled with some attention to academic aims. See "College Girl," *The New York Times Magazine*, December 2, 1956, pp. 16–17, 142–144.

[6] N. R. Maier, *Frustration* (New York: McGraw-Hill, 1949), p. 209, quoted approvingly in Maurice D. Woolf and Jeanne A. Woolf, *The Student Personnel Program: Its Development and Integration in the High School and College* (New York: McGraw-Hill, 1953), p. 54.

[7] William Graham Sumner, *Folkways* (Boston: Ginn, 1906), p. 79.

[8] Ruth Benedict, *Patterns of Culture* (Boston: Houghton, 1934); Melville J. Herskovits, *Man and His Works* (New York: Knopf, 1948).

[9] Burton P. Fowler, a consultant for the Fund for the Advancement of Education, said that he wished "to place great emphasis on the existence of both a barrier and a vacuum in a very large proportion of our liberal arts colleges — a barrier which, intentionally or otherwise, makes it seem as though the professor has little or no interest in the cultivation of social and moral values in his students." See *The New York Times*, May 26, 1957, p. E9.

[10] Charles W. Eliot, "The New Education: Its Organization," *Atlantic Monthly,* 23 (February 1869), p. 218.

[11] Huston Smith, *The Purposes of Higher Education* (New York: Harper, 1955), p. xiii.

[12] Sigmund Freud, *Totem and Taboo* (New York: Norton, 1952).

[13] Theodore Reik, *Ritual: Psychoanalytic Studies* (New York: International Universities Press, 1958).

[14] Erich Fromm, *The Forgotten Language* (New York: Rinehart, 1951).

[15] Hastings Rashdall, *The Universities of Europe in the Middle Ages* (New York: Oxford University Press, 1936), vol. 3.

[16] Ernest Earnest, *Academic Procession* (New York: Bobbs-Merrill, 1953).

[17] Edward Y. Hartshorne, "Undergraduate Society and the College Culture," *American Sociological Review,* 8 (1943), 321–331.

[18] It would prove provocative to attempt to develop the thesis regarding the role of "subcultures" and social class as found in Albert K. Cohen's *Delinquent Boys: The Culture of the Gang,* to the suggestions of Hartshorne.

[19] *Loc. cit.,* p. 323.

[20] *Loc. cit.,* p. 324.

[21] The modern university is often engaged in extension education, for example, which makes more ambiguous the claim that the university is a community. It also raises the question of the role, if any, of student activities in such extensions. See Frederick M. Rosentreter, *The Boundaries of the Campus* (Madison: University of Wisconsin Press, 1957).

[22] The common view, of course, is that communities arise whenever and wherever technical conditions and natural resources permit. Economic and political associations in this view are the first social derivatives of such material conditions. A publication of the Research Center in Economic Development and Cultural Change of the University of Chicago shows that this view is inaccurate. See Edward C. Banfield, *The Moral Basis of a Backward Society* (Glencoe, Ill.: The Free Press, 1958). Although Banfield's cultural explanation for community is an advance over the common estimate, it is not entirely synonymous with the symbolic approach employed in this section of the chapter.

[23] Ferdinand Tonnies described two forms of community, those based on natural relationships and those based on rational relationships. Obviously this distinction is similar to but not identical to those employed in this chapter. See *Community and Society: Gemeinschaft und Gesellschaft,* tr. and ed. by Charles P. Loomis (East Lansing: Michigan State University Press, 1957).

[24] A similar charge has been made traditionally in the United States regarding trusts. Both Woodrow Wilson and Franklin Roosevelt, for example, said that they were not opposed to trusts as such — as industrial mechanisms. They said they opposed trusts because they tended to self-magnification of their institutional power and to overshadow other legitimate interests in society. See Richard Hofstadter, *The American Political Tradition* (New York: Vintage Books, 1955), pp. 254–255, 341.

Chapter 9. Group Classification

[1] Ludwig Gumplowicz, *Outlines of Sociology,* tr. by F. H. Moore (Philadelphia: American Academy of Political and Social Science, 1899).

[2] Milton W. Horowitz and Howard V. Perlmutter have surveyed the historical and current views on the reality of the group and have shown that it is possible to assume a science of groups. See "The Concept of Social Group," *Journal of Social Psychology,* 37 (1953), 69–95.

[3] Robert E. L. Faris, "Development of Small-Group Research Movement," in

Muzafer Sherif and Milbourne O. Wilson, eds., *Group Relations at the Crossroads* (New York: Harper, 1953), pp. 155–184.

[4] Edward A. Ross, *Foundations of Sociology* (New York: Macmillan, 1905).

[5] John L. Gillin and John P. Gillin, *Introduction to Sociology* (New York: Macmillan, 1942).

[6] Raymond B. Cattell, "Concepts and Methods in the Measurement of Group Syntality," *Psychological Review*, 55 (1948), 46–63.

[7] Ludwig von Wiese, *Systematic Sociology*, tr. by Howard Becker (New York: Wiley, 1932).

[8] Pitirim A. Sorokin, Carle C. Zimmerman, and Charles J. Galpin, *A Systematic Source Book in Rural Sociology* (Minneapolis: University of Minnesota Press, 1930).

[9] Kenneth D. Benne and Grace Levit, "The Nature of Groups and Helping Groups Improve Their Operation," *Review of Educational Research*, 23 (1953), 289–308.

[10] Christoph Heinicke and Robert F. Bales, "Developmental Trends in the Structure of Small Groups," *Sociometry*, 16 (1953), 7–38.

[11] David G. Hays and Robert R. Bush, "A Study of Group Action," *American Sociological Review*, 19 (1954), 693–701.

[12] Edgar S. Bogardus suggests the term "groupality" to describe both the universal and unique aspects of groups. See "Group Behavior and Groupality," *Sociology and Social Research*, 38 (1954), 401–403. But it is difficult to see how any one term will suitably encompass both aspects of groups any more than a group classification system, needed and inevitable as it seems to be, can solve the problems of members and motivations.

[13] In this connection it is interesting to note the possibility of "leaderless group discussions." See Bernard M. Bass, "An analysis of the Leaderless Group Discussion," *Journal of Applied Psychology*, 33 (1949), 527–533; also, Heinz L. Ansbacher, "The History of the Leaderless Group Discussion Technique," *Psychological Bulletin*, 48 (1951), 383–391.

[14] Cohesiveness has been shown to be a significant factor in the influencing of group members by other members. See Kurt W. Back, "Influence through Social Communication," *Journal of Abnormal Social Psychology*, 46 (1951), 9–23. On the other hand, Robert S. Albert has questioned the need for the concept of cohesiveness in studying group behavior. See "Comments on the Scientific Function of the Concept of Cohesiveness," *American Journal of Sociology*, 59 (1953), 231–234.

[15] For example, *Campus Activities*, ed. Harold Hand (New York: McGraw-Hill, 1938), scarcely faces the problem and accepts the traditional descriptions, such as "campus forensics," "music activities," "men's athletics."

[16] The following throw light on status groups: Raymond E. Bassett, "Cliques in a Student Body of Stable Membership," *Sociometry*, 7 (1944), 290–302; Merl E. Bonney, Robert E. Hoblit, and Arnold H. Dreyer, "A Study of Some Factors Related to Sociometric Status in a Men's Dormitory," *Sociometry*, 16 (1953), 287–301; William Monroe Jackson, Jr., "Interactions in a College Fraternity," *Applied Anthropology*, 3 (1944), 16–21.

Chapter 10. Freedom

[1] E. Merrill Root, *Collectivism on the Campus: A Battle for the Mind in American Colleges* (New York: Devin-Adair, 1955).

[2] Robert M. MacIver, *Academic Freedom in Our Time* (New York: Columbia University Press, 1955). A companion volume in the same project, although of quite a different turn of mind, is Richard Hofstadter and Walter P. Metzger, *The Development of Academic Freedom in the United States* (New York: Columbia University Press, 1955).

[3] Several novels have been written about loyalty oaths on the American university campus. See May Sarton, *Faithful Are the Wounds* (New York: Rinehart, 1955), and Martha Dodd, *The Searching Light* (New York: Citadel Press, 1955).

[4] "Academic freedom" is not a term to be employed when discussing the freedom of students, for historically only faculties have been granted academic freedom. See Russell Kirk, *Academic Freedom: An Essay in Definition* (Chicago: Regnery, 1955). Similarly, it is inappropriate and illogical to speak of student freedom on the campus as "civil liberties," since freedom to act within the confines of a private or public organization is limited by the rules and regulations (the charter) of the institution. The American Civil Liberties Union unfortunately but repeatedly falls into this error. See, for example, *Academic Freedom and Civil Liberties of Students* (New York: American Civil Liberties Union, 1956).

[5] Helen C. White says that the university "is such a tempting field for what one may call an unlocalized crusading zeal." See "Freedom in the University," *The Key Reporter*, 21 (1956), 2.

[6] Walter Berns argues that the usual libertarian doctrine of civil liberties is false. He claims that virtue and justice must be the guiding principles of law and society. Freedom, to him, is of secondary importance. See *Freedom, Virtue, and the First Amendment* (Baton Rouge: Louisiana State University Press, 1957).

[7] Thomas Hobbes, *Leviathan* (New York: Dutton, 1940), pp. 49–50. Madison had a similar explanation for "factionalism." See *The Federalist* (New York: Modern Library, 1941), pp. 54–62.

[8] Marcel Proust, *Swann's Way* (New York: Modern Library, 1928), p. 270.

[9] Franz Boas, "Liberty Among Primitive People," in Ruth Nanda Anshen, *Freedom: Its Meaning* (New York: Harcourt, Brace, 1940), p. 378.

[10] *Letters and Speeches of Abraham Lincoln* (New York: Dutton; Everyman's Library, no. 206), p. 136.

[11] Mahatma Gandhi saw this truth and expressed it to UNESCO in the following manner: "I learned from my illiterate but wise mother that all rights to be deserved and preserved came from duty well done . . . From this one fundamental statement, perhaps it is enough to define the duties of Man and Woman and correlate every right to some corresponding duty to be first performed." See "The Rights of Man," *United Nations Weekly Bulletin*, vol. 3 (1947), p. 521.

[12] Leo Strauss, *Natural Right and History* (Chicago: University of Chicago Press, 1953), especially Chapter 3, pp. 81–119.

[13] The fate of freedom in the political community is discussed ably by Walter Gellhorn in *Individual Freedom and Governmental Restraints* (Baton Rouge: Louisiana State University Press, 1956).

[14] Eliot Freidson, ed., "Student Government," *Student Leaders and the American College* (Philadelphia: United States Student Association, 1955), p. 48.

[15] Samuel Eliot Morison appears to perceive this when he asserts after argument that he finds no "connection between democracy and political freedom." Freedom is not an achievable attribute of any political philosophy or form; it is a basic condition of the nature of man. See *Freedom in Contemporary Society* (Boston: Little, Brown, 1956).

[16] Paul Tillich, "Freedom in the Period of Transformation," in Ruth Nanda Anshen, *Freedom: Its Meaning* (New York: Harcourt, Brace, 1940), p. 123. I am indebted to Professor Tillich, my former teacher, for several basic categories of thought.

[17] Alfred North Whitehead, *Process and Reality: An Essay in Cosmology* (New York: Macmillan, 1930), p. 74.

[18] Aristotle commented upon the difficulty to define precisely the "moral actions." His ideas are relevant here. See *Nicomachean Ethics*, II, 1104a.

[19] Michael Polanyi, *The Logic of Liberty* (Chicago: University of Chicago Press, 1951), pp. 157–159.

[20] David Riesman upbraids intellectuals who "try to cope with their anxiety by telling each other atrocity stories about America." See *Individualism Reconsidered* (Glencoe, Ill.: The Free Press, 1954), pp. 124ff.

[21] Sidney Hook, "Education and Creative Intelligence," *School and Society*, 84 (1956), 6.

[22] Frank H. Knight has pointed out that anarchism, the absence of external restraint, has never been thoroughly practiced in any human society, is intolerable to those who say they want it, and is impossible in the light of the nature of human nature. See "Ethics and Economic Reform," in *Freedom and Reform* (New York: Harper, 1947), pp. 102–112.

[23] Perhaps "integrity" is the best word to describe the ability to use freedom constructively. At least it is that quality which General Robert E. Lee evinced when he had determined upon surrender at Appomattox. One of his officers remonstrated with him, saying: "Oh, General, what will history say of the surrender of the army in the field?" "Yes," replied the sobered Lee, "I know they will say hard things of us! They will not understand how we were overwhelmed by numbers. But that is not the question, Colonel: The question is, is it right to surrender the army? If it is right, then I will take all the responsibility." Carl Sandburg, *Storm over the Land* (New York: Harcourt, Brace, 1942), p. 227.

[24] *The New York Times*, May 25, 1956, p. 8E.

[25] William W. Brickman, "Higher Jinks and Higher Education," *School and Society*, 84 (1956), 11–12.

[26] William Temple has expressed this sentiment as follows: "Membership of family and nation is not an accidental appendage of my individuality, but a constitutive element in it . . . Membership, such as carried with it a share in a common weal and woe, is an essential element in our nature." *Nature, Man and God* (London: Macmillan, 1934), pp. 186–187.

[27] Elton Trueblood has written an appealing chapter on "The Achievement of Freedom." See *The Life We Prize* (New York: Harper, 1951), pp. 78–97.

[28] Paul Tillich, *The Courage to Be* (New Haven: Yale University Press, 1952), especially pp. 40–57. See also David Riesman's description of the problem in *Individualism Reconsidered* (Glencoe, Ill.: The Free Press, 1954), p. 118, and elsewhere.

[29] David Riesman, Nathan Glazer, and Reuel Denney, *The Lonely Crowd: A Study of the Changing American Character* (New Haven: Yale University Press, 1953).

[30] Walter Lippmann, *The Public Philosophy* (Boston: Little, Brown, 1955).

Chapter 11. The Curriculum and the Co-curriculum

[1] Bruce Barton, *The Man Nobody Knows* (Indianapolis: Bobbs-Merrill, 1925).

[2] Ferdinand Lundberg, *The Treason of the People* (New York: Harper, 1954).

[3] Ernest Havemann and Patricia Salter West, *They Went to College: The College Graduate of Today* (New York: Harcourt, Brace, 1952).

[4] A study of 13,586 employees of the General Electric Company who are college graduates indicates that they considered the prime purpose of a college education to be the development of the power to think, and to analyze successfully a large range of problems. Eighty-eight per cent of the liberal arts graduates and 93 per cent of the engineering majors said that they engaged in various student activities while in college and that they found them a valuable aid in developing for a business career. See *The New York Times*, December 2, 1956, p. E11.

[5] José Ortega y Gasset, *The Mission of the University* (Princeton: Princeton University Press, 1944), pp. 50ff. It has been said that "had its founders been lesser men, prey to some of the practical nonsense that plagues many a U.S. campus today, they [the founders of Harvard] might have set up a curriculum for Forest Clearing and

House Building, with possible electives in Indian Affairs and Musketry . . . The purpose of their college, they declared, was 'to advance learning and perpetuate it to posterity.' " See *Time*, 63 (March 1, 1954), p. 28.

⁶ Quoted by Burges Johnson, *Campus versus Classroom: A Candid Appraisal of the American College* (New York: Ives Washburn, 1946), p. 50.

⁷ Edward Caird, *The Critical Philosophy of Immanuel Kant* (New York: Macmillan, 1889), vol. 2, p. 164.

⁸ Paul Tillich, *Systematic Theology* (Chicago: University of Chicago Press, 1957), vol. 2, p. 66.

⁹ F. C. S. Schiller, *Studies in Humanism*, 2d ed. (London: Macmillan, 1912), pp. 127–128.

¹⁰ John Henry Newman, *The Idea of a University* (New York: Longmans, Green, 1947), p. 128.

¹¹ Fisk University in Nashville, Tennessee, embarked several years ago upon a striking reorganization plan by which many aspects of the traditional campus life will be changed. One aspect of the proposed change involves "the decentralization of the university into small study centers which will tend to erase the difference between classroom and non-classroom teaching. Students will live in groups of fifty with a headmaster and tutors." Features of this plan, of course, are already in effect in other universities in this country and may be found most frequently in British higher education. See *The New York Times*, June 3, 1956, p. E9.

¹² Walter Moberly, *The Crisis in the University* (London: SCM Press, 1949), pp. 40–41.

¹³ Abraham Flexner, *Universities: American, English, German* (New York: Oxford University Press, 1930), p. 22.

¹⁴ Georg Hegel, *Philosophy of Universal History*, tr. by J. Sibree (London: G. Bell and Sons, 1902).

¹⁵ Walter Moberly, *op. cit.*, pp. 40–41.

¹⁶ Regularly there have been reports that academic ability and social leadership go hand in hand in higher education. For example, a study made of the Amherst class of 1956 indicated that "students with high academic standing held the greatest number of campus offices, received the most undergraduate honors and are most active in extra-curricular activities." See *The New York Times*, December 9, 1956, p. E9.

¹⁷ George W. E. Russell, *William Ewart Gladstone* (New York: Harper, 1891), p. 22.

¹⁸ Algo D. Henderson, *Vitalizing Liberal Education: A Study of the Liberal Arts Program* (New York: Harper, 1944), p. 138. A similar conception was advanced by Burton P. Fowler, see *The New York Times*, May 26, 1957, p. E9.

¹⁹ In his *Ethics*, 1103a, Aristotle describes two excellencies, the intellectual and the moral. The one is composed of "pure science, intelligence, and practical wisdom"; the other, of "liberality and perfected wisdom." The challenge of this chapter is to perceive both excellencies as attributes of the unified individual and the university.

²⁰ The various disciplines as represented in the university have reminded Alfred North Whitehead in their disjointedness of "a rapid table of contents which a deity might run over in his mind while he was thinking of creating a world, and had not yet decided how to put it together." See *The Aims of Education* (New York: Mentor Books, 1949), pp. 18–19.

Chapter 12. Faculty-Student Cooperation

¹ The dividing line between the curriculum and the co-curriculum on such a point as compulsory and voluntary activities is becoming increasingly ambiguous.

Robert H. Bonthius, *et al.*, in reporting on undergraduate instructional methods, have analyzed twenty different types of independent study programs. Ten of these are compulsory and ten are voluntary. See *The Independent Study Program in the United States* (New York: Columbia University Press, 1957).

² Some evidence of such a doctrine may be found in Frances E. Falvey's *Student Participation in College Administration* (New York: Teachers College, 1952), although a discriminating effort is sustained throughout regarding the limitations which naturally rest upon student participation. Falvey discusses "the college as an institution of contemporary society" with thoughtfulness.

³ Edited by Eliot Freidson and published by the Association.

⁴ The late Professor Edgar S. Brightman of Boston University introduced the term "disvalue" into serious discussion. He wished it to be opposed to "value."

⁵ For a clear example, see Thomas Evans Coulton, *A City College in Action; Struggle and Achievement at Brooklyn College: 1930–1955* (New York: Harper, 1955), pp. 197–199.

⁶ *Op. cit.*, pp. 47–48.

⁷ *Op. cit.*, p. 39.

⁸ *Op. cit.*, p. 48.

Chapter 13. Professionalism

¹ Kingsley Amis, *Lucky Jim* (New York: Compass Books, 1958), p. 32.

² John Dewey defined the nature of a vocation as "nothing but such direction of life activities as renders them perceptibly significant to a person." See *Democracy and Education* (New York: Macmillan, 1916), pp. 358–359. This view, however, is absurdly shallow as will be made clear later in this chapter in the discussion of professions as self-centered activities.

³ Karl Marx, *The Poverty of Philosophy* (New York: International Publishers, n.d.), p. 145.

⁴ Adam Smith, *The Wealth of Nations* (New York: Collier, 1902).

⁵ The relationships between work and family are described by Everett C. Hughes in *Men and Their Work* (Glencoe, Ill.: The Free Press, 1958). Hughes also asks a significant question in terms of the historic changes in work motivation: Is work going out of style in America?

⁶ Émile Durkheim wrote instructively on the ethical relations of professions to the community. Contrary to some present-day opinion, Durkheim believed that the most highly developed systems of ethics are maintained by the professions attached to government. The least developed are related to business. See *Professional Ethics and Civic Morals* (Glencoe, Ill.: The Free Press, 1958).

⁷ In contrast, see Matthew 11:7–10.

⁸ Porter R. Lee, *Social Work as Cause and Function* (New York: Columbia University Press, 1937).

⁹ Mary E. Richmond, *Social Diagnosis* (New York: The Russell Sage Foundation, 1917).

¹⁰ Gordon Hamilton, *Theory and Practice of Social Case Work*, rev. ed. (New York: Columbia University Press, 1951).

¹¹ Jessie Taft, *A Functional Approach to Family Case Work* (Philadelphia: Pennsylvania School of Social Work, 1944).

¹² Mary J. McCormick, *Thomistic Philosophy in Social Casework* (New York: Columbia University Press, 1948).

¹³ Virginia Robinson has written a perceptive book on the changes in outlook. See *Changing Psychology in Social Case Work* (Chapel Hill: University of North Carolina Press, 1930). Of course many developments have occurred since she wrote.

[14] Paul L. Dressel makes this suggestion in "Editorial Comments," *Journal of Counseling Psychology*, 4 (Fall 1957).

[15] Graham Wallas, *Our Social Heritage* (New Haven: Yale University Press, 1921).

[16] Abraham Flexner, "Is Social Work a Profession?" *Proceedings of the National Conference of Charities and Corrections* (Chicago: University of Chicago Press, 1915), pp. 576–590. Another description, principally based on Flexner's, is given in Myron Lieberman, *Education as a Profession* (Englewood Cliffs, N.J.: Prentice-Hall, 1956), pp. 2–6.

[17] John G. Darley, "The Faculty Is Human, Too," *Personnel and Guidance Journal*, 25 (1956), 225–226.

[18] Actually licensing is very old, deriving from the licensing of professors in the medieval university. See C. H. Haskins, *The Rise of the Universities* (Ithaca, N.Y.: Cornell University Press, 1957), p. 11.

[19] Recent studies have developed this theme for other institutions. See Robert A. Brady, *Business as a System of Power* (New York: Columbia University Press, 1943), and Floyd Hunter, *Community Power Structures: A Study of Decision Makers* (Chapel Hill: University of North Carolina Press, 1953). Student personnel work awaits such an analysis.

[20] David Riesman, *Constraint and Variety in American Education* (Lincoln: University of Nebraska Press, 1956), pp. 54–56.

[21] A concept developed by David Riesman, *ibid.*, Chapter 2 especially.

[22] Darley, *op. cit.*, p. 226.

[23] The problems and possibilities of being neutral in relation to the power expressed within a social institution are discussed by Sylvia Selekman and Benjamin Selekman in *Power and Morality in a Business Society* (New York: McGraw-Hill, 1956), especially Chapter 3.

[24] F. C. Thorne, *Principles of Personality Counseling* (Brandon, Vt.: Journal of Clinical Psychology Press, 1950), pp. 64–65. Thorne says: "Counselors . . . have some responsibility to protect the interest of their employers."

[25] A pioneering study has investigated the problems encountered when a large organization, profit or nonprofit, seeks to alter its structure in order to improve its operations. At a number of points parallels to the situation of the student personnel worker are drawn. See Eli Ginsberg, Ewing W. Reilley, *et al.*, *Effecting Change in Large Organizations* (New York: Columbia University Press, 1957).

[26] See how the dilemma is described and resolved by Jane Warters, *Techniques of Counseling* (New York: McGraw-Hill, 1954), p. 314.

[27] A study conducted by Arthur T. Jersild indicated that sixty per cent of the 1000 teachers and graduate students studied over a five-year period admitted that their principal problem in personal living for professional effectiveness was a lack of meaningfulness. A similar study of student personnel workers as a group would be illuminating. See *The New York Times*, July 1, 1956, p. E9.

[28] Edward J. Shoben, Jr., "A Rationale for Modern Student Personnel Work," *Personnel-O-Gram*, 12 (1958), 11.

Index

198